In Business For Life

What Being in Business for Life Taught Me About the Business of Life

Brad Lindemann

Copyright ©2017 by Brad Lindemann
All rights reserved. No part of this book may be reproduced in any form or by any means, electronic or mechanical, including photocopying, recording or by any information storage and retrieval system, without the prior written permission of the Publisher.

Printed by Brad Lindemann

ISBN-13: 978-1540464453

ISBN-10: 1540464458

Unless otherwise noted, all bible quotations contained in this book are taken from the New International Version (NIV) by Zondervan.

Jacket design by Don Patton

Editorial and marketing support by Christopher Mann at PumpJack.me Thought Leader Marketing

www.InBusinessForLife.org

Brad Lindemann
In Business for Life

12400 N. Meridian Street
Suite 150
Carmel, IN 46032
317-691-6169
Brad@InBusinessForLife.org
Twitter: @blouis. @InBusiness4Life
https://www.linkedin.com/in/bradlindemann
https://www.linkedin.com/groups/6665766

Dedication

I wrote the following poem while driving to a sales call in northern Indiana. A few days prior, I had learned that my father had colon cancer. The poem came as quickly as I could write it down. It was finished by the time I arrived at my destination. Please don't try this in your vehicle.

Play On Piano Man

There's a piano man in the dessert,
Whose song has just begun.
A prelude he's been playing,
The words yet to be sung.

His gentle hands flow smoothly,
Across the ivory keys.
He hears each note before it's played,
No music does he see.

He plays songs from days of old,
With children all about.
Each note a precious memory,
But words he can't get out.

His melody progresses
Into more modern scores.
Beside him now his helpmate,
Whom he treasures and adores.

Hear his children singing.
The songs of yesteryear.
He strains to hear the lyrics,
From the ones he holds so dear.

He wishes he could sing along,
And run, and laugh, and shout.

He longs to sing them just one verse,
But words he can't get out.

There's a piano man in the dessert,
Whose song has just begun.
His bronze face brightly glowing,
In the blazing western sun.

A prelude he's still playing,
To a song of days to be.
The words he holds within his heart,
Are soon to be set free.

The piano man keeps playing,
Beneath the western skies.
His gaze turns toward the east,
The sun is on the rise.

Songs of faith, and hope, and love,
Abide in him these three.
His music and his lyrics
Now in perfect harmony.

Once again his family
Has joined him in his song.
In unison they're singing...
...play on, piano man, play on.

Brad Lindemann

Loving Son of the Piano Man (December 20, 1991)

Table of Contents

DEDICATION		III
TABLE OF CONTENTS		V
1.	INTRODUCTION	1
2.	BAD THINGS…GREAT PEOPLE…GOOD GOD?	9
3.	ON EARTH AS IT IS IN HEAVEN	13
4.	LEADING VS. TAKING A WALK	17
5.	HUBRIS: HOW THE MIGHTY FALL	19
6.	MY FATHER'S SON ONE	21
7.	YOU CAN'T DO IT…WE CAN'T HELP	29
8.	PACER, BUSTER AND THE JOHN MUIR TRAIL	35
9.	AMBASSADOR SOLUTIONS' CULTURE	43
10.	VALUES IN ACTION	51
11.	THE GET-OUT-OF-JAIL-FREE-CARD MYTH	71
12.	TAKE YOUR MARKS!	109
13.	BUSINESS LIFE LESSONS	113
14.	THE CHOSEN ONE	141
15.	LIFE-SAVING EXPERIENCES	143
16.	OUR GOOD MIDDLE CHILD	153
17.	LIFE WITH MY LOVELY BRIDE	157
18.	TELL YOUR GREATEST FEAR	161
19.	WHEN IT HURTS TO HUG	163

20.	HOPE FLOATS FROM THE BOTTOM UP	189
21.	WISDOM FROM ABOVE…AND BELOW	197
22.	COURAGE	215
23.	I'M FAILING AND I CAN'T GET UP	231
24.	IT'S A DOG WORLD…ADJUST!	239
25.	'TIL DEBT DO US PART	247
26.	WHY I'M IN BUSINESS FOR LIFE	267
27.	WHY ARE YOU IN BUSINESS?	273
28.	SO WHAT AND WHO CARES?	275

"…I press on to take hold of that for which Christ Jesus took hold of me."

- Philippians 3:12b

1. Introduction

Why I Wrote This Book

Think you have at least one good book in you before finishing your real-life epilogue? Of course you do…you, me and millions of other author wannabes.

Before rushing into it, however, you would do well to check your motivation and your material. So I asked myself, "What would motivate me to birth a tar baby affectionately known as 'My Book' for the next year or two?" Make that three.

My singularly sufficient motivator was the deathbed promise I made to my father in 1991 to write the book he never got around to. While mustering motivation and archiving material, Pop ran out of time. The gold watch my father received from Sears & Roebuck the previous year stopped ticking when he was 60 years young. Three weeks later, his only son turned 35 and feels like he's been aging in dog years ever since.

Material? Oh sure, lots of it. Been up in your attic lately? That's how your book material looks at the beginning of the birthing process.

Mind you, I've been a lost ball in high tech weeds since joining IBM's white shirt army in 1978. My contemporaries are Bill Gates and Steve Jobs, for crying out loud!

Thankfully, things got a bit less challenging when *their* children's generation came online. *Yeah right.* You know, pikers like Google's Larry Page and Sergey Brin and Facebook's Mark Zuckerberg. Seriously? These kids give every day billionaires *inferiority complexes*. What could *I* possibly say to a generation that defines success with a capital "B" and has every word ever written a mere click away?

"So What?" and "Who Cares?"

Two of the most illuminating questions I've found at the intersection of business and life are, "So what?" and "Who cares?" These questions have become the governor on my penchant for espousing profundities that mean little to anyone beyond the man in the mirror. So, while cradling my tar baby along with your favorite Starbucks venti, know that every word to follow has passed through the "So what?" and "Who cares?" filter.

We should probably put that filter to the test from the get-go. Know that I bring some strong biases into this project. I sincerely believe that everyone would benefit from experiencing the following at least once in their lifetime:

(a) Starting, owning and operating a business (for at least 2 years);

(b) Getting fired from a job and

(c) Spending the night in jail.

If you've already hit this trifecta, you might conserve your ammo and just download a copy of Brad Stone's fascinating book, *The Everything Store: Jeff Bezos and the Age of Amazon*. It's a great read and I'm sure Jeff would appreciate your business. Otherwise, check your mouthpiece and cinch up your gloves, because we won't be pulling any punches, though I sure wish I had on that fateful day in 2001.

If you're looking for another "How I succeeded in business and you can too" book, well, keep looking. My first book will likely disappoint you. It took me 27 years to complete this project, partly because I *falsely* believed that without a substantial business empire platform to stand upon, I had nothing worthwhile to say. I've come to believe just the opposite. My answers to the "So what?" and "Who cares?" questions have come at great cost on the battlefields of life and business. As such, they have "been tried as silver is tried" (Psalm 66:10). I now have the good fortune of sharing some of the lessons learned along the way.

Just prior to starting this little writing project, our humble enterprise known as Ambassador Solutions celebrated its 25th anniversary on April 1, 2014. In 2009, we "celebrated" our twentieth in the depths of The Great Recession. By God's grace, that marked the only money-losing year in our company's history. That also marked our second near-death corporate experience; 2001 was the first. The latter has been orders of magnitude more difficult to recover from. But recovering we are, albeit in a new fast and light condition.

While I've been in business my entire adult life and learned much about the business of life from it, I've not allowed my business to be my life. To which my lovely bride says, "Really? What about all those lost evenings spent brooding over deals gone bad and opportunities lost? What about all that whining over not being able to catch a break if it was dropped in your lap? What about all those ungrateful employees who just didn't seem to get it...whatever IT was at the time?"

Ouch. The lady has a point.

Okay, so let me dial-back a bit and distinguish how I have *wanted* to view my business versus how I have *actually* viewed my business. Over the last quarter century plus, I've spent way too much time and energy acting as if my business was my life. I hope this book helps balance the scales. There really was much more than just business going on during those years. In the end, the reader will be judge and jury regarding the value of the resulting wisdom contained herein.

With that, all please rise. The court of reader opinion is now in session. Please ignore anything that cannot pass through your personal "So what?" and "Who cares?" filter. If you neither get it nor care to, the fault is mine, not yours...move on. If something in my story connects to a dot in yours, I would be deeply grateful to hear about it. On the flipside, if I offend you in any way, I beg your forgiveness in advance and would be equally grateful to hear from you. I'm serious about both; in case you missed it, my full contact information is included at the front of this book. In the end, if something of what I've learned about the business of life enhances yours, it will have been worth the birthing process.

"My Book" is now yours.

Live Ammo With a BS-Free Guarantee

Throughout the book, you'll see references to "Live Ammo." Before telling you what that *is*, let me be very clear on what it is *not*.

Live Ammo does not compare the true heroes who have spilled their blood while protecting our liberty to those of us in the business world who fight most of our battles with keyboards whilst trapesing about cyber-space.

Like many, I don't appreciate the war/battle references often heard in our nation's athletic locker rooms. War can be a helpful metaphor, but offensive when seriously applied to the relatively safe games we play and desk jobs that we enjoy. Real war is no game. Comparing any other earthly activity to war potentially dishonors those who have sacrificed so much for the sake of so many. God forbid that anything contained herein would be so misunderstood.

For my purposes, I intend the phrase "Live Ammo" for guys like

Kurt, one of the more colorful members of my men's small group. For that group, the phrase actually has a dual meaning. First, it reminds us that within the spiritual realm, we really are at war. Second, it encourages us to keep things real—"*bring your live ammo to our meetings!*"—because we're committed to authentic relationships based upon truth and reality. No BS allowed.

As I began writing this book, it occurred to me that whatever came out of it must be based upon truth and reality. No BS allowed. Live ammo required. And, though not a Christian book per se, a book of my memoirs would be quite disingenuous without references to my personal faith journey—a journey that finds me increasingly more conscious of the spiritual warfare being waged all around us.

Rest assured, wherever your personal faith journey finds you, you should only find encouragement from this book. If not, then I've sorely missed the mark.

So, grab your weapon of choice and let's get to it. It's time for some Live Ammo...no BS allowed.

The Most Important Chapter of my Life

Spring time on a major college campus is pretty special. With new life blooming all around and the end of a long school year approaching, there's euphoria in the air. It's palpable. At least for most of the students. Not so much for me during the spring of 1975 on the campus of Indiana University in Bloomington. Academic pressures, fraternity pledgeship and my relationship with my girlfriend found me exhausted and gasping for air by early April. Something wasn't right in my spirit, but I had no idea what it was until I met Tom.

Tom showed up at my frat house during dinner one evening with an Olympic champion wrestler in tow. I can't remember what he said that caused me to join them in the living room after dinner. But, I'll never forget what he said once he got my attention. He told of a time during his college days when some of his friends started behaving rather strangely. Claiming to have found God, they stopped doing many of the things that college kids are wont to do and started acting all religious. When they started pressuring Tom to join in, he had to get away.

When school was out in the spring, Tom jumped on his motorcycle, kissed his mother goodbye and set out for Colorado, hoping to clear his head. Something wasn't right in his spirit and he had a growing sense that his friends may have found what it was. He hadn't gone looking for God, but rather God seemed to be looking for him. So, on a mountaintop in the Colorado Rockies, Tom looked up at the starlit sky and said words to this effect, "God, if you're real and if you want me to know you the way my friends do, then I'm all ears. If not, then please go away and leave me alone."

With that, Tom's life changed so radically that upon graduation a few years later he joined a campus ministry organization called Campus Crusade for Christ. Fortunately for me and many other students at the time, his first assignment was on the campus of Indiana University. After sharing his Rocky Mountain High story, Tom asked if anyone would like to meet one-on-one the following week. I was quick to accept his invitation. Maybe he would have some insight into my disquieted spirit? Maybe he could help me understand why I felt so empty while living a life that seemed so full?

Tom was blessed with Bill Clinton charisma and wisdom well beyond his years. He's was one of those rare people who could make you feel like you're the only one in a crowded room. The moment he entered my room number 18 at the Phi Kappa Psi house on North Jordan Avenue, I felt at ease and drawn to his dynamic personality. He quickly sized me up, and then eased into a conversation about spiritual things using a small booklet called The Four Spiritual Laws as a guide. As he explained things in a way I'd never heard them before, I started to realize that I knew *about* God, but I didn't really *know* Him.

The booklet starts out by saying, "Just as there are physical laws that govern the physical universe, so there are spiritual laws that govern our relationship with God." After Tom read that line, he looked out the window and pointed to the bell tower just behind our frat house.

"It's like this, Brad. Say you climbed to the top of that bell tower and stood teetering on the edge, shaking your fist at the sky and shouting, "Gravity I defy you. You cannot have an impact upon my life. And, then proceeded to jump. What do you think would happen?"

"I'd go splat," I said. Looking back, that was the splat heard round the world for me.

"Indeed you would, my friend" said Tom. "Because the law of gravity doesn't change based upon whether or not you choose to believe in it. And so it is with the laws of God. Make sense?"

It was starting to. He went on to explain all four of the spiritual laws:

1. God loves you and offers a wonderful plan for your life.
2. Man is sinful and separated from God. Therefore, he cannot know and experience God's love and plan for his life.
3. Jesus Christ is God's only provision for man's sin. Through Him you can know and experience God's love and plan for your life.
4. We must individually receive Jesus Christ as Savior and Lord; then we can know and experience God's love and plan for our lives.

When we got to the second law, Tom put it in terms that a swimmer like me could understand. "Imagine you, me and Mark Spitz lined up on the coast of California determined to swim to Hawaii. I might make it a few miles before going under. Maybe even 10 or 20, but before too long, I'm going to drown. You, being a swimmer, could probably go three times as far as me, but you too would eventually succumb to the sea. Mark Spitz could likely go much farther than you, but long before reaching Hawaii, he'd be shark bait just like us. It's impossible for anyone to swim from California to Hawaii and it's impossible for sinful man to bridge the gap that separates him from God."

Tom went on to explain that Jesus was the only one who could bridge that sin gap. But, just knowing that truth wasn't enough. Law Four states that you have to act upon that knowledge by individually receiving Jesus Christ as Lord and Savior.

And then he asked me the most important question that I've ever been asked, "Brad, would you like to ask Christ into your life right now?" He then showed me the following prayer on page 10:

> Lord Jesus, I need You. Thank You for dying on the cross for my sins. I open the door of my life and receive You as my Savior and Lord. Thank You for forgiving my sins and giving me eternal life. Take control of the throne of my life. Make me the kind of person You want me to be.

I prayed the above prayer on April 13, 1975. Lightning didn't flash and thunder didn't boom, but my life was radically transformed in that moment. Over 41 years later, I've doubted just about everything else at one time or another, but since that fateful spring day of my freshman year in college, I have never doubted the powerful presence of the living God in my life.

As my mother-in-law frequently reminded me, God didn't promise us a smooth ride, just a safe landing. We've had our share of difficult challenges, bitter losses and deep disappointments. Many of which are chronicled in this book. Becoming a Christian doesn't exempt you from life's trials and tribulations. In fact, the Bible builds a pretty strong case in the opposite direction. It even goes so far as to suggest that we should receive such trials joyfully (James 1:2-4). What's up with that?

The old adage, "What doesn't kill you makes you stronger" is not a direct quote from the Bible, but the underlying principle is replete throughout. One of the most thought provoking passages I've found along these lines is found in the book of Romans:

> *"... but we also glory in our sufferings, because we know that suffering produces perseverance; perseverance, character; and character, hope" (Romans 1:3,4).*

In essence, this suggests that the Christian life is the ultimate character-building experience. And, like the athlete who punishes his body to perform at his optimal level, the Christian is trained to be all that God wants him to be through suffering. Suffering that leads to hope. True hope that does not disappoint. Hope in the One who came to save us and who has gone to prepare a place for us (John 14:2).

So what's the point of all this Christian character-building? The athlete trains diligently to obtain the winner's trophy. What is the end game for the suffering Christian? I believe the character we gain through suffering is the transcendent key to seeing God's will be done "on Earth as it is in Heaven."

In other words, the more Christ-like our character becomes here on Earth, the more Heaven-like Earth can become.

Chapter 1

2. Bad Things...Great People...Good God?

Todd Erb

Not too long ago, I had lunch with a local businessman 10 months after his wife and daughter were senselessly and brutally beaten to death in their home by a disgruntled former employee of the man's company. As Todd anticipated the first anniversary of his tragic loss, his suffering was far from over. Yet, he was determined to persevere through it so that his character may continue to be refined by it and so that the living Christ within him, the hope of glory, will shine brighter because of it.

Impossible, you say? Todd would be quick to agree—by his *own* strength. He would also tell you, however, that he literally could not take his next breath but for the fact that "When I am weak, He is strong" (2 Corinthians 12:9).

Todd actually initiated our luncheon after hearing me share a prayer request in the small group Bible study where we recently met. Turns out one of Todd's children had been down a similar path to one of ours—the one who was the subject of my prayer request. He was anxious to share the story of his child's miraculous turnaround in hopes of encouraging *Elaine and me.*

Imagine that. A mere 10 months after losing his wife and daughter, this grieving husband/father is taking me to lunch to see if he can put a bit more pep in my step. Who does that? Someone who believes with all their heart:

For this world is not our home; we are looking forward to our city in Heaven, which is yet to come (Hebrews 13:14).

So I asked Todd, "As you're anticipating that painful one-year anniversary, I'm sure one of the voices that you're hearing is the one saying that to be anything but despondent around that time would somehow dishonor Marylyn and Kelley's memories. Right?" His answered surprised me.

"Maybe a little," he said, "but it's more knowing for certain that Marylyn and Kelley would not want me to be that way. They would want me to be joyful, knowing that they are experiencing perfect joy in Heaven right now and that we will be together again someday."

Wow. Joy in the aftermath of tragedy. Again, impossible but for His joy within us.

Doug Gripp

In the aftermath of another tragedy in our large church family, I realized how woefully ignorant I was of Heaven. Every August, we kick-off our Men's Ministry season with a big barbecue. Hundreds of hungry men gather to receive nourishment for both body and soul, the highlight of their year.

Less than an hour before the event was to start on Monday evening, August 26, 2013, I received a foreboding email from our senior pastor saying it had been cancelled. Shortly thereafter, I received a second email saying that the owner of the catering company providing the food was instantly killed when his massive gas grill exploded.

Doug Gripp, 52, was more than a caterer to Grace Church in Noblesville, Indiana. Having surrendered his life to Christ just a few years before his death, Doug was a very active member of the church. He saw his catering business as a ministry and often referred to his delicious food as "bait" to lure men into considering the claims of Christ. Doug lived out his new found faith with unbridled passion and contagious enthusiasm. His "Pit Crew" loved him deeply and would have followed him into combat. Little did they know that our own church parking lot would become Doug's personal war zone. Doug was survived by a wife and two daughters.

Comments about God needing a good barbecue chef in Heaven were certainly well intended by some struggling to make sense of the senseless, but they brought more pain than comfort. To satisfy his hankering for barbecue, did the God of the Universe horrifically kill his chef of choice in the presence of his closest friends, leaving a widowed wife and two fatherless children behind? I don't think so.

If that's the God we serve, then I'd seriously consider going AWOL. Such tragedies always lead to intense debates over God's omniscience, sovereignty and omnipotence. Whether He caused it or allowed it, those left in the tragic wake will invariably ask, "How could a loving God cause/allow such a thing?"

I can't possibly provide the full answer to this, perhaps the deepest of all questions, in these humble memoirs. I can suggest, however, that a better understanding of Heaven can lead to a more tolerable understanding of the sometimes tragic routes God's children take to get there. It did for me.

Chapter 2

3. On Earth as it is in Heaven

Randy Alcorn, author of 40-some books and the founder and director of Eternal Perspective Ministries, has quite possibly studied and written about the vast subject of Heaven more than anyone ever has. That's why I sought out his writings in the aftermath of the BBQ tragedy. Alcorn's 560-page tome is simply and appropriately titled, Heaven (Tyndale House, 2011). Whatever your question about Heaven might be, you're likely to find the answer in this book. Alcorn painstakingly clarifies what the Bible says and doesn't say on the subject.

Then, with biblical fact as his foundation, he paints a wonderfully comprehensive picture of a Heavenly future bright beyond comprehension. I was thrilled to learn that harps and clouds weren't in it:

> *I am convinced that the typical view of Heaven – eternity in a disembodied state – is not only completely contrary to the Bible but hides from our imaginations the far greater truth of Scripture, the far richer eternal destiny of redeemed life, relationships, culture and physical activity on the New Earth. –* Randy Alcorn.[1]

The more I read Alcorn's writings on Heaven, the more stunned I became over my previously woeful ignorance on the subject. I took some solace in knowing that I was far from alone. From my personal experience, most Christians have a very shallow and shaky understanding of where and how they're to spend eternity. Before being too hard on them (or yourself) for what appears to be the ultimate "bet on the come," realize that the bet has been placed on the risen Christ and the loving Father who gave Him to save a dying world that He loved above all things. Having placed the bet on this dynamic duo, most believers (heretofore me included) trust that their eternal home will suit them just fine. But, as he is wont to do, the Devil is in the details of our fuzzy thinking about Heaven.

Think about it. If your mission was to keep as many people as possible out of Heaven, wouldn't launching a negative publicity campaign against it be a great strategy?

---

[1] Why You Can Live Free from the Burden of YOLO, "You Only Live Once," by Randy Alcorn, October 1, 2014. http://www.epm.org/blog/2014/Oct/1/yolo-you-only-live-once

"Why in the world would you want to go there?" Lucifer whispers. "Do you really want to leave Monday Night Football or Ladies Night Out Tuesdays behind? No beer, no chocolate, no fun. Just floating around the throne of God as a wispy spirit singing the Alleluia chorus for eternity. Yippee! Best to grab all the gusto you can now, my friend. Take that hot little number over there for example...."

Thankfully, the Bible doesn't leave us defenseless to this satanic sophistry. The big idea about Heaven is that it's coming to Earth, new and improved, fully redeemed from sin and Satan's temporary rein. The Scriptures are very clear: Heaven can hardly wait to get to Earth. This truth is revealed to the Old Testament prophet, Daniel, in chapter 7. Alcorn writes:

> *In contrast to the tenuous and temporary rule of the nations, we're told that the Messiah's dominion — in context, a kingdom on Earth — will be "everlasting" and "will not pass away" and "will never be destroyed" (v. 14). Christ will not merely destroy the Earth where fallen kings once ruled. Rather, He will rule over the same Earth, transformed and new (Alcorn, Heaven, 2014).*

At Daniel's request, an angel provides an interpretation of his vision:

> *"The four great beasts are four kingdoms that will rise from the Earth" (v. 17).*

Then the angel makes an extraordinary statement:

> *"But the saints of the Most High will receive the kingdom and will possess it forever — yes, for ever and ever" (v. 18).*

This statement makes clear both the kingdom's location (Earth) and its duration (eternal).

God has never abandoned His original plan that righteous human beings will inhabit and rule the Earth. That's not merely an argument from silence. Daniel 7:18 explicitly reveals that "the saints of the Most High will receive the kingdom and will possess it forever." What is "the kingdom"? Earth.

Earth is unique. It's the one planet — perhaps among billions — where God chose to act out the unfolding drama of redemption and reveal the wonders of His grace. It's on the new Earth, the capital planet of the new universe, that He will establish an eternal kingdom.

I know what you're thinking. "So, let me get this straight. Are you telling me that I could be drinking beer at Buffalo Wild Wings while watching NFL football in Heaven?"

Why not? Yes, I know this can be hard to square with our image of clouds, gates, harps and halos, but let's let scripture guide an understanding of Heaven rather than medieval painters and modern cartoonists.

Jesus, however, already tipped his hand regarding sipping wine in Heaven (Mark 14:25). And, with regards to the games we love to play/watch and the related gathering places, there's no Biblical basis for believing that such things won't be with us in Heaven.

But if they aren't, it's safe to say they'll be replaced be something far better. For example, being a Sunday afternoon couch potato while watching Peyton Manning destroy the New England Patriots with his fully redeemed laser rocket arm may still be an option.

(Be honest Patriots fans. You weren't buying the book anyway.)

But, you may prefer to put on your Luke Skywalker by hopping in your personal X-Wing and zooming off to play Star Wars, while exploring galaxies previously unknown with your forever friends. When it comes to Heaven, the possibilities truly are staggering, and so much more joyful than the eternal choir caricature that gets popularized.

Having a clear picture of Heaven does much to clarify how we should be spending our time on Earth — the first time around. Christians are properly focused upon doing all they can to help as many people as possible find their way to Heaven. What's often lost in that passionate pursuit, however, is the importance of the training that Heaven bound sojourners are receiving in the here and now — training that goes far beyond how to get one's ticket to Heaven punched. As a leader, I'm particularly interested in what God will be looking for in the rulers He will appoint on the new Earth:

> *"Then the sovereignty, power and greatness of the kingdoms under the whole Heaven will be handed over to the saints, the people of the Most High. His kingdom will be an everlasting kingdom, and all rulers will worship and obey him" (Daniel 7:27).*

Now, let's juxtapose the above passage with what Jesus taught us about Heaven during His Sermon on the Mount as recorded in these select verses from Matthew 5:3, 5 and 10:

> *"Blessed are the poor in spirit, for theirs is the kingdom of Heaven." (Matthew 5:3)*
>
> *Blessed are the meek, for they will inherit the Earth. (Matthew 5:5)*

Blessed are those who are persecuted because of righteousness, for theirs is the kingdom of Heaven (Matthew 5:10).

Note that the poor in spirit and the persecuted because of righteousness receive the kingdom of Heaven, while the meek inherit the Earth. Are the meek getting short-changed? Hardly. Once the new Earth arrives, the kingdom of Heaven will reside upon it. Heaven and Earth become one, thereby fulfilling what Jesus intimated in the Lord's Prayer when he said, "Your kingdom come, your will be done, on Earth as it is in Heaven" (Matthew 6:10).

I confess to being mildly disappointed that our ultimate eternal destiny is right back here on planet Earth. As wondrous as it is, I've hoped for more…and believe there is much more. It just warps my brain trying to grasp it. I can somewhat grasp Heaven on Earth. So, to inherit the Earth is to receive the kingdom of Heaven.

Chapter 3

4. Leading vs. Taking a Walk

As a leader, I'm keenly interested in how my life on this Earth is preparing me for life on a new Earth under Jesus' reign. The Sermon on the Mount strongly suggests those things that seem to be holding me back today are the very things that are preparing me for ultimate leadership in God's kingdom.

Take persecution, for example. Precious few American Christians today, though increasingly discriminated against in their workplaces and the hallowed halls of government, can claim to be the bona fide victim of persecution, at least not relative to our brothers and sisters in less tolerant countries such as those in the Middle East. To the horror of a watching world, the evil Islamic State of Iraq and Syria (ISIS) has been terrorizing Christians in Northern Iraq and Africa since 2014, forcing many followers of the Cross to choose between death and converting to Islam. This, while beheading their children. It would not surprise me in the least to find some of these martyred saints in very high positions of leadership within the kingdom of God. Meek fathers and mothers cut down with their children on the old Earth could very conceivably be charged with leading millions of lesser persecuted saints in the new Earth. The meek shall indeed inherit the Earth.

Credit leadership guru John Maxwell with the following quote that has haunted me in recent years:

> *"He who thinketh he leadeth and hath no one following him is only taking a walk."*

Since the Great Recession hit in 2008, my tribe has systematically decreased. Ambassador Solutions has struggled to find a new way through the highly competitive jungles of I.T. At many points, my confidence has been shaken to the core. While hacking through those high-tech jungles with a dull machete, I've often turned around to find no one following, leaving me to wonder if I was merely taking a walk. Had I lost my leadership mojo?

When a leader just can't figure out what hill to take or how to take it, he begins to doubt everything he thought he ever knew about himself, at least every good thing. Ever the early riser, while waiting for his life giving first cup of coffee, he notices the all too familiar sign on the fridge—Same S*#t, Different Day. He stares at the stranger in the mirror and proceeds to shave the dumbest American. His fruitless days end in anxious exhaustion. He mutters pitiful sounding prayers and repeats well-worn verses into his sweat-soaked pillow.

    Being a leader can be very challenging. Being a lost leader can be devastating.

Chapter 4

5. Hubris: How the Mighty Fall

In his book, How The Mighty Fall, Jim Collins describes the Five Stages of Decline that once-mighty companies go through on their way out of business. Stage 1 is "Hubris born of success." Collins' research team observed that "Luck and chance play a role in many successful outcomes, and those who fail to acknowledge the role luck may have played in their success — and thereby overestimate their own merit and capabilities — have succumbed to hubris."

Collins' research strongly suggests that the end of a great business begins when its leaders become overly full of themselves. While the road to humility is paved with humiliation, the road to hubris is adorned with palm branches, confetti born of press clippings and starry-eyed sycophants. Trips down this corporate version of Wisteria Lane (think Desperate Housewives) often end badly for both the businesses and their leaders who take them there (think Merrill Lynch).

I'm certainly no former mighty, now fallen titan of business. Our humble company was far from making Collins' research list, and Jim didn't ask me which companies should be on it. However, I think all business leaders (all leaders, for that matter) should pay close attention to both sides of the success coin. Most exhaust themselves getting their companies from survival to good, to great, while ignoring the telltale signs that a company could be headed the other way. As I ponder telltale sign #1 (hubris), the loud voice of my former boss still rings in my ears.

You'll hear later about how I went from hero to goat in my former job and was subsequently fired. In a meeting with my boss just a few weeks prior to that, he got very exasperated with me. The question he asked me at the height of our emotional exchange — Why are you so damned arrogant? — is one I've asked myself many times since. The seeds of hubris are apparently planted deep within my seemingly humble heart. It never ceases to amaze me how a little taste of success can find me strutting around our office like the only rooster in the barnyard.

Mind you, this isn't *entirely* a bad thing. Like Babe Ruth before them, every true sales guy knows that strike-outs are prerequisite to home runs…and more plentiful. So, celebrating the singles in between is appropriate and healthy. But, when we celebrate the singles as if they are home runs, we realize that hubris can spring up like a weed at any time, choking the life out of our team.

From the diamond to the gridiron, consider who's lined up on the other side of the ball when our foolish pride finds its way into the playbook:

"God opposes the proud, but gives grace to the humble" (James 4:6).

Pride is like calling an end-run around the God of the Universe—a play that will not likely end well. Humility, however, is like calling a "flea flicker" while telegraphing the play to the opposing defensive captain (a.k.a. God of the Universe). He then directs all of the defenders to gang tackle the halfback just after he's lateralled back to the quarterback. With no defenders near him, the humble QB has all the time he needs to throw a perfect pass to the wide-open receiver for the game-winning touchdown. And the crowd went wild!

That, football fans, is grace in action. And that is something truly worth celebrating. Who wants to join me in the "Super Bowl Shuffle"?

Why is pride a problem? Because it puts you and God on opposing sides. Humility, however, puts you in position to receive much more than you could ever deserve. That's called grace. Without grace in large daily dose, you're toast.

Understanding this in the depths of his soul, the late Brennan Manning chose to entitle his last book, All Is Grace. Manning was a passionate Christ follower who struggled with alcoholism his entire life. The central theme of his preaching and writings was simply that God loves us just as we are…not as we're supposed to be. I've come to believe that there's more life-transforming power in this single truth than perhaps any other. With it, Manning hit the nail on the head…the one that pierced the Savior of the world. My favorite of Manning's books is Ruthless Trust.

Sidebar: Hubris on the Gridiron

A current sports example of hubris that annoys the tar out of me is when NFL football players celebrate their every move as if they'd just won the Super Bowl. Why would a defender whose team is down by three touchdowns late in the fourth quarter celebrate a tackle as if it was a game changer? And why does his coach put up with such self-centered nonsense? I'm all for celebrating points on the board and the occasional spectacular play, but when nearly every play ends with one or more players strutting around like peacocks on the prowl, it detracts from the game. At least it does for me.

6. My Father's Son One

> *When a man's father dies, any excuse the son has clung to for not being the true man he was meant to be, dies with him.*

I was the first of the four children to leave our father's deathbed. The doctor told us he could linger as long as two weeks. My sister, Marilee, was a college professor on summer break, so she volunteered to stay with Mom and Pop until the end. The rest of us returned to our homes in various states to begin our grieving process and contemplate a life without father. Here's one of Marilee's last journal entries before our father died:

Dad was apparently restless all night long, his confusion increased by the fact that seemingly every nurse who passed through the house was named Mary. In the middle of the night he finally decided this particular Mary [the hospice nurse who stayed overnight that night] was Mary Mulvaney, which seemed to please him immensely, though Mom had never heard of such a person and will wonder forever who the hell she was and why she showed up at my father's deathbed. He babbled quite incoherently that night, whether in response to questions and promptings from Mom or because he was hallucinating I can't know because I wasn't there. Mom claims he was frantic about some thirsty children, insisting they had to have water. She was also saying rosaries over him, which still infuriates me but may explain why one of the Marys he talked about was a Virgin and why he announced in the middle of the night that "those Catholics are wrong." Amen, Papa.

"Those Catholics are wrong"? What an odd thing to say as the sun was setting on his life. These, some of his last words, were spoken a few days before his death on August 1, 1991. And, ever true to the script, my father died as he had lived, leaving yet another unanswered question behind. Had he lived beyond his 60 short years, I strongly suspect some answers would have been forthcoming.

Just *what* those Catholics were so wrong about is anybody's guess. My father never was a Catholic nor did he speak ill of those who were. I suspect this odd confession stems from Pop's teenage years when his spiritual pilgrimage took him into a study of Catholicism. Mom says he was close to converting until his father found out what he was up to. His father, Herman Louis Lindemann, known to us all as Hermie, would have none of it. He shamed my dad into renouncing his new found faith. From that day forward, Pop pretty much kept his religious views to himself.

I loved my father dearly and miss him greatly. As an only son, I immediately felt the burden of filling his void upon his passing. I haven't viewed my mother or my three sisters the same since. However, I can no more fill the void Pop left in the hearts of those he left behind than take his place at the piano bench.

My Dad was a very accomplished pianist, though he couldn't read a single note of music. He would endlessly play Broadway tunes, by ear, to the sheer delight of his family and friends. Our fondest memories are of gathering around the piano while Dad played rhapsodically, often into the wee hours of the morning. While we all sang, the girls would add some choreography for dramatic effect. This was our family at its very best.

When the oncologist described Pop's insides as having an "oatmeal consistency," we knew it wouldn't be long. We could prolong the inevitable or we could take him home to die in peace and dignity. We chose the latter.

Cancer is an insidious killer that touches nearly every family at some time or another. The only good news that comes with the bad news of cancer is that there is usually time for its victims to settle accounts, make amends and, hopefully, make peace with their Maker. Yet, to no one's surprise, Pop lived his final days as he had lived his entire life — quietly.

Pop's body could no longer process food. Without IVs and a feeding tube, death would likely come by starvation. Oddly enough, in the interim, before a morphine-induced coma commences, many victims can function amazingly well. Pop certainly could.

My father did not require an ambulance when he came home to die. He rode in the front passenger seat alongside me, the driver. The following morning, as usual, Pop was the first one up making coffee and watching the sun rise. This man who had been issued a death sentence to be carried out roughly one week hence was padding about the kitchen as if it were just another Saturday morning. It was eerie, very eerie.

Accounts to settle? Amends to make? Not my Pop. This self-effacing accountant had balanced books to the bitter end and had no enemies. No debts. No enemies. No risk. That was my Pop.

His love for his wife and children was well-affirmed, although each longed to hear him reaffirm it in ways he was incapable of. Since he talked little of his imminent death, it only followed that he would have few parting words for those he would be leaving behind. It was, nonetheless, disappointing to hear Pop offer his last words to the apparently wrong-headed Catholics rather than his heart-broken wife and progeny.

Apparently, Pop wanted to let his fingers do the talking. Once home and comfortably medicated, Pop took his rightful place at the piano for one final curtain call. Delirious from the morphine, my dad could still play the piano better than anyone I'd ever known. He played, while between sobs, we sang. Is it true that one day our mourning will be turned into dancing? There was no dancing that day, yet Pop did go out in glory doing what he did so well and loved so much.

Peace with his Maker? I think so. Like I said, since being run off the road towards Catholicism, Pop would never again be caught for speeding on his spiritual journey. We did talk about such things, while sharing our last ever beer together on his back porch. I somehow delicately asked him if he was sure that he'd make it to Heaven and he somehow gave me the assurance I was looking for. After so many years of silence on such matters, it was awkward and uncomfortable.

When words fail, it's often easier to steal the thoughts of others. Pop seemed particularly moved as I read the following song lyrics to him that day:

Home, by Rich Mullins

And everything You sent to shake me from my dreams,
They come to wake me in the love I find in You.
Now the morning comes and I can see the things that really matter
Become the wings You send to gather me to my home.

I'm going home.

"Hey Pop...."

July, 1991

"Hey Pop, remember that time we went crow hunting on the Ohio River?" I asked to break the tension.

He got a far off look in his eyes and slowly said, "Yes, yes son, I do remember that."

"I'll never forget how silly you looked in that funny hat and that old hand-me-down corduroy coat of Grandpa's. It really didn't matter that you never fired a shot. I just appreciated your willingness to take me even though hunting wasn't exactly a passion of yours."

"I was happy to do it, son."

"I know you were, Pop. I know you were."

"Hey Pop, remember that time we went fishing on that lake about an hour north of town? We rented a row boat. Just the two of us. Did we catch any fish that day, Pop?"

"I don't know, son. I can't remember."

"Me neither. No matter. Just being with you on that lake amongst the lily pads was enough."

Truth was, Pop didn't really take me hunting or fishing. I took him. He truly could not have cared less about such things, yet he loved his only son enough to be dragged along for the ride. I loved him for that.

As Pop sipped his beer, I watched it run down a tube coming out his side and into a bag hanging by his leg. The lump in my throat was so large; I could barely swallow my own beer. Is this really happening? Is my father really dying? Is this really the last beer we'll ever share together? Although my heart was breaking, I somehow managed to keep it together…until it was time to say goodbye.

The last time I saw my father was when he walked me to my car parked in the driveway of his Phoenix home. As we said our final goodbyes, there was no holding back the tears.

"I love you, Pop."

"And I love you, son."

Choking on emotions, I said, "I don't know what to say, Pop."

"How 'bout… 'see ya' later'?"

"Yeah, I guess that's right. See ya' later, Pop."

"See ya' later, son."

I'll never forget that day. That was the day the music died in my life. Pop was 60 years old. I was 34. Neither of us was old enough.

We took Pop home to the sleepy Southern Indiana river town he grew up in. I also grew up in New Albany until we moved north near the end of my eighth grade. Every time I return, I'm reminded of what a true hick

Chapter 6

from the sticks I used to be, or perhaps still am.

Before moving to Phoenix, Mom and Pop lived in a condominium on the eastern shore of Lake Michigan in the quaint harbor town of Safe Haven. One of Pop's favorite pastimes was to walk the beach collecting "beach glass." To qualify, beach glass had to be sufficiently worn by the sand and the water so that it no longer had any sharp edges. It came in a variety of colors with green being the most common and cobalt blue being the most precious. Pop kept his treasures in a large, hollow glass sculpture of a whale. When it came to collecting beach glass, my Pop was the master.

The Dunayczans were some of my parents' best friends at the lake. I wasn't surprised to see them at the funeral home, and only mildly surprised when Paula pulled a small plastic bag filled with beach glass from her purse. With both a tear and a twinkle in her eye, Paula took the glass out of the bag and placed it in Pop's sport coat pocket. She gingerly patted the pocket and walked away from the casket.

In passing, she placed a consoling hand upon my shoulder and, with a tearful wink, said, "Buried treasure." I looked over to see her husband, Fred, balling like a baby. I don't recall having ever seen a grown man cry so uncontrollably. Perhaps he was grappling as much with his own mortality as the loss of his friend? Odd. Funerals are indeed quite odd.

My wife of 15 years had never met Robin, a southern flame from my junior high days. I suppose she came to Pop's funeral to see just how much she had missed out on. After all, I do believe it was she who had flamed out on me.

"Hey honey, there's someone I'd like you to meet. Elaine, this is Robin, an old friend from my junior high days. Robin, this is my wife, Elaine. My lovely bride of 15 years."

"Hello, Robin. Thank you for coming. It's nice to meet you."

"It's my pleasure, Elaine. I was so sorry to hear about Brad's dad, I just had to come. How long has it been, Brad? 20 years?"

"Yes, I suppose it's been at least that. But, time has been kind to you, Robin. You look as lovely as ever."

"Oh Brad, you always knew how to get to a girl's heart."

"Is that so? That's not exactly what you told me 20 years ago," I said with a chuckle.

"Well, times have changed, Brad. Looks to me like time has been pretty kind to you as well."

Growing uncomfortable with the direction of this conversation, I clumsily try to change the subject.

"Hey honey, I just noticed the strangest thing, you and Robin look very much alike. Why sure enough, you two could be sisters. What do you know about that?"

With that astute observation, I proceeded to parade my wife and my old girlfriend around the funeral parlor, pointing out their many similar features to anyone who would listen.

Looking back, I must have been in shock. I don't think even *I* am that dim-witted under normal circumstances. Robin seemed amused, if not flattered. Elaine, on the other hand, began planning another funeral....

During the grieving process, you long to remember the good times and forget the ever-present ache surrounding the hole in your heart. You can't do enough of either. While the memories fade, the heartache lingers. What did Pop smell like? How did his whiskers feel against my face? Dear God, will I ever feel whole again?

When a man's father dies, any excuse the son has clung to for not being the true man he was meant to be, dies with him. Along the masculine journey, there are many milestones, but only a few defining moments. The death of a man's father is one such moment.

How does a boy become a man in 21st-century America? Many American boys have been set adrift on a cultural sea, continually running their manhood aground on effeminate shores of shifting sands. While working on their softer sides, American males have either forgotten, or increasingly, never been taught, how to become a man.

Our great hunters and strong protectors have been hunted down, captured and encaged in human zoos called office buildings. It's no more natural for a man to spend his days there than it is for a lion to live in a cage. Truly, much of the American dream becomes a nightmare for the American male.

My father was "the man in the gray flannel suit" although he didn't start out that way. Out of college, he went to work for his father in an auto supply business. With little interest in things mechanical and even less in living under his father's shadow, Pop left the business and went back to college for his MBA.

He actually lived on the Indiana University campus in Bloomington for two years, coming home on weekends. I was too young to realize what a gutsy move this was and how great the sacrifices were along the way. I do, however, remember attending his graduation ceremony on a beautiful spring day on the IU campus. I knew I was proud of my Pop that day, but I didn't really understand why.

Pop took his MBA in International Business to Sears Roebuck & Company in the mid-1960s. His first job was that of furniture salesman. On our rare shopping trips, we would stop by to see Pop in the furniture department. I would always ask him what he had sold that day.

One time, Pop told me he had only sold a baby stroller the entire day. Even back then, I'm sure the commission on a baby stroller didn't go very far towards feeding our family of five. Although Mom taught school, I'm still not sure how we managed to make ends meet. But we did and we never felt lacking for anything.

With a penchant for numbers, Pop soon turned his Sears career towards accounting. He hit the road as a traveling auditor in his VW Beetle. He'd arrive home on Friday nights, hot and tired from a hard week on the audit trail. How Mom managed alone through those years, I'll never know.

My baby sister, PJ, was conceived during these difficult times and named after Mom, Patricia Jane. No doubt, Mom and Pop got a bit careless one Saturday night between auditing assignments. They always called PJ the best mistake they had ever made.

Dad's accounts always balanced. I think that's why he gravitated towards accounting. As a business discipline, it was the most predictable and controllable. You might not always like what the numbers tell you, but the numbers, unlike people, never lie.

Whatever a "man's man" is, I'm reasonably certain that my father wasn't. Nor am I. My father never seemed entirely comfortable with his manhood. Don't get me wrong—I'm not referring to sexual orientation. I'm talking about becoming a real man in a real sense and knowing it—for real. I don't think Pop ever quite got there. Many men don't, although my father certainly had his moments, at least from his son's perspective.

Pop was never more of a man to me than when he was swimming in the ocean. He would venture out further than I'd ever dare to, then swim parallel to the beach with seemingly no effort and, to my amazement, no fear. His stroke was flawless. His bronze body glistened in the summer sun. He was brave. He was my father. I was proud of him.

After one such swim in Fort Lauderdale, I remember sharing a chocolate malt with Pop in the hotel coffee shop. It was a rare treat, both the ice cream and the time alone with my dad. I have no idea what we talked about. It didn't matter. That day, it was just me and my dad, together on the soda fountain stools. Nothing else mattered to an eight-year-old son.

As the years went by, what Pop said (or most often, what he didn't say) began to matter more and more to me. With life's stakes getting higher, I sought more fatherly advice than Pop was comfortable dispensing. While Pop "just wanted me to be happy," I had higher aspirations, but was often at a loss for how to get there. He would always hear me out, but in the end, he'd say little to dissuade me from my assumed position.

There were times in my teen and young adult years when I verily wanted to shake my father in hopes of getting some guidance from him. What college to attend? What to major in? What job to take? How to invest? How to raise children? The questions were endless. "I don't know, son" was invariably the answer. Mind you, my father was brilliant. I guess he just never quite believed that what he said really mattered…but it mattered. He mattered. I mattered.

Ironically, the one time that Pop stepped completely outside his comfort zone to give me some advice, he could not have been more wrong. It was when we were in the process of adopting our fifth child, Bradley Louis II. Pop called and, with a quiver in his voice, begged me to reconsider this life-changing decision. He was convinced that I was about to make the worst mistake of my life.

For a brief moment, I was completely undone by Pop's uncharacteristic pleadings. How could God lead us down this stream and then allow my father to so thoroughly muddy the waters? How could Pop strike out the time he stepped up to the fatherhood plate in such a big way?

"God please," I prayed. "After agonizing over this decision, we finally had peace, and now *this*. Talk about mixed signals."

As quickly as they had come, the doubts passed. God had made it abundantly clear to both Elaine and me that her sister's biological child, Samuel, was destined to be our son. So, I was able to accept Pop's advice for the ultimate act of love that it truly was. Though the advice was errant, the love behind it was pure and powerful. I was deeply touched by it.

Pop's early exit from his masculine journey made my own seem interminably long at times. Like an impatient child on a long road trip, I incessantly ask my Heavenly Father, "Are we there yet?" Like most parental road warriors, His response is inevitably the same: "Almost son…almost."

Chapter 6

7. You Can't Do It...We Can't Help

Try as I may, I can't remember a single time during my childhood when my father purposely taught me something. Mind you, I'm quite sure that I've forgotten a few things, perhaps many. One sure example is the fact that he taught me how to swim. However, I was so young at the time that I have no recollection of it. What I do recall is often being left to figure things out on my own.

Before proceeding, I must ask Pop's forgiveness for my poor memory.

"Pop, I'm sure you taught me much more than I can recall. My purpose in writing about it is in no way to cast aspersions upon you. But rather, to shed light upon what it was like growing up as the only son with a self-effacing father who was content to let me find my own way. Now that I'm as old as you were when you went to the great piano bar in Heaven, I am continually amazed at how difficult this masculine journey can be. So Pop, I proceed with love and respect that grow deeper with each passing day as my father's only son."

During our early married years, whenever we'd visit my parents, I would spend the first day playing handyman around their house. I'd grab Pop's tiny red toolbox and set about fixing doorknobs, leaky faucets and whatever else looked like it needed some attention. I'm not sure if Pop didn't notice these things or didn't know how to go about fixing them. But, I was happy to apply what little mechanical expertise I had. Mom always appreciated my efforts, while Dad seemed to have no problem with Son One coming to the rescue.

There weren't a lot of tools in Pop's toolbox and many were 50 plus years old. Mom would occasionally add a screwdriver or a pair of pliers as she was attempting one of her own home improvement projects. I'm not sure Pop ever bought a single tool himself. I am sure that one of the most memorable gifts I ever received was a Craftsman tool box full of wonderful tools with a lifetime guarantee. Though I knew little of how to use them, one of my very favorite things to do on a Saturday morning was to putter around the garage pretending that I did. After getting my driver's license and my grandfather's 1960 Rambler American, those Saturday mornings became turbo-charged.

By that time, I was thoroughly smitten with my bride-to-be. So, while she'd sleep in on Saturdays, I would spend hours transforming my beloved Rambler into one of the sweetest rides in Kokomo, Indiana. At least it was in my mind. After a morning of performing mechanical miracles, I'd shine up the "Oola Mobile" (Oola was my high school nickname for reasons I'm too embarrassed to mention) and drive over to Elaine's house. With a straight six-cylinder engine, my sweet ride wouldn't win many drag races. But with fully reclining bench seats, it was a love boat on wheels. I have very fond memories of Elaine and me reclining while listening to Mac Davis sing "Baby, Baby Don't Get Hooked On Me" on the eight track. Looking back, she may wish she had heeded his advice, though I hope not.

Ah yes, that reminds me of the sacrifice I made to get that eight track tape player rockin' my Rambler. By my low standards, it was one of my bigger projects. To install the speakers under the metal rear deck, I had to drill holes in it. That entailed lying on my back directly beneath where the metal shavings were falling as I drilled. Don't try this at home without eye protection; metal shavings in your eye are no fun. Though it was kind of fun to go to school for the next week with a big ole patch on my eye making up all kinds of stories as to what happened.

I'm pleased to end this chapter by reporting on a recent home improvement project that pushed my craftsman skills several levels beyond cleaning out the garage. My lovely bride the artist has found a new medium that she's very excited about — glass mosaics. To encourage her in this new artistic direction, I repurposed our former guest bedroom (a.k.a. dog room) into a mosaic studio, complete with a four-by-eight-foot craft table custom built by yours truly. Elaine has been over the moon happy with the entire set-up, bragging about her artisan hubby to whoever would listen.

Generational Lessons

You might think that I would have worked hard to teach my three sons many of the things my father never taught me. The truth, however, is that I did little more than my father had done. It's a sad confession, I know. There were probably two primary reasons as to why I repeated the "sins" of my father. First, being self-taught, I didn't think I had much to pass along to my boys. Second, with five children and the prevailing chaos that defined our family for many years, it was just easier to do things myself than it was to take the time and exercise the patience to teach my sons. I deeply regret this sad fact.

Seeing this pattern, I would occasionally seize a teachable moment in a clumsy effort to make up for lost time. On one such occasion, our youngest son, Bradley, had a bunch of his fellow 13-year-old buddies over for a swim. I was having trouble keeping one of our pool umbrella stands from falling over until I came up with the brilliant idea of securing the umbrella stand by attaching it to the outdoor couch leg with a bungee cord. I was feeling pretty proud of my improvised solution and then it dawned on me. I could not only teach these boys the art of improvisation as it related to things mechanical when one lacks both experience and the proper tools, but I could also teach them a new vocabulary word — *improvisation*.

"Hey boys, come over here, I want to show you something. See that bungee cord wrapped around the umbrella stand. You know what that is an example of?" I asked, as if I'm about to unveil the secret of the universe.

"Uh well, Mr. Lindemann, it looks like a bungee cord to me. Am I missing something?" asked Bradley's best friend, Andrew.

"Look closer boys," I said. "There's much more than a bungee cord going on here. What is that bungee cord an example of?"

I paused for dramatic effect. They all looked at the bungee cord, shrug their shoulders, looked at one another as if Bradley's father had ventured a bit too far off the reservation, and then in unison said, "We don't know. What is it?"

"*Improvisation*, gentlemen. That bungee cord is a perfect example of it. 'What's improvisation?' you ask. Well boys, improvisation is what you do when you have a problem to solve but you lack the proper experience and tools to solve it in a traditional way. So, you improvise. If you learn how to improvise, you'll be able to do things that others cannot do. Got it?"

That was over thirteen years ago. To this day, whenever I see one of those boys he invariably reminds me of this goofy lesson in life and vocabulary. "I got it, Mr. Lindemann."

I've always envied guys that were good with their hands. Guys who can actually build things. Prior to Elaine's new craft table, the closest I've ever come to truly building something was when Bradley and I built a go-kart from a kit we bought online. We got-r-done, but within a few months, Bradley had outgrown it. Determined to redeem our all-too-rare project, I took the cart to a welding shop and had them extend the frame by about a foot. Bradley got a couple of years of fun out of that project before we gave the cart to the son of one of our employees.

Elaine and I have often wondered what life would have been like had we moved to the gentlemen's farm that we frequently talked about. Had I felt the least bit prepared for such a venture, I think we would have done it. But, who was going to teach me how to milk the cows so I could teach our kids? What would I do when the tractor broke down or the fence needed mending? It just seemed like too much of a stretch, so we never got terribly serious about our Green Acres notion. I do, however, think that kids who grow up on farms have a distinct advantage over us city slickers. Though farmers are generally well prepared for most eventualities, they can improvise with the best of them. If a farmer doesn't know how to get-r-done, he knows someone who does.

Most days, my idea of a big project is cleaning out the garage. I usually save such projects for those frustrating times when I can't seem to make any progress in other areas…work, family, finances etc. You know, the small stuff that we tend to sweat profusely over. When I seem to have moved out of life's fast lane and onto a shoulder knee deep in quick sand, cleaning out the garage always helps me to course correct. After a couple hours of garage keeping, I can see tangible results…sometimes for the first time in days, if not weeks. Sounds pretty pedestrian doesn't it? Now you know why I'm so envious of the craftsmen and farmers of the world. I suspect building a backyard shed or mending the fence on the back 40 is infinitely more satisfying than tidying up one's garage. Perhaps I'll find out some day when I take up that hobby Elaine has been pestering me about for a decade or two.

When I drive through our neighborhood, I rarely see children playing outside. Not because there aren't any. There are plenty of kids comfortably ensconced within their suburban McMansions. They're gaming, texting and tweeting their way through their hyper-connected days. Kids today are more likely to suffer from carpel tunnel syndrome than skinned knees or bloody noses. As a grandparent, this is concerning to me.

When my baby boomer generation was growing up, we rode the wheels off our bicycles and only came inside after our exasperated, hoarse mothers called us for dinner. Vacant lots quickly became football fields and baseball diamonds. Driveway basketball hoops were worn out by constant play, often in the dead of winter. If there wasn't snow on the driveway, we were hoopin' it up. If there was, then we were off to the nearest frozen pond for a pick-up game of ice hockey.

Today, according to KidsHealth by Nemours, one out of three American kids is considered obese. Inactivity and poor diet are the primary culprits. Certainly this physical health toll is cause for alarm. However, I'm even more concerned about the mental, emotional and social development issues these digitally isolated kids are likely to face. What becomes of a society whose citizens would rather text than talk to one another? How will we then live when our youngsters prefer personas to real people? If infants die for lack of human touch, what happens to entire generations of children who never learn how to engage in productive face-to-face dialogue?

Since 1978, I've supported a large family by riding the waves of technology that have roared through the American economy. And of course, there's nothing inherently evil in that technology. I'm all for it.

But I'm also all for our kids taking their hands off the keyboards long enough to get some dirt under their fingernails. Every kid needs a regular dose of the great outdoors whether it comes via organized sports or just good dirty fun around the neighborhood. Most parents will have to work pretty hard to see to it that their children balance their digital diet with regular doses of physical activity. What once came naturally is now counter-cultural.

As a grandfather, I intend to focus increasing amounts of time and energy to helping my grandkids enjoy wholesome outdoor physical activities like hiking and camping. Never having done such things myself growing up, I've been slow to the campfire. But, I'm picking up speed and look forward to making some great outdoor memories with my grandkids.

Chapter 7

8. Pacer, Buster and the John Muir Trail

When my best friend, Tim (trail name Pacer) told me he wanted to hike the entire 210-mile John Muir Trail (JMT) in California, I thought he'd already spent too much time at high altitudes. I frankly couldn't see the fun in going three weeks without a shower and eating every meal out of a foil dehydrated food pouch, while torturing a body that's already seen its better days.

To prove my point, I agreed to join Tim and his wife, Kathy, for a one-week warm-up hike during the summer of 2013. I left that mini-adventure convinced that Pacer needed to check the JMT off his bucket list and add something a little less rigorous and time consuming. Something like, oh I don't know, like climbing the Matterhorn, perhaps?

Ever the gluttons for punishment, Tim and Kathy stayed on the trail several days beyond my departure point. I'll always remember my torturous solo hike down to Yosemite's lower valley on my way back to civilization. Between my overweight, ill-fitted backpack and the brand new hiking boots that all the reviews said didn't need to be broken in (not!), every descending step sent shock waves of pain throughout my body.

And of course, I missed a critical turn and ended up mistakenly going down the very steep Mist Trail along the Vernal Falls just as the day hikers in their flip flops were coming up from the valley. As I passed one such father with two kids in tow, he looked at me and said to his kids, "Look guys, there's the original John Muir himself." I briefly fantasized about tossing Dad over the falls, but snapped back to reality when I then realized that would leave me responsible for getting his orphaned kids back down the trail. At that late stage of the adventure, my body of misery didn't want that kind of company.

You would think that the world's most famous hiking trail would be easier to get to and from than it actually is. Once down to the lower valley (which, by the way, is sweltering during the peak summer season), I had to catch two buses and a train to get to the nearest airport in Fresno, so I could catch my flight home the next morning. It made for a very long day.

At least I got to enjoy free entertainment during the train ride. I sat next to three unsupervised, screeching adolescent girls who couldn't have been more annoying if they had spent the entire hour scratching a chalkboard with their neon-colored fingernails. I felt older than John Muir and more likely to sprout wings and fly home than to return to the JMT in this lifetime. Pacer was going to have to find another aimless wanderer to share that bucket list adventure with.

Did I mention that Tim was an early retired Cisco sales exec? Like all good ones, he had mastered the art of "dripping" on his prospects until the stars aligned in sales Heaven and it was time to move in for the close. He also understood that half a loaf was better than none at all. So, when it became clear that I wasn't about to join him for his entire three week JMT trek, he started selling the idea of merging in for the final leg of the journey. As my resolve weakened with each drip, Mr. Sales Guy decided to play his ace.

"By the way, brother," Tim said. "Did you know that the JMT ends on top of Mount Whitney, the highest peak in the lower 48 states?"

"Really?" I said, piqued. "How high is it?"

"14,505 feet," he replied, knowing that he had me at "by the way." I suppose more dumb and dangerous things have been attempted in pursuit of petty bragging rights.

Like all great adventures, our JMT sequel was not without its challenges. Our solar charger proved inadequate, so we missed a lot of great photos due to dead batteries. When our phones were charged, we had no cell coverage, so we were quite literally off the grid for 12 full days. Pacer lost his reading glasses and broke his Kindle, so he had no reading material or means to read it. Buster (my trail name) was plagued with constant neck stingers and toe blisters that made each step a painful one. Two days and 29 miles from the trail's end, those steps became even more painful when I accidently spilled boiling water on my foot.

Don't try this at home.

The Power of Team Goals

The JMT trek was Pacer's rodeo from the get-go. It was on his bucket list, not mine. I was just the last member of a support team of six who accompanied him at different stages, albeit the longest and most challenging stage. Booyah! Yet, as we pressed on, we became more determined to attain "our" Whitney summit goal than either of us ever would have been had it merely been a personal goal. I found this very compelling and relevant to the business of life.

Chapter 8

There could be many reasons why you find yourself leading an under-performing team. They might be lacking challenging team goals and/or have an abundance of conflicting personal goals. Personal goals are great, but Pacer and Buster would tell you that team goals will lead to higher overall performance. I feel certain that I would have left the trail after burning my foot, but for my intense desire to summit Mount Whitney with my best friend. We started our trek in pursuit of his personal goal. But, as his goal became our goal, nothing was going to stop us from attaining it.

The Longest Day of My Life

The longest day of my life started at one o'clock in the morning on July 21, 2014. Our last night in the tents was a short one at our campsite around Guitar Lake in Sequoia National Park. We wanted to get a very early start on our Whitney summit attempt, hoping to reach the highest peak in the lower 48 by sunrise. This was the first time we had been out and about after dark the entire trip, excepting an occasional need to use the "restroom" in the middle of the night. As we broke camp and hit the trail, I was surprised at how dim Pacer's headlamp was. It was a bit unnerving to see my trail boss inching his way up the mountain aided by the luminous equivalent of a kitchen match.

My fears were well founded. We lost the trail within the first 30 minutes. During the day, no big deal. During the night, while schlepping your way up a very big mountain perilously close to precipitous drop-offs, it's a big deal. So, we did what any self-respecting mountain men would do; we sat down. Fortunately, we didn't have to wait long for brighter lights and brighter minds to arrive.

As we sat waiting in the dark, it occurred to me that as embarrassing as it was, sitting down on the job in the wee hours of our summit morning was probably one of the smartest moves we made during the entire trek. How often do we lose our way in life, then make matters worse by redoubling our efforts despite being misguided and ill-equipped? It's far better to call a time-out, reevaluate the situation, then make the necessary course corrections.

As we approached Mt. Whitney that morning, the attainment of our lofty goal loomed just below the clouds before us. But, at a critical juncture we found ourselves ill-prepared to continue moving towards it. We had to either turn back or find a way around our dangerous dilemma. Turning back was out of the question. It was, after all, our final summit day. So, we sat and waited for the Calvary to arrive.

And arrive they did in the form of a single trekker decked out in all the latest European climbing gear. He was chugging along like the Little Toot That Could with a headlamp that could have illuminated The Grand Canyon. In a mild British accent, he graciously gave us the assurance that we needed and invited us to follow him. In less than a minute, we were back on the trail and Little Toot was back in high gear. It didn't take long for us to lose sight of him.

The whole scene reminded me of another one in the classic film Butch Cassidy and the Sundance Kid. While being hotly pursued by an unknown posse, with a puzzled look on his face, Butch turns to Sundance and asks, "Who are those guys?" Though we never got his name, we'll be forever grateful to Little Toot and his brilliant headlamp.

The Trail to The Top Is Never Straight Up

When you hike the John Muir Trail from north to south, the average elevation is constantly increasing until you reach the highest point at Mt. Whitney. At many points along the way, however, you have to descend in order to continue your ascent. Giving back those hard-earned feet of elevation can be frustrating. Like a good marine, once trekkers take a hill, they want to keep it. But, as with the business of life, the trail to the top is never straight up.

In life and in business, we often have to take a few steps backwards (sometimes quite a few) in order to continue our journey forward. Such times of reassessment and recalibration can be painful, but usually yield long term benefits, making the pain worth the gain. Steve Jobs understood this when he reassumed his CEO role at Apple in 1998. He eliminated far more products than he retained, realizing that the company he founded had lost its way along the high-tech trail. Jobs knew Apple had to descend before it could ascend to the Mt. Everest of business. Some 15 years later, Apple would become the world's most valuable company with a market capitalization just under $600 billion.

If life's trail finds you in perpetual descent mode, don't fight it—right it. First, reassess it. Then, recalibrate it. Then, right it. Along the way, glance upward to see the summit and be reminded that the trail will ultimately take you to the top…though never straight up.

Life's Secret Serendipitous Sauce

Isn't it funny how life's great adventures are so often best remembered by the silly serendipitous moments that occur along the way? I feel certain that when Pacer and Buster reflect upon their JMT trek from their rocking chairs in years to come, top of mind will not be the top of Mt. Whitney. Oh, we'll remember that summit moment for sure (assuming our marbles remain intact), but that won't be the story that we'll tell over and over again. The truly epic stories will be more about *getting* there than *arriving* there.

We were in the middle of our warm-up trek during the summer of 2013. It was the eve of our Half Dome climb, so we made an early camp in Little Yosemite Valley and took a very refreshing dip in the Merced River. Pacer strung a clothesline between the trees where we could hang our wet gear to dry. Prior to the trip, he had highly recommended some high-tech underwear to me, ex officio. He was particularly impressed with their odor eliminating "Microbe Shield" fabric. Pacer made a compelling case, so I purchased three pairs of those odor-eating boxer shorts for the trip—blue, green and black.

As we were milling about the campsite strategizing our big Half Dome climb the next day, I looked over and saw Pacer taking a whiff of my black boxers hanging on the line.

"Dude, you just whiffed my shorts," I said.

"Uh-uh" said Pacer. "Those are *my* shorts."

"No, I'm pretty sure your shorts are over *there* on the other line."

As he looked over to see his fresh-as-a-daisy black ex officio shorts hanging on the other line, we laughed until we cried. To commemorate our trip, I made Pacer a three-dimensional collage that includes a two-headed picture of us wearing a single pair of those now famous black boxers. Yep, I suspect that story will be told 10 times for every one we tell about our Whitney summit experience. Thanks to the secret serendipitous sauce of life.

Life Is a Journey and a Destination

I think Ralph Waldo Emerson was only half right when he said, "Life is a journey, not a destination." It's really both.

As a Christ-follower, I look forward to reaching my ultimate destination in Heaven. Along the way, however, I don't want to be among those who are so Heavenly-minded they're no earthly-good. The Bible makes it crystal clear that what we do with our brief time in this world is vitally important in the one to come. I truly want to make the most of it. In so doing, I want to embrace the joy of the journey. Be it a true mountain top experience or a laugh out loud moment of sweet serendipity, I don't want to miss any of it.

Mom's Journey Ends in the Middle of Mine

Most people believe in some form of after-life. No one this side of it truly knows what it's going to be like. And, there's no shortage of opinions as to how one goes about getting there. There are, however, in my humble opinion many indicators pointing us to a spiritual realm that is as real (if not more so) than anything we experience during our time on Earth. One such indicator came to light about halfway through my second JMT trek with Pacer.

One night while lying in my tent contemplating the fact that we were completely cut off from family and friends, I pondered the fact that I wouldn't even know if a member of my family died while I was on the trail. It was a disturbing thought. In going down the family tree, I realized that my soon-to-be 83-year-old mother with Alzheimer's was the most likely member to take her last breath while I was on the trail. That logical thought was immediately followed by a far more mysterious one — Mom would, in fact, die while I was on the JMT. It was a clear and sacred moment. So much so, I didn't even mention it to my best friend.

Five or six days later, when I was finally able to call my wife from the Whitney Portal at the end of our journey, she said, "I've been trying to reach you for days. I'm sorry to have to tell you this, but I have some bad news."

I said, "I know what it is. Mom died, didn't she?"

"Yes," she said, "I'm so sorry. How did you know?"

"God told me," I said, my voice quivering.

With that, I hung up from the first phone call I'd made in 12 days and officially stepped into my new life without parents. Having lost his own mother in her late forties to brain cancer, Tim fully appreciated the import of the news I shared with him. He gave me a big mountain man hug and

Chapter 8

then the space I needed to cry quietly on the picnic table outside.

Once home, Elaine told me that before I left she had a premonition about Mom dying while I was gone. She didn't mention it because she wasn't fully confident in what she had "heard" and not sure how I'd react to it. With both of us receiving the same message at different time, I'm confident that it was beyond coincidence. I believe it was the Spirit of God communicating in both cases. But why? Did God try to keep me from going on the trip by giving Elaine her premonition? Once there, what was the purpose in letting me know that I'd never see my mother alive again? I wasn't so much troubled by these questions as I was curious. Knowing the answers to these questions could give me some keen insight into the character of God and my relationship to Him.

As I mentioned, learning of my mother's passing was one of many reasons that this day deserved the distinction of being remembered as the longest day of my life. We hiked for 15 hours over 17 miles of very difficult terrain. After that, we paid a young couple $200 to drive us the remaining 120 miles to reach Tim's car.

We were both nearly delirious with exhaustion, but also exhilarated at having checked a big box on Pacer's bucket list. Though bone-tired mountain men, we were mountain men nonetheless. It was an epic celebratory moment, destined to be forever muted by the news of Mom's passing. None of this was a surprise to my Heavenly Father. I call Him Papa.

So, why the double "heads-up" from Papa regarding Mom's death? Let's see...He knew the fragile condition of my mind and body. He loves me beyond words. He didn't want to see our mountain man moment completely spoiled by my melting into a blubbering puddle when Elaine confirmed the news I had already received. That's the kind of thing loving fathers do for kids they're crazy nuts about. That's the kind of thing my Papa does for me. To make sure we knew it was Him, He told both Elaine and me.

Rich Mullins got it so right—our God is an awesome God.

Chapter 8

Chapter 8

9. Ambassador Solutions' Culture

The uniquely inspiring culture of Ambassador Solutions is built upon a firm foundation with a rich history spanning five decades. Our corporate family tree dates back to 1973 with the birth of our "grandparent," Ambassador Steel, in Fort Wayne, Indiana. One of their early partners was also an early partner in our original parent company, Ambassador Leasing. Beyond common ownership, Ambassador shareholders over the years have shared a common commitment to the deep spiritual meaning behind the namesake of each related Ambassador entity. The following describes the owners' deeply held personal convictions and may not apply to any other employees of Ambassador Solutions.

Ambassadors for Christ

The name Ambassador was derived from a verse in the Bible and is the cornerstone of the personal business philosophy that my partner, Max Frodge, and I have embraced for many years:

"For we are ambassadors for Christ, God making His appeal through us" (2 Corinthians 5:20).

Simply stated, this verse says that those claiming to follow Jesus Christ (as Max and I do) are also called to represent Him (as ambassadors) in whatever walk of life they find themselves, including the marketplace. God may then choose to speak and act through His ambassadors to accomplish His purposes. If that sounds the least bit haughty, it certainly shouldn't. Accepting the Ambassador for Christ mantle is one of the most humbling acts anyone can ever do.

Since 1973, Shareholders in every Ambassador entity have sought to serve as "Ambassadors for Christ" — within the marketplaces they served. Today, Max and I truly see our ownership of Ambassador Solutions as a divine calling. However, we are quick to eschew the "Christian company" label that so many ascribe to us. There is no such thing, as only people (not companies) can be Christians. Ambassador Solutions is simply a company owned by Christians, and one that embraces and employs people of a variety of faiths and no faith. We wouldn't want it any other way.

Our Basic Beliefs

Since our founding in 1989, Max and I have periodically pondered the question, "What does it mean to be an Ambassador for Christ?" We've always concluded that the answer begins and ends with people. So, after much debate over many years, in the mid-1990s we adopted what became known as our Basic Beliefs, stating that people:

- Last forever
- Are of immeasurable worth
- Are created in the image of God

Given the religious origins of these beliefs, we knew that they needed further translation. Like IBM, Ambassador needed a set of values to which all employees would be expected to subscribe. So, a few years later, we formulated our **Core Values** (Dignity, Integrity, Excellence). In 2006, we created our **Values in Action** to illuminate our Core Values by illustrating four practical applications of each. While our company Namesake and Basic Beliefs emanate from our deeply held personal convictions as owners, our Core Values and Values in Action must be embraced by all Ambassador Solutions' employees.

Core Values

The Core Values of Ambassador Solutions are etched in Indiana limestone on the lobby wall of our former corporate headquarters. As such, they represent the distilled essence of our uniquely inspiring culture:

- **Dignity** — Nurture the Dignity of All People
- **Integrity** — Pursue uncompromised integrity
- **Excellence** — Deliver excellence

To be an Ambassador teammate is to wholeheartedly embrace our Core Values. They are non-negotiable values to "D.I.E." for. These values serve as our guiding light. While all else might and should change, these values will never change. That's why we etched them in limestone on our lobby wall.

All of our employees know that the quickest way to gain my attention is to challenge our practice of these Core Values. Questions such as, "Will this nurture that person's dignity?" are routinely asked during management meetings. When faced with a particularly difficult decision, we have been known to go into our lobby and literally make the decision while standing in front of the wall with our Core Values upon it. Those values are not on that wall as an outward advertisement, but as a constant internal reminder of how we are supposed to do what we do. Towards that end, every employee is expected to hold every other one accountable to our Core Values...and they do.

The seeds of our Core Values were planted deep within me early in my career. The following three very humbling experiences are not only evidence of that, but did much to shape who I am today.

Values in Action: Dignity

1. Embrace the whole person
2. Humbly serve others
3. Liberally seek and offer forgiveness
4. Recognize weaknesses as strengths taken to extremes

Nurture the Dignity of All People

It was the Thursday before Easter of 1989—the day my boss and former partner handed me my "pink slip" and my head on a platter. As soon as Don came into my office, I knew from the look on his face what he was about to tell me.

"What's up, Don?"

"It's not good, brother."

"What do you mean?"

"I mean...it's not good. I couldn't stop it. Pierre sent me here to tell you that your job has been eliminated."

"You mean I'm fired."

"Yeah," he said forlornly. "You're fired, Brad. I'm sorry."

"It's OK, Don. It's not as though I couldn't see it coming. Pierre hasn't spoken to me since he became president last month. You might say we share a mutual disdain for one another. Besides, this place is going down the tubes, so everybody's going to lose their jobs eventually. I just wish Pierre hadn't gotten to me before I got out of here on my own terms."

"So what are you going to do?"

"I'm close to a deal with some guys back in Indy. If we can finalize things, I'll join them and we'll move back home. Speaking of terms, what are mine?"

"You mean severance?"

"Yeah, what's my package?"

"There is no package, Brad."

"Are you telling me that after five years with this company and the millions I've made for them, they're giving me no severance?"

"I'm afraid so, partner. I know it's not right. I tried everything to convince Pierre that we owed you something, but he wouldn't budge."

"True to himself to the bitter end. When do I get my last paycheck?"

"That's the worst part. You already got it."

"What? Do you mean to tell me that he's going to stiff me out of salary I've already earned?"

"He doesn't exactly see it that way, but yeah, you got it right. He just doesn't care."

Talk about adding insult to injury. I couldn't believe what I was hearing. Just a few years earlier, having won the Eagle Award for salesman of the year, I received a letter from Pierre's boss, the CEO. He was effusive in his praise for me, saying how fortunate they were to have me on their team. Now, I was being ruthlessly terminated in absentia by his arrogant hatchet man. Layoffs are never easy, but it is possible to do them without robbing people of their dignity. I felt more than robbed. I felt raped. A feeling I would never forget.

In fact, I really couldn't forget it, so I wrote the CEO requesting a meeting in a sincere effort to understand why I had been fired. Looking back, it was a naïve thing to do. It was effectively an engraved invitation to the French man with a Napoleon complex to kick me while I was down. Kick me he did…hard. To this day, the cold-hearted and mean-spirited reply I got back from him remains the cruelest thing anyone's ever done to me. I still have the letter, though I'm convinced the Lord hid it from me for many years.

I used to reread the letter occasionally when I was in a self-loathing funk. I'm not sure if I was trying to use it to climb my way out of the mire or drown in self-pity. Either one was a bad idea, so God just "misplaced" the letter for a decade or so. Having recently found it, my hope is to use the letter for more redemptive purposes. I thought about reprinting it here, but couldn't bring myself to do it. Memorializing the letter itself won't help others deal with their own pain and it could clearly add to mine.

What about your pain? What wounds from your past remain open, holding you back like anchor lines on a ship? A few years ago I had the privilege of spending a day with two of my modern day heroes, Pastor Bill Hybels of Willow Creek Community Church and renowned psychologist, Henry Cloud. I vividly recall Dr. Cloud's crude drawing of a ship with many anchor lines tied to things hidden below the surface of the water. He said that those things need to be brought to the surface of our lives one at a time and dealt with in a redemptive manner. If not, we'll eventually find ourselves unable to make any forward progress in life because we remain tethered to too many things holding us back.

By way of a sneak preview, one of our company's Values in Action states that "holding grudges only holds us back." Rest assured, when I penned those words in 2006, the painful letter and its author were in the forefront of my mind. I've confessed my anger towards the author many times over the years. And yes, I've repeatedly forgiven him in prayer. But, I must confess to yet some remaining bitterness that, no doubt, is hurting no one but myself. Perhaps that lingering bitter aftertaste is just God's way of assuring that I never return the favor at someone else's expense? I truly don't know. I do know that even a healed wound can hurt on occasion, no matter how much time has passed.

Our 12 Values in Action essentially put "feet" to our three Core Values (Dignity, Integrity, Excellence). They provide practical guidance for how we can consistently operate in harmony with our values.

Values in Action: Integrity

1. Listen with understanding
2. Speak the truth in love
3. Encourage healthy conflict
4. Do the right thing…every time.

Pursue Uncompromised Integrity

I knew it was the wrong thing to do. But, I wasn't willing to pay the price for doing the right thing. Besides, I gave the customer exactly what he asked for—a fair market value lease extension. Just like we'd done many times before. This time, however, I noticed a purchase option within the original lease granting them the right to buy the equipment for $250,000 less than the cost of the lease extension. I would soon learn that integrity cannot be bought, but it can be very expensive.

It was easy to rationalize not telling the customer about their purchase option. After all, they leased all their computer equipment, not wanting to carry such assets on their books. And of course, when I told my colleagues about my moral dilemma, they were quick to add fuel to my fire of rationalization. "Are you crazy? You would be a fool to tell them," they said. So, I went back to calculating my commissions and never said a word…until 15 years later.

The guilt had become unbearable. Rarely did a day go by without being reminded of my transgression. I knew what I had to do, but the thought of doing it made my knees weak. My former customer was now the CFO of a Fortune 100 company…a very rich and powerful man. What if he demanded restitution…with interest? That would be well over $500,000 dollars! No matter. It was time to pursue uncompromised integrity.

I picked up the phone with trembling hands and made the call. "Hello "Andy," it's been a long time…." Andy was far more gracious than I deserved him to be. He readily forgave me, excusing my actions as "business as usual" for the fast-paced times we were in back then.

Though I knew my ultimate authority wasn't so dismissive of my transgression, I was beyond grateful for Andy's response. As the weight I'd carried for 15 years was lifted from weary shoulders, I lost control of my emotions. Like my Heavenly Father, Andy then became far more concerned with consoling, rather than punishing, me.

Had I not confessed my sin to Andy, it would have continued to rob me of the joy of my salvation, as it had done for 15 long years. The pursuit of uncompromised integrity will lead you to a clear conscience. A priceless commodity that cannot be bought, though it was paid for in full on a cross 2,000 years ago.

Values in Action: Excellence

1. Learn continuously
2. Put team before self
3. Do your best
4. Discover, Invent, Innovate

On Not Delivering Excellence

As is the IBM way, success is typically followed by greater challenges. Having earned Regional Rookie-of-the-Year honors in 1980, I was sent on a mission impossible in 1981. I failed miserably. Worse yet, I copped a major attitude along the way. In the aftermath, the wise words of my branch manager made an indelible impression upon me.

"Brad, I'm disappointed in you, but not because you failed. I'm disappointed because instead of taking a bad situation and making it better, you made it worse. Remember, no matter what situation you find yourself in, you can always find a way to make it better." That wise IBM manager was Dave Thomas who, not surprisingly, went on to become one of their top executives. I have used these same words many times in talking with employees I've managed over the years.

Chapter 9

10. Values in Action

Nurture the Dignity of All People

> *Had I reported to myself over the years, I would have fired employee number one annually given the level of dysfunctionality he brought to the office some days.*

Embrace the Whole Person

We embrace the whole person for both practical and philosophical reasons. On the practical side, we find that no one ever truly leaves their "baggage" at the door, so we help them carry it in. Philosophically, we celebrate the personal and professional growth of all teammates and work with each to overcome obstacles that might stifle that growth.

Had I reported to myself over the years, I would have fired employee number one annually given the level of dysfunctionality he brought to the office some days. Baggage? Are you kidding me? Some mornings I needed a Skycap just to get through the front door. Knowing this about myself has helped me empathize with a wide variety of employees' personal problems.

I recall interviewing a single mom who tearfully told me about the travails of her teenaged son. He had gotten so out of control that she had no choice but to put him in one of those very strict private boot camp like facilities. She was desperately trying to keep him out of the legal system, knowing that once he went down that slippery slope he may never come back.

Having our fair share of experience with rebellious teenagers, my wife and I are very sympathetic and empathetic to parents in such situations. We've felt the self-incrimination and the harsh judgments coming from the "perfect kids" parents. We know how it feels to be loathed by the ones you love so deeply that you'd gladly trade your life for theirs. And as a business person, I well know how difficult it is to focus upon the business at hand when you have a child with one foot over a cliff.

That's why we embrace the whole person…bags and all. Sometimes it helps just knowing that you're not alone and that others have gone before you. Sometimes your co-workers (even your boss) can be the best support system available, particularly in broken family situations. Sometimes it just helps to talk about the things that trouble you the most. Not so much because your listeners will be able to solve your problems. But rather, having been listened to with understanding, you will be better equipped to solve them yourself.

Don't confuse "embracing the whole person" with minding someone else's business. We've been very careful over the years to respect the personal boundaries of our employees. We don't force transparency. We simply make it a safe and sensible way to be should our employees want or need to be so. Otherwise, the burden of keeping one's personal baggage hidden becomes yet one more rock in an already very heavy bag.

You can't expect those around you to be transparent if you're not. People become comfortable with transparency when they become comfortable with and trusting of those around them. In organizations, that only happens when the leaders demonstrate transparency themselves and prove trustworthy to those who follow suit. This aspect of leadership comes quite naturally to me, though like any strength, it becomes a weakness when taken to extremes. To this point, Elaine once asked me, "do you ever have an unspoken thought?" That was many years ago and I'm still trying to come up with my one unspoken thought so I can speak it and remove all doubt.

A former employer once brought his "alcoholic bag" to my attention. His addiction had cost him dearly, but he was on the road to recovery and seeking a new job as a software developer. He could have tried to hide the truth, but his 12 Steps training had taught him otherwise. Because we had a history of trust and transparency with one another, he asked if I would advocate for him with one of our best clients. I gladly did and the client gladly gave him the opportunity he was seeking. That was many years ago and he's been gainfully employed ever since.

Speaking of addictions, this is a problem that impacts every employer of almost any size. Substance abuse is rampant in our country. From alcohol to illegal drugs to illegal use of prescription drugs, increasing numbers of Americans are coming to work in a self-induced fog that renders them marginally effective and poses great risks to their employers. And, these problems are not limited to those in the lower economic strata.

Chapter 10

Billionaire Indianapolis Colts owner, Jim Irsay, was arrested in 2014 for illegal use and possession of prescription drugs. Just weeks before, a female friend of Mr. Irsay's died of a drug overdose in a condo he had purchased for her. Similar tragic tales are playing out in the lives of employees every day, leaving employers with the challenge of how to handle such difficult situations.

According to the Centers for Disease Control and Prevention, nearly 60 percent of the drug overdose deaths in 2010 involved pharmaceutical drugs.[2] This steadily-rising number should send shivers up the spine of employers and employees alike. It's truly hard to believe that more people die every year from prescription drug overdoses (primarily pain-killers) than from hellish illegal drugs like heroin and crystal meth.

This one hits painfully close to home. Several of our children have battled Opioid and Benzodiazepine addictions, while chronic back pain has forced Elaine to use pain-killers far more often than she'd like to. That's why I often pause and pray whenever I hear the current PSA on the radio stating that someone in the United States dies every 20 minutes from a prescription drug overdose. But for the grace of God, there go one of my own.

During our early years, we encouraged each employee to have a Personal and Professional Development Plan (PPDP). It was a sincere effort to meld each employee's personal goals with those of the firm. And occasionally, it was the means by which we identified the impossibility of doing so. Such was the case with Dave Burns, our original People First Director.

Dave did an outstanding job handling the HR function at Ambassador Solutions during the week. But on weekends, he traveled throughout the Midwest as a track announcer on the American Speed Association (ASA) circuit. While going through the PPDP process himself, Dave realized that motorsports was his true passion. So, he sold all of his personal belongings that wouldn't fit into his tiny new apartment in Charlotte where he moved to be near NASCAR's headquarters. Today, Dave covers NASCAR as a pit reporter for ESPN. Though we lost a great employee in the exchange, Dave Burns is proof positive that the PPDP

---

[2] "Opioids drive continued increase in drug overdose deaths," by the Centers for Disease Control and Prevention, February 20, 2013. http://www.cdc.gov/media/releases/2013/p0220_drug_overdose_deaths.html.

process worked quite well.

Humbly Serve Others

We are people serving people. We believe that our best interests are ultimately served by putting the interests of others before our own. Such service includes the giving of our time, talents and treasures (individually and corporately) to those less fortunate. We do this in hopes of improving their quality of life today and their odds for a better life tomorrow. We do this in hopes of doing what we can to change the world for the better.

Since that memorable April Fools' Day in 1989, we've run our business with the absolute conviction that our best interests are served by putting the best interests of our clients, candidates and employees before our own. This can only be done consistently by taking a long-term view of every relationship and every decision. Today's expedient move can lay the traps for tomorrow's unforeseen setback. Maximizing short-term profit can minimize long-term growth.

It's not always easy to determine what's best for all parties. Realizing this some years ago, I started thinking in terms of *God's* best versus *the* best. They are, of course, one in the same, yet framing the issue from God's perspective has really helped mine. After all, most matters of substance call for wisdom that only He can provide, so why not start there?

To humbly serve others, to lead by serving, is a counter-intuitive concept, but one that's been around for millennia. However, the modern concept and phrase "servant leadership" was first articulated by Robert K. Greenleaf in 1970. With the publishing of Greenleaf's first essay entitled "The Servant as Leader," a global counter-cultural leadership movement was born. Today, the Robert K. Greenleaf Center for Servant Leadership is located in Westfield, Indiana, about a mile north of our home in Carmel-By-The-Retention-Pond.

As an employer, I've found servant leadership to be an invaluable and essential practice, though by no means an easy one. To keep my bearings, I simply try to avoid asking employees to do anything that I'm personally unwilling or unable to do.

Pedestrian examples would be:

- If I want folks in the office by 8:00 a.m., then I should be there by 7:59 (I fail miserably here).

- If I expect everyone to take care of their own dirty dishes in the break room, then mine should never be left in the sink. Better yet, while tending to mine I'll also take care of the dishes others have left behind.
- If I need to bum an occasional ride from an employee when my car's in the shop, then I should be willing to return the favor.
- You get the idea.

Some years ago, I crashed and burned while attempting an act of servant leadership. Tom, our CFO, was going in for oral surgery and his wife was out of town. He asked if I'd mind giving him a ride home after the procedure. He couldn't drive due to the anesthesia's after-effects. Since all of my financial affairs have been in Tom's able hands for eight years at that point, agreeing to chauffer him home was as much about self-preservation as it was servant leadership. Tom was appreciative nonetheless.

Tom came out of the dental office looking like he'd been on a three-day bender at a Grateful Dead concert still very much in need of a miracle. (For all you former "deadheads" who got the miracle reference, where were you when I was trying to scalp tickets in my younger days at our local amphitheater?)

Did I mention Tom's a teetotaler? That's why I took such pleasure in the rare opportunity to see him completely schnockered. I think I quipped something like, "I'll have what he's having," to his dental assistant escort. She handed him off to me along with his briefcase, telling me to be sure to hold onto him because he was a bit wobbly.

"Ya' think?" I said as we walked out the door and into the hallway. Tom instinctively reached for his briefcase and just kept right on going, doing a full face plant on the hallway floor. Had it not been carpeted, we would have gone straight from the dental surgeon's office to the ER. I felt terrible, but ole Tom never felt a thing. Much to my chagrin, the next day He did remember falling. But hey, I said I only practiced servant leadership. I never claimed to be very good at it.

Liberally Seek and Offer Forgiveness

When we make mistakes and sometimes offend others, we keep short accounts by liberally seeking forgiveness. When offended, we liberally offer forgiveness to those who have wronged us. Holding grudges only holds us back.

I'd like to say a word about the most famous line from the 1970 movie, Love Story. Before ruining all your fun, however, go ahead and say the line then give yourself a pat on the back if you said, "love means never having to say you're sorry."

To which I say…baloney! Anyone who's been married more than 24 hours knows it just isn't so. It would be more accurate to say, "Love means having to say you're sorry every day of your life and twice on Sundays." At last count, Love Story co-stars, Ali McGraw and Ryan O'Neal, have five divorces between them. Fairly low by Hollywood standards, but likely sufficient to leave them both questioning the wisdom of the line they made famous so many years ago.

While Staples has their "Easy Button," I've got my "Sorry Button." I find myself apologizing to people so often I should probably just tattoo "I'm sorry" on my forehead. Seriously, if there was a prize for most apologies per day, I'd win hands down. But, simply saying you're sorry only gets you halfway back to relational health. A contrite apology needs to be followed with a much more difficult question, "Will you forgive me?"

If you've ever held a grudge against someone for a long period of time, you'll likely agree that "holding grudges only holds us back." It's true that some people are successful in using their grudges as powerful motivators to achieve something they might otherwise have seen as unattainable. But, it's also true that grinding an axe over time will eventually grind you down. For long term health and well-being, it's hard to beat the old "forgive and forget" adage.

A word of caution as you enter into the fragile business of seeking and offering forgiveness. If the other party is unaware of the offense, your attempt to bring healing to the relationship may only bring more hurt to one or both parties.

Say someone has hurt you deeply but is oblivious to that fact. If you offer them forgiveness, their response may only add to your hurt. They might get defensive or attempt to invalidate your feelings by saying something like, "you're just overreacting." If it's something you can't move beyond without some help, then before offering forgiveness, you need to let the offending party know of their offense. Not an easy thing to do, but a necessary first step towards true forgiveness.

What about the reverse situation when you see yourself as the offending party, but the offended one doesn't necessarily see it that way? Or, they're simply not aware of what you did? Like before, the path to forgiveness may require at least two steps. The first step is confession. You start by letting the other party know what you did or clarifying that you think what they know you did was wrong. Then, and perhaps after some time has passed, you can seek their forgiveness if it hasn't already been offered. You'll need to be discerning in these situations to know how much progress towards full relational healing you can make in one exchange.

Recall my story of being ruthlessly fired in 1989 by my former employer, then receiving a cold-hearted letter from the CEO shortly thereafter. I've struggled mightily with forgiving that CEO over the years. I can't honestly say I fully have. To this day, I'm sure he would dismiss the notion that he'd done anything wrong to me. Worse, were I to approach him, he'd likely reopen the wounds he inflicted 27 years ago and add some fresh ones.

If you, like me, need to forgive someone who's hurt you deeply but believes they've done nothing wrong, then do just that. Forgive them. There are three practical steps you can take that may help.

- First, ask a trusted to friend to be a surrogate for the offender. Tell the surrogate how they hurt you and how it made you feel. Then forgive them with no strings attached.
- Second, do the same thing by writing a letter to the offender, but don't send it.
- Third, take your pain to the One who has forgiven you for every wrong you've ever done or ever will do. Exchange your pain for the forgiveness that He freely gives, then in prayer and in your heart, offer it to your offender...no strings attached.

Recognize Weaknesses as Strengths Taken to Extremes

It's easier to overlook and overcome weaknesses when you realize that most often they are merely strengths taken to an extreme.

This is far from an original thought, but one that has proven immensely helpful to me over the years as a manager, husband, father and friend. The reason I like it so much is because it draws us back to positive common ground after a weakness lands us in the mud puddle. Here's how...

Since I'm such an easy target, I'll pick on myself. Truth is, I've got a pretty limited skill set. So, I can do a couple of things fairly well, then there's a steep drop-off in competency.

Most who know me would say I'm a decent, perhaps even gifted, communicator. Yes sir, given enough time, I can talk the chrome off a trailer hitch. And given the right ingredients, I can whip up a pretty mean omelet. Beyond that, there's a long list of better qualified people to do whatever the situation calls for.

So, how might my communications strength become a weakness? Zig Ziegler tells a related story that I often tell on myself. It's about a little boy who asks his Dad a question to which Dad replies, "I really don't know, son. Have you asked your Mom?" The son deadpans, "I really didn't want to know that much about it." It probably won't surprise you to know that I'm much more like the mother than the father in Zig's story. My leaning is towards the whole loaf when a single slice would have suited you just fine.

To illustrate the power of the "extreme strengths = weakness" formula, pretend you're my manager and we've just gotten out of a meeting during which I talked the chrome off of three trailer hitches and a nice set of mag wheels. Feeling you can't let this teachable moment pass, you pull me into your office and say, "Brad, how do you think the meeting went?" Still on an adrenaline high from having just summited Mt. Gushmore, I say, "Geez boss, I don't think it could have gone any better. The team really seemed engaged and fired up. How 'bout you?" Just the opening you were looking for. "Have a seat, Brad. I've got a few things I'd like to share with you."

"Brad, you're one of the most gifted communicators I've ever known. Our firm has benefited greatly from those gifts. The way you rallied the troops during our last annual meeting was truly awe-inspiring.

"The meeting we just got out of however…not so much. The team was fired up all right, but not in a positive way. They were mad because you talked so much they couldn't get a word in edgewise. You were so mesmerized with your own words, you had no interest in what anyone else had to say. I'm afraid your communications strengths were taken to extremes today, Brad. I just wanted you to be aware of it, so you can dial it back a notch or two next time. Make sense?"

You bet it makes sense. It makes perfect sense to take someone who's fallen into the weakness mud puddle back to their point of strength before attempting to work on their weakness. After all, it's much easier to throttle back something you're really good at than to muster a strength from something you're not so good at.

I've used this approach during many coaching sessions with employees over the years. It makes otherwise difficult conversations much easier, leaving the employee feeling valued instead of chastised. I won't go into it here, but the applications to other relationships are obvious. The next time your spouse does something that makes you want to put a fork in your head, retreat to his/her underlying strength and start moving towards marital harmony.

Listen with Understanding

We believe that the highest compliment we can pay to someone is to listen with understanding, while listening poorly can be highly offensive.

I've heard my friend, Dr. Tim Gardner, speak on many occasions. I wholeheartedly agree with his thought-provoking mantra—"The heart cry of every person is to know and be known and to love and be loved." I further believe that knowledge of and love for another human being begins by listening with understanding to their heart cries.

We "gifted communicators" have to work extra hard at listening with understanding. Though God gave us two ears and one mouth to be used in proportion to on another, we're prone to enter most conversations with earplugs and a megaphone. Talk truly is cheap, while listening is priceless. To truly listening with understanding is some of the hardest work you'll ever do.

Recall my story about the man who led me to Jesus. Tom was a very gifted communicator. Though an eloquent and powerful speaker, it was Tom's superbly tuned listening skills that truly set him apart. He was one of those rare people who could make you feel like you were the only person in the room...make that on the planet. To have a conversation with Tom was to be the center of his universe. As a result, we became very close friends during the year that I was privileged to be under his tutelage. That was 41 years ago. I can say without hesitation that I experienced more personal growth during that year than any since. Why? Because Tom listened to me with understanding, then spoke the truth in love into my heart, mind and soul. Speaking of...

Speak the Truth in Love

To speak the truth in love is to communicate accurately with proper motive and with the best interests of our listeners at heart. There is no middle ground between honesty and dishonesty—to deceive is to be dishonest.

Ambassador Solutions had some healthy conflict amongst the management team regarding the wording of this Value in Action. Some felt that using the word "love" in a corporate context was inappropriate. Others objected to the fact that "speak the truth in love" was a direct quote from Ephesians 4:15 in the New Testament. Heretofore, we had purposely avoided scripture references. We needed to be able to hold our employees accountable for upholding our values without fear of religious discrimination accusations. But, try as we may, we simply couldn't find a better way to say what we wanted to say.

In crafting this Value in Action, we wanted to address two primary concerns. First, we wanted to dismiss the notion that there are shades of the truth. We don't see it that way. We believe that only shady people shade the truth. Secondly, we wanted to embrace the notion that communicating the truth properly often calls for great sensitivity and wisdom. Many factors are to be considered, such as timing, location, method, body language, presence of others, etc.

Long before we codified "speak the truth in love" I had an opportunity to put that value into action. "Michelle" was very warm and compassionate person. She truly loved people and went out of her way to help them in any way she could. As a recruiter, she had the prerequisite heart for people that the job requires. However, it also requires a head for business, something Michelle had, but too often allowed her big heart to override. She would spend far too much time with sub-par candidates who were often out of work for good reason. Michelle was costing us precious time and money that we couldn't afford to lose. It was time to speak the truth of termination to this highly valued employee.

I thought it best to have this tough conversation outside the office. So, we took a short drive around the lake nearby. Knowing of Michelle's strong faith, I played a song for her that had deeply impacted me. The title seemed apropos enough: "God Is In Control." I told Michelle how much I appreciated all she had done for our firm and for me personally. We talked about the heart/head balance needed for recruiting success and how her heart was actually holding her back. I encouraged her to follow her heart to a career that would be a better fit. After a few tears and a prayer, we ended our employee/employer relationship.

That was 22 years ago and I haven't seen Michelle since, though we do stay in touch via Facebook. She went on to spend some time in the mission field, got a degree in counseling and became a licensed therapist. My sense is that it hasn't been an easy road for Michelle. Putting one's heart on the line for people rarely is. However, I have no doubt that it was the road she needed to go down and speaking the truth in love helped her do it.

Encourage Healthy Conflict

We encourage an open exchange of ideas and the healthy conflict that naturally follows from discussing matters of substance. We believe that unanimity is rare and therefore rarely required; while unity is essential once an issue has been fairly debated.

In his seminal book, The Five Dysfunctions of a Team, Patrick Lencioni contends that the absence, not the presence, of conflict is the death knell of any organization. I couldn't agree more. The reason is simple yet profound. Absence of conflict indicates the absence of caring. Why argue about what's going on within the organization when all you really care about is what you'll be doing after the five o'clock bell?

A few years ago, a major client hired us to build a mission critical system for them. Given the high-profile nature of the project, the client's executive sponsor was monitoring our progress very closely. One day he called me to strongly suggest I should attend the next project status meeting. I said I'd be happy to and asked him why he wanted me there. He said, "Well, we're going to be speaking the truth in love and more than likely we'll be engaging in healthy conflict."

I said, "You're talking my language, Mike. I'll see you at the meeting."

As it turned out, the meeting went just as Mike had predicted. At issue was a six-figure change order on the project. The client very much wanted our company to perform the additional work at no additional charge. However, what they were asking us to do was clearly beyond the original scope. Once both parties spoke the truth in love and engaged in some very lively healthy conflict, the matter was settled. The client agreed to approve the change order. Would they have still rather had the additional work for free? Of course, who wouldn't? But, this is a great example of our values truly in action when the stakes were very high. It's also a great example of how important communicating your values to your customers can be…assuming you're operating in harmony with them.

Do the Right Thing . . . Every Time

We are committed to doing the right thing every time with our Core Values and Values in Action as our guide. When we fall short and do the wrong thing, we make it right.

It may sound a bit extreme to say that we virtually always know what the right thing to do is, but we do. And, I'm including you in "we." I'm not referring here to typical business decisions like what new products to launch, what markets to enter or exit and who to hire to make it all happen. No, I'm referring to matters of ethics, morals and values. So long as you're clear on what your ethics, morals and values are, what you should do is usually pretty clear in light of them. In our experience, the proverbial "moral dilemma" is a rare occurrence once your morals have been clarified, memorialized and agreed upon.

This Value in Action was put to the test in several ways after making a very poor consultant hiring decision. This particular mistake was all on me and once again validated a lifelong pattern; most of my mistakes have been made in a hurry.

In our rush to meet the client's need, we forgot to do a background check on our new consultant. Had we done so, law enforcement later assured me that we would not have hired this individual. Enter part B of doing the right thing: "When we fall short and do the wrong thing, we make it right."

When we provide a consultant to perform staff augmentation work for a client, supervision of that consultant is the client's responsibility. Such was the case with the deeply disturbed consultant we had unwittingly introduced into our client's environment. So, when they refused to pay for two months' of billable work, we could have challenged them on the basis that supervision was their responsibility, not ours. However, but for our inexcusable hiring mistake, their supervisory challenge would not have existed. Ergo, writing off the entire two months of billings was the right thing to do, so we did.

That decision was much easier than those regarding our troubled consultant's termination process. Mind you, this person had just caused me the most professionally embarrassing situation of my entire career. I was more than a bit upset by it. So much so that I'm uncharacteristically leaving out many details herein. I would literally break out in a cold sweat whenever I checked the email folder reserved for the frequent e-missiles launched by our troubled employee at me and our client. It was a nightmare.

Our first Core Value, "Nurture the Dignity of All People" was immensely helpful in my efforts to end this nightmare. Though this person had made major withdrawals from my personal dignity account, I was determined to make some deposits in theirs. While those e-missiles often contained very derogatory names for me and our client, we resisted the urge to return fire. Sticks and stones break bones but words can destroy a soul. To engage in name calling would have been a blatant violation of our Dignity value.

We did, however, face one of those rare moral dilemmas when it came to our troubled former employee's unemployment claim. Since we had terminated this employee for multiple causes, we could have denied their claim to unemployment. However, since this person was either mentally ill and/or had a very debilitating addiction problem with no support system around them, they were going to be receiving state and federal aid for the foreseeable future. Unemployment would be the first and least expensive form, so after much discussion with our CFO, we decided to let the claim go through. If we made a mistake, we did so erring on the side of grace and compassion, so we have peace with the decision.

Deliver Excellence

Learn Continuously

We believe in lifelong learning for teammates and clients alike. We consider "teaching our teammates/clients to fish" (rather than fostering an unhealthy dependency upon us) to be an important part of the work we do.

One of the many benefits of being a lost ball in high tech weeds all these years has been to be surrounded by true IT pros for whom lifelong learning is a way of life. You can't survive in the technology industry without continuing education along the way. However, outsiders would be amazed at how little sales guys like me understand about the underlying technology they're selling. Those who know me aren't the least surprised to hear me say that.

Since entering the IT industry in 1978, I've actually never sold one byte of technology. I've simply been selling the services of really smart folks who understand the technology whilst remaining comfortably clueless as to the ingredients within the acronym soup du jour. I understand people who understand technology.

Have you ever been around brainiacs who think the way to make themselves irreplaceable is by hoarding their knowledge? Getting useful information out of them is akin to lancing a boil. Yuck!

I find such people insufferable. That's why I tell our clients that they're paying us for everything between our consultants' two ears. And, I tell our consultants it's their responsibility to share whatever useful knowledge they have with our clients—everything. Withholding knowledge from clients creates an unhealthy dependency that inevitably leads to bitterness and resentment. By giving them more than what they're paying for, we hope to leave them with a sweet, not bitter, taste in their mouths at the end of an engagement.

To date, I've been unable to provide anything akin to my IBM educational experiences for our own employees. I truly hope our second quarter century will afford us more opportunities to do so. Turnover within the traditional IT consulting industry is such that we're forced to recruit folks who already have the knowledge and training we need versus providing it to them. We're happy to fill in the gaps for those whom we believe to be in IT with us for the long haul, but they need to have most of the prerequisites coming in. As such, we rarely hire someone fresh off the college campus, though I long for the day when we can.

I received my MBA from Taylor University in 2008, 30 years after receiving my BS in Business from Indiana University. It was the achievement of a longstanding goal and one of the most fulfilling things I've ever done. I did it for pure joy of learning and for the great fun of mixing it up with fellow students who were the ages of my children. It's true—to feel young, hang out with those who are. The highlight was a required 10-day trip to Great Britain (Ireland, Scotland, England) during which we visited six different companies, including my personal favorite, Waterford Crystal in Ireland.

Elaine joined me on our MBA class trip, though I nearly lost my lovely lass in Ireland. To this day, we have conflicting stories as to how she ended up walking the streets of Dublin alone at night with no money, credit card or any form of ID. You know the kinds of stories I'm talking about. The ones where the villain (that would be me) gets more evil with each version and the scene gets ever more frightening. I suppose the final version will cast me as the Anti-Christ and Dublin as "Ground Zero" for Armageddon.

Truth be told, the lass walked away from the lad on that ill-fated

Dublin night. Just sayin'. Glad you made it back safe and sound, sweetie!

Put Team Before Self

We believe that we can accomplish more together than any one of us could ever accomplish alone. While we do not believe that winning is everything, we do believe that consistently doing our best in a winning effort is vital to long term success.

You may not yet believe in miracles, though one day you will. But, if you're a hockey fan and old enough to remember the 1980 Winter Olympics in Lake Placid, New York, you witnessed a "Miracle on Ice." Perhaps you've seen the movie by that title chronicling the amazing story of Team USA capturing the gold medal against all odds? Sports Illustrated named this "one freezing moment" Top Sports Moment of the 20th Century in 1999.

So, without checking your smart phone, can you name one player on that gold medal winning hockey team? I doubt that one in 100 Americans can. Why? Because the "Miracle on Ice" was perhaps the greatest team effort in the history of sport...and there is no "I" in team.

Everyone loves to be part of a winning team. That's why tonight I'll be glued to the tube watching our beloved Indiana Pacers take on the Atlanta Hawks in a "do or die" game seven of their first-round NBA playoff series. Never mind the fact that the number one-seeded Pacers should have dispensed with their southern nemesis in no more than five games. So, why are there so many rabid sports fans around the world? Because even when we're losing at home or in the office or in the classroom or in relationships, our favorite teams give us a shot at winning. And, everyone loves to be part of a winning team.

As a swimmer, I grew up idolizing Mark Spitz. How appropriate to my story that he made Olympic history by winning seven gold medals in the 1972 Munich Olympics, the summer I met my lovely bride-to-be. Spitz's record would stand until the 2008 Beijing Games when Michael Phelps grabbed an unbelievable eight gold medals. But for Jason Lezak's epic anchor leg on the Men's 4 by 100 Freestyle Relay, Michael Phelps would be forever tied with Spitz with seven golds.

I've watched the video of that amazing relay dozens of times and still can't get through it without getting teary-eyed and a lump in my throat. What's up with that?

With 25 meters to go, the announcers had all but hung the silver medal around the necks of Team USA's relay members, predictably succumbing to the trash-talking French team. After all, their arrogant anchorman, Alain Bernard, was the current world record holder in the 100-meter freestyle. But then, the Frenchman starts to fade and Jason Lezak starts to look like a human hydro-plane powered by rocket fuel. He swims the fastest 100 meters in history, out-touches Bernard by .08 seconds and then fades into the background as Michael Phelps is soon immortalized as the greatest Olympian in history. Most Americans know who Michael Phelps is. Few could tell you who Jason Lezak is. I'll never forget either, because both inspire me to go for the gold even when it looks like I'll have to settle for silver. That's what's up with that.

"Winning isn't everything. It's the only thing." This famous sports quote is widely and wrongly attributed to Vince Lombardi, legendary coach of the Green Bay Packers. The quote actually originated with UCLA Bruins football coach, Henry Russell "Red" Sanders, who first said it in 1950.

Regardless of who said it, I couldn't disagree more, though I recognize that it has often been used as an effective locker room motivational tool. Just because a statement is motivating doesn't make it true.

It's equally untrue to say that "winning doesn't matter." Winning matters greatly in many walks of life well beyond the athletic field. Like many, I believe that the greatest benefit of pursuing athletic victories lies in what one learns from such pursuits and how those lessons can be applied in other walks of life.

Perhaps the most valuable lesson of all is…put team before self.

Discover, Invent, and Innovate

We believe investigating our curiosities leads to discoveries, inventions, and innovations that improve the world around us. To unleash individual and collective creativity we must have the courage to test new ideas, confront possible failure, and discard obsolete ideas.

Back in the dot-com crazy days, I was determined to leverage our technical prowess into the next Google. I started thinking about how technology might be used to relieve some of the bottlenecks within our business. One of the biggest was the reference-checking process. It's the bane of every recruiter's existence. Chief among the many problems within the reference checking process was the fact that most employers have policies prohibiting employees from giving references on former employees. So, we came up with a solution to most of the reference checking problems. We called it 3references.com—the world's first and only clearinghouse for job references via the Internet.

3references.com represented our "field of dreams" so we built it, but they didn't come. To this day, I think it was a pretty darn innovative idea. The idea was to record reference giver voice responses to a list of standardized questions, then give prospective employers online access to both their verbal and numerical rating responses.

So, if out of 15 questions, a reference giver rated the candidate 9 out of 10 on all but one question rated a 5, the reference checker could go straight to the 5-rated question to determine if it's worth the time to listen to the rest of the responses. Slick huh? We tried selling it to Monster.com and CareerBuilder.com, but never got very far. I've been looking for the next field of dreams ever since. Even spent some time praying about it.

FocusOnPrayer.com never got built, but we did a pretty thorough analysis of the possibilities while coming up with a rough design. The vision was huge and the life-changing potential was incalculable. Just think about something in your own life that you prayed fervently for…or perhaps still are. It could be for the health of a loved one or the strength to survive their loss. It could be for that big promotion or for a desperately needed job. It could be for relief from chronic pain or the will power to overcome the debilitating addiction that came with it. It could be for the future spouse of your dreams or the end of a marital nightmare. When it comes to prayer, it could be for an infinite variety of things.

I don't profess to fully comprehend the mystery of prayer. And, I'm pretty skeptical of anyone who does. The notion that my feeble requests can literally prompt the creator God of the universe to action is beyond mind-boggling. Yet, my own life experiences and the well-documented experiences of millions over millennia suggest prayer may well be the most powerful force on the planet. If so, how far-fetched is it to think that we could use technology to wield our powerful prayer weapon in a more effective way?

Referring to prayer, Jesus said, "If two of you agree on Earth about anything you ask, it will be done for you by my Father in Heaven" (Matthew 18:19). Entire books have been written on the theology packed into that single statement. I won't attempt to unpack it here. But, the notion that the only thing more powerful than prayer is when two or more people pray together was foundational to FocusOnPrayer.com.

Its 2:00 a.m. and your third sleepless night in a row. You can't get your 14-year-old son's face out of your mind. You don't want to. No parent should have to bury a child like you did three days ago. Your next-door neighbor who came to the door with the police officers to give you the horrible news has been a great comfort to you. But, she's never been where you are. You don't know anyone who has. Desperate for something you can't even articulate, you get on your laptop and Google "parent grieving loss of child."

That's when you discover FocusOnPrayer.com. With a few clicks, you're connected to another mother on the other side of the world who's been where you are and is available to join you in prayer.

But there's a third party to this transaction. Jesus followed His previous statement with this, "For where two or three are gathered in my name, I am there among them" (Matthew 18:20). So, while your grieving husband sleeps off the scotch he pours to temporarily deaden his pain, you pour out your heart with your new cyber friend to the mysterious One who promised to be present, to listen and to act upon your request. 15 years later, I still get goose bumps thinking about the life-changing possibilities of FocusOnPrayer.com.

By far, we have less experience with our Discover, Invent and Innovate Value in Action than any of the others. In saying this, I'm probably unfairly discounting a great deal of innovation that we bring to each and every client engagement. But, the *big* ideas (and hence the biggest innovations) originate with the clients who then bring us in to help execute their plans. During our firm's next quarter century, we'll be much more focused upon bringing our own innovations to market. I can't wait!

Do Your Best

Doing your best means giving your best effort with the best possible attitude, recognizing that both are always within your control. Doing your best means working hard *and* smart, while living a balanced life. Working hard does not mean over-working to the neglect of one's health, family and other higher priorities. Working hard does mean that, for brief seasons, life balance may be impossible to maintain, but we are deeply committed to restoring it as soon as possible.

Much of what I've said to our five children during my 39 years of fatherhood has fallen upon deaf and distracted ears. There is one thing, however, that to this day each of them can recite at gunpoint. I can see them now with their eyeballs rolling back into their heads whenever I would ask them my favorite question, "What are the only two things that you can always control in life?" They'd bemoan their reply (think Eeyore to Pooh), "Yeah Dad, we know...effort and attitude." "That's right, kids!" I'd say. "Everything else is partially or completely out of your control."

I've thought about my 1-2 effort-attitude punch a great deal over nearly four decades now. It may be slightly overstated, but not by much. I like it for two primary reasons. First, it takes away any excuses for not giving your best effort while having the best possible attitude. It's simply unacceptable to do otherwise, because both are completely in your control. Second, it helps you stay laser-focused on that which you can control, so you don't have time or energy to worry about the myriad of things you can't.

Life Balance

Can we talk about life balance? Or, perhaps better stated, is there any way to avoid talking about life balance? It's all the rage you know. Just ask the nearest Millennial (born between 1981 and 2000) their thoughts on work and you'll soon hear something akin to "I work to live...I don't live to work."

This may be one of the few things that Millennials and their employers consistently agree upon. The other being that Millennials are "special." Yep, not many in my children's generation "work for the man." They seem to prefer to work for themselves on the man's dime. Unless of course, they're working to become the next dot-com billionaire, so work-life balance gets tossed out with last night's leftover pizza stepped on while rolling out of their cot at the office.

Despite the preceding remarks, I actually strongly believe in life balance. We would not have survived the raising of five children without it. One of the ways we maintained it was to have dinner at six o'clock every week night. And, if I was in town, I was there.

Another key to parental survival was consistent and early bedtimes commandeered by the King of Cleanliness. Following in my father's footsteps, I would sing, "Stand up, stand up for Daddy and let him wash you off" whilst the kids squirmed under the torrent of water pouring out of a large cup or, better yet, a bucket. Cleanliness cannot be next to godliness until the little buggers' first layer of skin is rinsed clean off of them. Gently pat dry, read a bedtime story, say prayers and put the last one down for the night no later than eight o'clock. This affords Mom and Dad a sacred two hours of peace and quiet before their bedtime.

When I'm out of town on business trips, my family's work-life balance suffers. When the kids were young, Elaine had some very long days filling in for the King of Cleanliness. At times she was tempted to do what our neighbor did with her three young children. I think she got it from a Roseanne Barr comedy routine. The neighbor lady would combine meal time with bath time by feeding the kids in the tub. For real. Unless you have three or more children of your own, please withhold judgment. Like I said, Elaine was tempted. Speaking of Roseanne, I'm reminded of her line about child-rearing, "if the kids are alive at the end of the day…hey, I've done my job."

There are many things companies can do to help their employees maintain work-life balance. To be sure that we're maintaining it over time, we never ask employees to do anything that management isn't willing to do. As our Value in Action states, we go out of our way to restore balance as soon as possible. We also do something that many companies in our industry don't. We pay our consultants for any billable overtime. So, if we bill the client 50 hours in a week, we pay the consultant 10 hours of overtime. Many firms seize this opportunity to add to their profits at their employees' expense. One of my personal favorites is to give employees who have been working long hours a "Dinner-for-Two" to a nice restaurant as a way of restoring some work-life balance to the home front. For extraordinary efforts, we've occasionally given employees extended weekend getaway "Trips-for-Two." The possibilities are endless.

A few closing (hopefully affirming) comments for my Millennial friends. In the not too distant future, I will be leaving my enterprise in your very capable hands. As one born smack dab in the middle of the Baby Boomer generation, I will do so with some trepidation. Hopefully, you will have had ample opportunity to show me and our clients how truly special you are…in every positive sense of that word.

Hopefully, I will have had ample opportunity show you that working to live is an honorable pursuit that occasionally calls for more than that which you would normally be willing to give. On such occasions, I would simply ask that you do just that…*give*. Give more of yourself than you're comfortable in giving. For you see, your personal comfort should rarely be your primary pursuit. Rest assured, it is not that of your employer. More importantly, it is rarely that of your God.

Chapter 10

11. The Get-Out-of-Jail-Free-Card Myth

"My God, it's my wife," I thought, looking down at her crumpled body and bloody face lying next to the soccer field. "I've hit my wife. Where did she come from? I never saw her." She never saw it coming. I didn't even feel the prescription sunglasses that I smashed into her face. Was that crunching sound the glasses, her nose or her eye socket...or all three? Whatever it was gave way to a fist that hadn't seen such action since fourth grade.

Steve Henry was the "Baby Huey" of Miss Carlisle's fourth grade class at Mt. Tabor Elementary School. A loveable lug who was also a neighborhood friend of mine. I can't recall what provoked my rage during our daily "square ball" ritual. But, I'll never forget hitting young Steve's face with my fist. Although immediately remorseful, I also felt a sense of conquest as though I'd completed some tribal rite of passage that I didn't really understand. Fortunately, during high school, when the "loveable lug" became a veritable battering ram, my family had moved out of town.

While kneeling down to check on my fallen bride, I looked over my shoulder to see my provocateur. He has the fiendish look of a fallen angel upon his face.

"Who is this demonic version of an adult Dennis the Menace?" I thought. "Where did he come from? Why, for God's sake, did this perfect stranger accost me?"

When it comes to youth soccer Midwestern style, few rivalries equaled that of the "Dynamite" versus "Fire" (team names changed to protect the guilty). These cross-town rivals loathed each other since anyone can remember, although no one is sure just why. While Dynamite was the more dominant team, The Fire won just enough to fan the competitive flames into a raging inferno, one that didn't always stop at the sidelines.

Dynamite led The Fire 2-0 in the second half of the State Cup championship. Both goals came on penalty kicks in the first half, indicative of the "foul if beaten" coaching strategy The Fire was infamous for. It hadn't been pretty, but Dynamite seemed to have the game under control and was cruising to a "three-peat" State Cup victory...or so it seemed.

All soccer hell broke loose after one of The Fire's players was given a yellow card with about 15 minutes to go in the game. As the penalized Fire player is arguing the call and brazenly refusing to release the ball, our son knocks the ball out of his hands and kicks it into play. The referee stopped play and gave Caleb a yellow card. As a team captain, he was permitted to talk to the ref. While he respectfully attempted to explain his actions, the ref gave him a second yellow card resulting in his ejection from the game. Under the rules of soccer, this meant that Caleb would also be unable to play in the next game, a devastating blow to Dynamite's regional tourney hopes.

I stared at the field in disbelief. Our son had just been ejected from the biggest soccer game of his young life, thanks to the worst sequence of officiating I'd seen in nearly 20 years. Turning away from the field, I saw every Fire fan on their feet cheering as if they'd just won the World Cup. I guess the next best thing to winning is getting your opponent's star player ejected.

Oh well, fans will be fans. Besides, I'd been known to say a cheer or two when our Indiana Pacers managed to foul "Shaq" out of a playoff game. But, aren't these our children we're cheering for…and against?

Knowing trouble when I see it, I lowered my head and walked away from the field. As I stepped between two blue chairs belonging to Dynamite parents, I looked up to see a man about my size within 12 inches of my face. He's beside himself with glee over what's just taken place on the field and clearly wants to make sure that I know it. I'll never forget his fiendish grin.

Why would my child's pain bring him such great joy? He's clapping his hands right in my face and saying, "Ha, ha, ha. He got just what he deserved!"

Deserved? What game was he watching? Caleb didn't deserve one yellow card, much less two. And why is the Fire player who instigated the whole thing still in the game?

What happened next has never happened before and, hopefully, will never happen again. Without thinking (truly, without thinking, as an instinctive paternal reflex took over), I put my best right hook forward on this most deserving soccer dad.

"What were you thinking?!" you ask?

I promise you, I wasn't thinking. That swing came as automatically as the Patellar Reflex when a doctor taps you knee with a rubber hammer. Not even for a millisecond did I stop to think, "I'm gonna hit this guy." Taking that swing came as naturally as my next breath.

My wife and I didn't typically stand or sit together on the soccer sidelines. Suffice it to say, she took a little more laid back approach to the game than me. So, it was normative that I wouldn't have known where she was as this conflict emerged. She happened to be nearby. When she saw me making a fist at my side, she made a fateful decision to intervene — fortunate for me, very fortunate for my accoster, but very unfortunate for her.

My nemesis pulls his head back just in time to avoid a direct hit. My ego wants to believe that Elaine or someone else sent my punch astray by grabbing me. I'll never know for sure. It wasn't a total swing and a miss, as I did manage to break his sunglasses as well as Elaine's. Unfortunately, the damage could not be confined to two pairs of sunglasses.

On my follow-through, my right fist landed squarely on Elaine's left eye, smashing her sunglasses into her face. With that, I win my one and only fight as an adult by a knockout…of my own wife. The longest year of my life had just begun.

I was trapped between the woman I loved and the overzealous soccer fan I had just met, yet already loathed. Should I stay by her side or go maim the one who (in my view) truly caused her pain?

She was surrounded by soccer moms who seemed to know more about what to do than I did, so I followed my savage instincts. Blind rage subsided into uncontrollable anger, yet I did sense a few brain cells slowly beginning to function once again. Instead of pounding my adversary into the turf like a corner flag, I called him every name I could think of while begging him to hit me.

Correctly assuming I was already on the wrong side of the law, I incorrectly thought I could strengthen my case by provoking him to hit me back. So, I got nose-to-nose and screamed, "Come on you stack of s***, just one time. Come on, hit me, just one time."

Before proceeding, I'm compelled to remind you of our "no BS allowed" policy.

In lieu of granting my request, I think he said something about pressing charges. Little did I know, he was well-acquainted with how to handle such legal matters. Of course, he was a lawyer. Thank God, he didn't hit me back. He would have gone to the hospital and I might still be in jail.

Unsuccessful in my counter-provocations, I retreat to check on Elaine. She's conscious now, but her face is a bloody mess. I'm reminded once again why my mother was never meant to have a son who was a doctor. "Dear God, I can't believe I did this to my own wife," I'm thinking. Then the power of rationalizing kicked in and I was right back in the soccer dad's face…." Just one time, you stack…." Nothin' doin.' He had me dead to rights and he knew it. He wasn't about to risk releasing me from his well-set trap.

I'll be forever grateful to the Dynamite dads who pulled me away from this altercation before I dug my hole any deeper. Joe in particular will forever be known as my "wingman" for his heroics that day. It wasn't long before the deputies showed up and started taking statements from anyone who would give one. After taking my statement, the officer asked me to stand by the patrol car while the two officers continued talking to bystanders. Not sure just how hot-wired I really was, they took turns circling back regularly to check on me.

"Officer, what is the legal definition of provocation?" I asked, as the magnitude of my dilemma started coming into focus. I'm not sure exactly what he said, but whatever it was didn't bode well for me.

"And officer, please note the fact that my wife is lying on the Dynamite spectator's side of the field." I'm no lawyer, but I'd watched enough crime shows to know that the location of the body is usually a key piece of evidence. "See where she is officer. Obviously, he came onto our side of the field to get to me. What about my personal space, officer? He was 12 inches from my face. The body, officer, write it down. Her body was on the Dynamite side of the field. That's important," so I thought.

To my horror, I look over to see our 23-year-old son approaching the police car, clenching both fists at his side with a look of utter anguish upon his face.

"Josh, what are you doing here? Please, I'm begging you to stay away." Then I realize that for nearly 30 minutes now, he's been thinking that the other guy hit his mother.

"Josh, it was me. I hit your Mom, not him. It was an accident, but he didn't do it."

I could almost hear the groan coming from the depth of his tortured soul. He turned and walked away as if freshly skewered on the horns of a moral dilemma he couldn't comprehend. It was as though in some twisted way he blamed himself for what had happened. I sensed he felt like only *his* father could be involved in such a bizarre accident, while only *his* mother could be the victim of such injustice. Only *his* life could be so screwed up so often. But why?

The game continues, though with no fans on the sidelines. They had been ordered away from the field. Ironically, I had a front row seat from the side of the Sheriff's car, as the officers continued taking statements. As

I begin coping with the very real possibility of going to jail, I'm also thinking, "I must really be over the edge, because I still care about who wins this game. Dang, they scored. It's now 2-1."

I risk a look across the way at my nemesis. He's still there. "Officer, can't you charge him with provocation? He started all this."

Respectfully and apologetically, the officer said, "No sir, I can't, but I sure would encourage you to try. I know he provoked you, but that doesn't justify taking a swing at him. I'm sorry sir."

Dynamite's third and final goal went unaccompanied by the usual wild cheers from the non-existent fans on the sidelines. When the Dynamite boys accepted their State Champion medals, no parents and fans were there to celebrate. They had been banned from the awards ceremony as well. No, what should have been the sweet "three-peat" for the Dynamite U14 boys, instead became a bitter defeat for parents on both sides of the field that day. Everyone who attended that fateful game sensed something very ugly and shameful had happened.

The ambulance arrived and the paramedics took over tending to my wife. I have no idea what her condition is, as none of her many attendants seemed to think I'm owed an update. Go figure. They strap her into a gurney along with a head and neck brace, hopefully only as a precaution, but then again I don't really know.

Our oldest daughter, Emily, never left her side. We exchanged glances as she walked alongside her mother's stretcher, now nearing the ambulance. Her face showed no real expression, although I detected a subtle disdain for her father. While her lips were silent, her eyes seemed to scream out, "How could you do this to her?"

"Sir, I'm sorry, but I'm going to have to take you in." said the deputy. "It's policy. Whenever battery occurs, somebody's going to jail. Today, that somebody is you, Mr. Lindemann."

"I'm going to jail. I can't believe it. I'm actually going to jail," I said to myself. Several of the Dynamite soccer dads are standing by offering to help in any way they can.

"Brad, whatever you need, just ask, my friend. We'll take care of it for you," said Jim, father of John "Junkyard Dog," one of Dynamite's best defenders.

"Jim, here's the keys to my car. It's over there somewhere. Can you make sure it gets home? Bradley's home alone. Please tell Josh to go get him."

Freedom as I had known it every day of my life for 44 years was about to be taken away from me. My wife. My children. My home. My car. Gone. I was being sucked into the vortex of the American judicial system from which no one emerges unscathed.

At this point I was incessantly muttering, "I'm going to jail. I'm going to jail. I'm going to jail...."

"Sir, please turn around and place your hands on the car," the officer said. "I need to search you. It's policy."

I thought, "Oh my..., I'm being frisked by a police officer in the middle of a soccer field for all of soccerdom and two of my sons to see. Could this be any more humiliating?"

In fact, it could be and would be.

"Mr. Lindemann, before I put you in the car, I need to put these on you," said the ever-polite but firmly-spoken deputy, holding out a pair of handcuffs.

"Is that really necessary, officer? I've been completely cooperative with you. Do you really have to put those things on me?" Of course, I already know the answer to that question.

"It's policy, sir. Please put your hands behind your back. I'll put them on as loose as they'll go, but I have to put them on."

Loose? If they were any tighter those handcuffs would have sliced my slender, city slicker wrists to ribbons. With that, I was cuffed and stuffed into the squad car, forced to sit upon my shackled wrists, greatly exacerbating the pain.

My arms quickly fell "asleep" and were completely numb by the time we reach the jail about 20 minutes later. I soon understand why in all those cop shows the first thing criminals do when their handcuffs are removed is vigorously rub their wrists. Five more minutes of that torture device and I would have needed a tourniquet to stop the bleeding. Mercifully, the cuffs were quickly removed once I went inside the jail.

"I'm in jail. Imagine that," I thought to myself. The only other time I've even seen the inside of a jailhouse was over 30 years ago. They nabbed us for skinny-dipping in the Kokomo Country Club pool. Must have been a slow night in Howard County, as evidenced by the four or five squad cars dispatched to chase our bare backsides out of the pool and send us scampering across the 10th fairway. Not sure which group I would have rather been caught with. The six buck naked banshees upon whom the bright lights of the law fell or the two who escaped into the night. The

Chapter 11

streaking escapees must have been quite a sight, as they ran between the houses hoping to reach home before their indecency was further exposed.

Dad wasn't smiling when he entered the station, but I bet he and Mom had a good laugh afterwards. I suppose we were trespassing, but they never charged us with anything other than being young, foolish and in need of testosterone. Nothing a full dose of adolescence wouldn't cure. I've often wondered if the deputies ever surmised that what few brain cells we had going into the evening had been eradicated by copious quantities of Boone's Farm wine. It took me 20 years to re-acquire a taste for wine of any kind.

Officer "Nice" lets me know that he's only booking me on a single count of battery, although he could easily hit me with at least three charges. I thank him, bid him adieu and continue the perfunctory booking process with the deputy at the front desk. As he's taking a print of all 10 fingers, I ponder how amazing it is that I am the only person on the planet with those particular fingerprints. I'll keep that in mind if I ever feel the urge to go on the lam. Yeah, right.

I wonder why they don't tell you to smile when taking your mug shot. As the mug shot of every serial killer arrested since circa 1965 flashes through my mind (could they possibly look any guiltier?), the deputy says, "Look into the camera."

"Should I smile?" I'm wondering. If I do, will the prosecutor misunderstand and think that I think this is all a big joke? Will my friends and family be less sympathetic when they see what a rollicking good time I was having in jail? What about my wife? After all, I did lay her out like a rug. She probably wouldn't take too kindly to my pearly whites beaming as though I'd just won the Publisher's Clearinghouse Sweepstakes. I really can't win on this one. I'm either just another "Bubba" being booked for his latest run-in with the law or I'm a psycho soccer dad who thinks the real game started when they hauled me off to jail.

I don't smile. I can't. Nothing's funny at this point. No doubt, my black tee-shirt will provide a fitting frame for my guilty mug. Maybe they'd like a shot of the back of my shirt too. A real collector's item, this one is. Got it at Planet Hollywood. You know, the bankrupt chain of theme restaurants owned by all those starlit entrepreneurial wannabes, such as Sylvester Stallone?

I confess to smiling faintly, after the mug shot of course, when I realized that on the back of my shirt was a silk-screened picture of none other than Rocky Balboa — the Italian Stallion, boxer extraordinaire. I think the irony is lost on Officer "Perfunctory." He's too busy going over the checklist for my very own jailbird goody basket.

That's basket, as in laundry. When staying at "The Hamilton County Hilton," if you don't wear it in, you carry it in a laundry basket. For the duration of your stay, all of your worldly possessions are contained within a single, averaged-sized laundry basket. Once your rolled-up sleeping mat (not to be confused with a real mattress), blanket and sheet go in, there's not much room for anything else.

I was given the opportunity to purchase a small plastic bag of toiletries for $2. They threw in a roll of toilet paper, courtesy of the county (God forbid I should need it before my release) and, most importantly, a "spork." If I have to explain what a spork is, then you're probably also wondering why they don't issue knives to the inmates. Beyond that, my basket contained some booking paperwork, a commissary order form and a list of jailhouse rules (which oddly, I never got around to reading. I must have been too absorbed in my first ever Jerry Springer Show).

After relinquishing my 10th wedding anniversary Rolex and my wallet containing all of $52 (seems my life is a perpetual paradox of late), I was pleasantly surprised to be told I could keep my wedding band on. This, only after confirming that it was indeed a wedding band versus any other type of ring.

"How interesting," I thought, "that this institution housing so many home wreckers recognizes the sanctity of the marriage institution in such a tangible way." I just hope my wife feels the same when I get out.

It stands to reason that many folks show up at the jail looking and smelling a might gamy. So, before entering your cell-block for the first time, you are required to enter *the* shower.

You don't want to ponder this too long. Yes, there's only one and, yes, every new inmate takes a shower in it. Just before entering *the* shower, I'm informed that I would have to relinquish my boxer shorts. In exchange, I receive a free pair of county-issued, paper thin, disposable white boxers.

Officer "Perfunctory" was quick to point out that "it beats going commando." Roger that, so I emerge from my communal shower donning a fresh pair of crepe paper skivvies underneath my brand new, tangerine orange, "jailhouse jammies." Booked and bathed, it's time for me to enter Cell Block A.

Chapter 11

On Raising Your Star Athlete

Before beginning our tour of Cell Block A, now's a good time to talk about the pitfalls to avoid when raising a star athlete. If parents aren't careful, they will allow their rising stars to grow up with the false belief that the world revolves around them. Elaine and I were admittedly guilty of this in raising our star athlete, Caleb (a.k.a. "C Monster"). Thankfully, the Lord knew better and put the C Monster on a steady diet of humble pie starting just before he entered high school.

When it came to soccer, Caleb had the whole package — speed, strength and skill. As his parents, it was easy for Elaine and me to get caught up in the accolades that came his way. More specifically, as his father, it was seemingly impossible to avoid vicariously living out my shattered athletic dreams through my son (see Chapter 12, "Take Your Marks!").

Looking back, I know I was far too wrapped around the axle of Caleb's soccer career. But for that fact, I probably would have never seen the inside of a jail cell. But for that fact, Caleb would have never been allowed to miss his sister's wedding so he could play in a soccer game. But for that fact...when I told Caleb to get a job between college semesters he wouldn't have told me that soccer was his job...you get the idea.

Caleb is named after one of my favorite Biblical characters. He was one of the 12 leaders of the tribes of Israel sent to spy out the Promised Land before entering. 10 of the 12 came back quaking in their sandals. Caleb and Joshua were the only ones who returned with a positive report. I love the way Caleb summed it up: "Let us go up at once and occupy it, for we are well able to overcome it" (Numbers 13:30 NSRV).

Though very tough on the outside, Caleb also had a very tender heart toward God. This resulted in a rich inheritance for his family when they entered the Promised Land "because he wholeheartedly followed the Lord" (Joshua 14:14 NSRV). Watching our Caleb grow up, it was amazing to see the similarities between him and Caleb of old.

Looking back, the trajectory of Caleb's soccer career began tilting downward after the unfortunate altercation that sent his Mom to the hospital and his Dad to jail. Many took great delight in what they saw as a well-deserved comeuppance, not only for Caleb, but for Elaine and me as well. Some were quite vocal about it, even sharing their sadistic glee via hateful signs in the stands.

As my buddy Murph often reminds me, when it comes to our

problems, half the folks are glad we have them and the other half couldn't care less. Truer words were never spoken. Our entire family was deeply and repeatedly hurt following that fateful incident. We were constantly reminded of those bad memories. Opposing players ruthlessly taunted Caleb with snide comments about the day his father punched out his mother, breaking his tender heart.

While sitting in the back of the Sheriff's car on my way to jail, an Old Testament verse came to mind. It's what Joseph said to his brothers who had left him for dead a few years prior, only to later find their lives in his hands.

As for you, you meant evil against me, but God meant it for good…" (Genesis 50:20 ESV).

In my darkest hour, I believe God gave me that verse to give me the perspective that I desperately needed from a vantage point I've never had. It wasn't only applicable to me, however. Our entire family would be better for this miserable experience, including Caleb. In the years to come, he would often find himself on the road to humility…paved with humiliation.

Caleb did go on to play Division One college soccer, first at the University of Dayton and then at IUPUI in Indianapolis. Despite one disappointment after another, he persevered through four miserable years on the pitch, then graduated. From a soccer perspective, it was a bitterly disappointing premature end to what many assumed would be a long professional career.

It capped off with a poorly placed penalty kick in the last minute of his last college game. When the ball went right into the hands of the opposing goalie, I was inconsolable on the sidelines. "Really God? After all he's been through, couldn't you at least give him one shining moment before his soccer dreams are dashed forever?"

Answer: "No, he needed this moment much more than the one you had in mind." Indeed he did.

Elaine and I often talk about how glad we are that Caleb never lived up to his soccer press clippings. We both firmly believe that it would have been the worst possible thing for him. As difficult as it was to watch him suffer through the death of his soccer dreams, we now know that it was for the best. Caleb affirmed this a couple of years ago when he emailed his former coach at Dayton to thank him for all he had done for him…or at least tried to.

Mind you, this was the guy who squeezed Caleb so hard his

sophomore year that he felt he had no choice but to transfer elsewhere. To Coach's credit, he responded in a very classy manner. And, Dad was far more proud of his son for having sent that email than I would have been had he nailed that PK in the final minute of his last college soccer game. Both father and son have come a long way since the days when our world revolved around the beautiful game.

So, what's the parent of a rising athletic star to do? Know the difference between supporting your child's sports endeavors and allowing your world and theirs to revolve around them. I'm writing this a few weeks before the start of the 2016 Summer Olympics in Rio. Michael Phelps, the most decorated Olympian in history, will be there for an unprecedented fifth time. No athlete has more dominated their sport than Michael has. Yet, somewhere between the 2012 Summer Olympics in London and the road to Rio, Michael lost his way.

Alcohol abuse landed Phelps in jail and then rehab. He lost his will to live and seriously considered taking his own life. Fortunately, he found his way back, but only after finding meaning in life beyond swimming. His name is Boomer, Michael's son. You probably saw him in the stands at Rio cheering for his star athlete father. You know, the guy who would give every medal he's ever won just to spend one more day with his son — Michael Phelps, Boomer's dad. There is indeed life after swimming for the greatest swimmer of all time.

As to our former star athlete, Caleb's well on his way to a very successful sales career at SalesForce.com. He's happily married to his college sweetheart, Lena, whom he would not have met but for transferring from Dayton to IUPUI. They're the proud parents of two canine kids, Bert and Ernie, and plan to increase our gaggle of grandkids in the not too distant future. Right Lena? Caleb still enjoys playing the beautiful game in some adult recreational leagues. As fate would have it, he incurred his most serious sports injury a year or so ago when he torn his Achilles tendon during an indoor game.

My Longest Day in Cell Block A

I enter Cell #101 in Cell Block A of the Hamilton County Jail at around 2 pm on Sunday, May 20, 2001. There's only one door in the entire cellblock and no bars anywhere. No bars? I thought all jails had bars, but not this one. Each cell measured about 12' x 12' and housed four to six inmates. The cells were actually more like alcoves, all feeding into a central common area containing stainless steel tables bolted into the concrete floor. There was one small TV hanging from the wall. There were also two cigarette lighters built into the walls. How odd that you retain the right to systematically kill yourself by smoking in jail whilst relinquishing nearly all other rights.

Cell #101 is the first cell on the left. There are two bunk beds lined up end-to-end along one wall and a single hard rubber pallet-type bed along the other wall. Two young white men are playing cards on the lower bed of the first bunk. On the lower bed of the next bunk, an Afro-American man appearing to be in his forties is intently foraging through his laundry basket while making notes in a small notebook. The inmate lying on the single pallet has his blanket pulled up over his head. He appears to be sound asleep wearing a bicycle helmet.

"Don't mind ole Horse there. He had a rough night last night," said my new bunk mate sitting on the edge of the lower bunk. The only bunk not taken is the one above him, so I introduce myself to Tony and start to settle in to my new home. I'm still not sure this is really happening and hoping to soon wake up from the nightmare.

My first challenge was how to make up my bed and get into it without disturbing my bunkmate. Tony seemed determined to hold his position on the edge of the lower bunk, so I had to gingerly maneuver around him, being careful to neither encroach upon his personal space nor disturb the bountiful stash in his laundry basket. Tony apparently ran his own commissary, offering such tasty treats as dunkin' sticks, peanut butter, crackers, cookies, dry soup mix…M'm, M'm good. Thinking I might fast during what I hope will be a very brief visit, I turn down Tony's gracious offer of a dunkin' stick. I begin to sense that Tony is not just another inmate in Cell Block A.

"So what's in the notebook?" I ask with no small amount of trepidation. While Tony ponders his response for what seems like an eternity, I look up to see one of his dunkin' stick boxes flattened out to cover the register from the ventilation system. Not hard to figure that it wouldn't take much AC to turn our cozy little cell into a walk-in freezer. Soft, warm spots are hard to come by in jail.

"It's my book, man. You know. It's how I know who owes me what. Just about every bastard in this joint owes Tony something," he says while flipping through page after page of pencil-scrawled debits and credits.

Yes, the entrepreneurial spirit is alive and well in the Hamilton Hilton and Tony appears to be the jailhouse equivalent of Sam Walton. I'm bettin' if you can't find it at Tony's, then it can't be found. Something tells me he

Chapter 11

may have cornered the market on jailhouse sundries and snacks.

In some ways, being in jail was just like another day at the office. For example, when I got bored and needed a break, I got up to go to the restroom. But come to think of it, that's where the similarities ended.

"You can't be out there, man," groused one of my younger white cellmates looking up from his bunk bed card game. "It's lockdown."

"Oh," I sheepishly reply feeling like the new kid in grade school. "How long does that last?"

"Until three o'clock."

Oh well, just like at the office, I really didn't have to go that badly. Less so than normal, since I hadn't enjoyed my usual morning tankard of Starbucks. Can't wait to quaff some jailhouse java in the morning. However bad it may be, no doubt it will be the best part of waking up. That's assuming, of course, I can manage to get some sleep. I'm bettin' this Hilton doesn't offer turn down service? Just as well. If I had a pillow, which I don't, I certainly wouldn't be eating any chocolate that might appear upon it.

15 minutes until we're free to move about the cell block. Funny how quickly one's definition of "freedom" can be redefined. Might as well take a nap. Yeah right. I can count the naps I've taking in my entire life on one hand with fingers left over. My odds of winning the lottery are better than enjoying an afternoon siesta in this place. Guess I'll just lie here and ponder how humiliated, angry, frustrated, embarrassed and all-around miserable I am. That I can do. No doubt about it, today…it sucks to be me.

Over one-third of a century ago (circa 1962), the three o'clock bell signaled the end of my school day. Free at last, we would burst forth from Mt. Tabor Elementary in Southern Indiana. We had more pent-up energy than a NASA rocket on the launch pad at Cape Canaveral. Of course, we walked home from school, dissipating some of our "rocket fuel" along the way. But, there was always plenty of time and energy before supper to play a few games of whatever happened to be in season—football, basketball, baseball. It didn't matter. Whatever ball game it was, we had a ball playing it. No soccer back then. Guess we were much too civilized for that.

Time and energy. An unbeatable combination. When you're a prisoner, you have nothing but time. Yet, you have no energy whatsoever. It's as though you checked it at the desk along with your valuables. Perhaps this is just as well, since there are so few positive outlets for one's energy within a jail. Yet again, I was intrigued by the eight or so inmates who gathered in a circle to go through what I presume to be their daily exercise regimen. I'm thinking, if I were here for the duration, I would keep my sanity by exercising relentlessly until my body was as hard as the cellblock floor.

Concrete. Cold, hard, solid, low maintenance, drab, durable, strong…and cheap. Up, down and all around me. All I can see and feel is concrete. Poured on the floor. Stacked up the walls. Hanging ominously overhead. Is it protecting me from the world or the world from me? Imagine that, a world that needed protection from me. What has the world come to? What have I come to?

Freedom doesn't exactly ring at the Hamilton Hilton. The signal that we were free to move about the cellblock was more like a muted siren chirp than a ringing bell. Seems only fitting, as many of my cellmates, no doubt, arrived with sirens blaring. The chirp serves as a constant reminder that more trouble is never far away from Cellblock A.

As my new "homeys" shuffle from their cells into the common area, mingling is the last thing I want to do. A good stiff drink would sure come in handy about now — the proverbial "shot of courage." Why not? They get their cigarettes. Why can't I have a daily allotment of a nice single malt scotch? Before crashing the party, I close my eyes and lick my lips, imagining that I've just polished off my favorite scotch on the rocks. OK boys, it's party time!

I make my way over to one of the steel tables near the television. I take a seat and proceed to feign intense interest in the Oprah Winfrey Show. Soon, I begin to alter my gaze between the TV and the hollow faces of the inmates. Most seem to have a sickening pallor like someone suffering a terminal illness. Perhaps their countenance is a reflection of the hopelessness within? Hopeless, not because they'll never get out, as nearly all will. Many sooner than they deserve. No, hopeless more due to the ever-present reality of what life holds for them outside these walls, not within them.

"Why are you in here?" I ask the well-scrubbed young man sitting next to me. He looks pretty harmless and, like me, has that "I don't really belong here" look on his face.

"Probation violation," he says.

"Really, so what did you do to get put on probation in the first place?"

"Underage drinking. I got really drunk at a party in high school and the cops busted the joint. They found me passed out in the backyard where my friends had left me when they ran away. While I was on probation, they nailed me with a DUI, so I had to do six weekends in here. This is my last one."

"Wow," I say, "ya' gotta feel good about that."

"Yeah, I don't ever want to come back here. This place really sucks. I try to sleep as much as I can. Just before coming in on Friday night, I take a double dose of cold medicine. I usually sleep for the first 15 hours or so. Then, there's only 33 to go."

"What about the showers? Have you ever taken one here?"

The kid looks at me like I have two heads.

"Are you kidding? I wouldn't get in those showers if my life depended on it. You never know what's in there. Can you imagine what some of these guys do in those showers?"

Unfortunately, I could, but I sure didn't want to.

"Yeah, I guess you're right. Hopefully, I won't be in here long enough to care."

Back to Oprah. I have no idea what the show's about. It's just much safer to stare at the TV than any of these guys. Having broken the ice with this one, I can't resist asking him, "Do you wanna know what I'm in for?"

He unsuccessfully tries to hide his fear. His eyes nearly pop out of his head. I can almost feel the sweat dripping down his spine. Momentarily, I'm feeling a bit sinister, rather Anthony Hopkins like. What a hoot. Had I been a seasoned jailbird, I could have had this kid going for quite some time. Yet, the real me was dying to let someone in there know who the real me really was. So, I recounted my sad soccer story and graciously returned my young friend's eyeballs to their sockets.

DUI. Driving Under the Influence. Hamilton County Indiana is as tough as they get on such offenses. There are nearly 17,000 alcohol-related traffic fatalities in the United States every year. Hamilton County has no interest in getting its fair share. This is one county where drinking and driving not only doesn't pay, but it can cost you…big time. My young friend would be wise to stay sober behind the wheel. If not, the next time he enters the Hamilton County Jail could be under the extended stay plan

Come to find out, most residents of Cellblock A are in for some kind of probation violation. It seems that once you're "in the system," it's very hard to get out. One too many beers, an ill-timed toke on the evil weed and…BAM! Its slammer time all over again. I'm struck by the chronic nature of the petty crimes that keep recycling many of these jailbirds. Are these chronic criminals really stuck on stupid or is the system stuck in its Byzantine ways? Should society really care if a 40-year old accountant still likes to smoke marijuana now and then? From where I'm sitting at this moment, I sure couldn't care less.

It's near six o'clock. It must be getting close to dinnertime. Inmates begin shuffling into their cells, emerging with sporks in hand and empty peanut butter jars in which they mix a variety of jailhouse concoctions. Slowly and quietly they begin lining up along the wall. I'm in no hurry to sample Hamilton Hilton cuisine, so I stay seated until about two-thirds of the guys are in line. I grab my spork out of my laundry basket and do my best to merge in without drawing undue attention to myself. Do I look as different from them as I feel? Like the new kid in class, I'm agonizing over the decision of where to sit in the lunchroom.

I spot one of my cellmates and decide to grab a seat at his table. It's apparent that most inmates know right where they're going to sit, probably sitting in the same place at every meal. What if I'm in someone's seat? What if that someone takes exception to my trespass and decides to teach me a lesson in jailhouse etiquette? His right hook is sure to be more accurate than mine. Nobody seems to mind my presence. But then, nobody acknowledges it either. Fine by me. I won't be sending any friend requests to these guys after I'm released. What's for dinner?

Just as I'm about to take my first bite of what vaguely resembles chicken fried steak, Tony sets his tray down beside me and, as he always does, takes charge. No one else seems to be eating. I soon learn why. Tony extends his fists from either side. Everyone at the table follows suit and gets fist over fist with those next to them. Then, with every head bowed and all eyes closed, the self-ordained Reverend T asks a blessing upon the meal. Good thing too. From the looks of it, this grub needs all the prayers we can muster. Bon appetite!

In addition to our tasty entrée, we have cold corn, tasteless paste-like mashed potatoes and chocolate pudding. I'd liken the pudding to ground up chalk with a small amount of stale cocoa thrown in. There's quite a bit of food bartering taking place at every table. After one taste of the chalky pudding, I offer mine to the new friend next to me. To my surprise, he actually said, "thanks," then quickly sporked it from my plate to his. There aren't a lot of leftovers at the Jailhouse Cafe. To complete the full meal deal, you wash it all down with some putrid "bug juice" that makes the summer camp variety taste like a top shelf margarita. Yuck! I should've stayed with that fasting idea. At least then I could have escaped this deli from hell a few pounds lighter. Can't wait for breakfast.

Waiting. When you're in jail, you're always waiting on something. To

Chapter 11

get out, of course. But, you're waiting on so many more mundane things as well. You wait for lockdown to be over. You wait for Thursday, so you can place your commissary order. You wait for mealtimes—6 AM, 12 noon, and 6 PM. You wait for your wife to be home, so you can call her collect (you can't call cell phones from jail). You wait for The Jerry Springer Show to end. You even wait for your next bowel movement, because it could be the highlight of your day. Yes, jail time is wait time. God, I can't wait to get outta here. Has it really only been six hours?

It's seven o'clock in the evening. Guess I really am going to spend my first night in jail. If I was home with my bride, we'd be quaffing a nice Pinot Noir about now, as I settled in with my Wall Street Journal. As it is, my homeys and I look to be settling into an evening of TV and cards. I'm not about to get into a card game with these sharks, so I cozy up to a nice steel stool and watch TV. Still wanting to minimize the risk of engaging anyone in conversation, I continue my mindless stare. I'm really not interested in repeating my soccer story nor do I particularly care to hear theirs. This adds to my guilt, knowing that I really should care more about my fellow man. But, I really just wish I could lapse into a nice, quiet coma until my release.

The evening is interminably long. Boredom hangs in the air like a toxic cloud, choking the life out of everyone in Cellblock A. At least if I was rubbing shoulders with a serial killer or two, it would keep my blood flowing. As it is, I'm not sure I still have a pulse. Speaking of blood flow, I suspect hemorrhoids could be a real problem for those on the extended stay plan. I have to get off the stool every half hour to restore the feeling in my backside. I walk down cell row towards the restroom (no doors, of course), catch a glimpse of myself in the stainless steel mirror over the sink, and then head back down the row. Once in a while, I'll arrive at the restroom to find an inmate squatting on one of the four toilets. Each toilet is separated by a concrete block wall about four feet high. There are no doors on these half stalls. It's not a pretty picture. There is no such thing as privacy in jail.

With three more hours to "lights out," I've got to do something besides grow hemorrhoids and pace this joint. What the heck, that guy leaning against the wall looks harmless enough.

"So, what brings you to the Hamilton Hilton?" I ask in my most nonchalant veteran jailbird voice.

"The evil weed. Got me the second time while I was still on probation for the first and sent me straight to The Big House."

"The Big House?"

"Michigan City Penitentiary. This place really is a hotel compared to that. Trust me. You don't wanna go there. I spent six months in that hellhole and I don't ever want to go back. Guys in there would just as soon kill you as look at you."

Feeling emboldened for some insane reason, I ask, "So, you must have been dealing the stuff pretty big to catch all that heat, huh?" (As if I had a clue.)

"Dealing? Hell no, I wasn't dealing. Never have. They found less than a nickel bag on me the second time. Judges round here hate two things more than anything—DUI's and the evil weed. I think that's how they pay for all the road improvements."

"Sounds like they ought to name a street after you. What do you do for a living when you're not helping to pave the roads in Hamilton County?"

"I'm an accountant. Got a good job, at least I did, until this crap hit the fan. Might still have it when I get out. Not sure. My boss is pretty cool, so it's possible. What about you? What do you do?"

"I run an IT consulting business. Don't know much about the stuff, but have some really smart guys on my team who do. Always tried to make myself as dispensable as possible. Comes in real handy during times like these, not that I'm in familiar territory or anything."

"So, what brought ya' here?" he asks.

To which I reply, "Ya' got any kids?"

"Yep. Two. A boy and a girl."

"They ever play soccer"

"Oh yeah, my boy's a pretty good soccer player."

"Really, then you know how interesting things can get on the sidelines at a kids' soccer game."

"You better believe it. Those damn parents get crazy sometimes."

"Ya' got that right. Let me tell you just how crazy they can get...."

Thanks to my new laid-back accountant friend, the last hour has gone by faster than any of the previous seven. Conversation definitely helps pass the time in jail.

This one also gave me some food for thought regarding our country's marijuana laws. Unlike President Clinton, I did inhale in college, but never since then. I have seen firsthand the true evil that chronic use of this weed

Chapter 11

can bring into kids' lives. Despite this, it occurs to me that our criminal justice system has bigger fish to fry than weekend-tokin,' otherwise law-abiding, citizens. It's a quandary I'm not sure what to do with. Like alcohol, should marijuana use be legal after a certain age? I really don't know, but Hamilton County sure seems dead set against it. After all, somebody has to use (and pay for) these plush accommodations. Might as well be the potheads, right?

A Man Called Horse

Its 11 pm. "Lights out" time at the Hamilton County Jail. Mercifully, sleep approaches...I hope. It won't be easy, given the accommodations. The thin bedroll offers little cushion between my weary body and the solid steel bed frame. With no pillow (I suppose jailhouse pillow fights can get pretty ugly), I have to choose between comfort and cold. If I use my rolled-up blanket as a makeshift pillow, then I'll be cold with only a threadbare sheet covering me. If not, I'll be uncomfortable with my head "resting" on the vinyl bedroll.

It's dark and eerily quiet now. There is some bunk chatter going on and a few cross-cell exchanges, but I can't make out most of what's being said. I'm mentally muttering something from the Book of Psalms regarding the Lord giving sleep, when suddenly Tony bolts out of bed and into the common area.

"Ya'll ▆▆▆, listen up or I'll come in there and kick every one of your sorry ▆▆. Who the ▆▆ you think you are, talking about an old man that way? This man's old enough to be your father. ▆▆, he's old enough to be most of your sorry ▆▆▆ grandfather. I been lying in here listening to you young ▆▆▆ talk about ole Horse here like he ain't nothing. Waddn't long ago he'd kick your ▆▆ himself, but Tony will ▆▆ sure do it for him iffin' I hear one more word outta you sorry mother ▆▆▆. You unnerstan' me? This man deserves your respect and you no good ▆▆▆ are gonna give it to him. What the ▆▆ wrong with you? Didn't your mamas teach ya' nothing? Now, shut the ▆▆ up and go to sleep."

Whoa! I didn't know whether to say "Amen," "Good night, John Boy" or just go to bed. Man, that was one heck of a speech and, quite predictably, you could hear a pin drop in Cellblock A when it was over. Nobody said a word. Not even Horse, our elderly cellmate with the bicycle helmet. In fact, Horse may well have slept through Tony's entire performance. I'll never know. I do know this—my bunkmate is no average Jailhouse Joe. He's Mr. T to me and he's got my respect.

Lying there contemplating what had just taken place, I recall a conversation with Horse earlier in the day. He had sheepishly approached me and asked, "Are you who I think you are?"

"I don't know," I said. "Who do you think I am?"

"Basketball. You have anything to do with basketball?"

"Well, I play it now and then. Does that count?"

"Ever coach?"

"I've coached our kids' teams at various times."

"You're not him, are you? You know, the General?"

"You mean Bobby Knight? No, not hardly. Why?"

"That's good, cause if you was him I was gonna ask to be moved to another cellblock. I don't like him."

"Why don't you like Bobby Knight?" I ask.

"I don't like the way he treats those young boys. It ain't right. He's a bad man." Peering through street worn steely eyes, he asks again, "You sure you ain't him?"

"I'm sure, Horse. I don't like him either."

I turned like a rotisserie all night long, sleeping only intermittently. Things remained quiet, too quiet, in fact. With no bathroom exhaust fan providing white noise (ah, the comforts of home), I could hear every snore, belch and flatulent throughout the cellblock. Imagine sleeping in a concrete barn filled with animals suffering from a myriad of respiratory and gastro-intestinal afflictions. Understandably, nobody asked me the proverbial "how'd you sleep?" question in the morning. In jail, everybody gets up on the wrong side of bed.

It's 6 am, Monday morning, May 21. I should be starting my second cup of homebrewed Starbucks and trading my daily newspaper in on my Bible. Oh how I wish this was "just another manic Monday," but far from it. Nope, the best part of waking up this morning is…well, waking up, I guess. After all, some folks didn't and I'm seven hours closer to freedom than when I went to bed. I don't see how breakfast could be any worse than dinner and if the coffee's drinkable, I'll be good to go. Any edible food will be considered a bonus. Jail quickly changes your perspective on a lot of things, especially food.

Chapter 11

After picking up my tray from the food slot in the door, I hit the coffee urn. The cups are like small plastic tea cups, so I anticipate multiple re-fills. Not only am I desperate for the caffeine, but I'll need something stout to wash down my powdered eggs and pasty grits. Edible? Could go either way.

Having staked my claim at dinnertime, I don't have to consternate over where to sit. In fact, after last night, right next to Tony looks like "position A" to me. Being a little slow to rise this morning, the good Reverend T is making his way from the back of the chow line. Of course, we must wait for his blessing before eating. If I was convinced these were really eggs, I might be perturbed that they're getting cold waiting on our main man of the cloth. I'll just sip my coffee until Tony arrives.

"Ugh, I thought I'd already tasted all the bad coffee the world had to offer. This crap's awful," I say to whoever might be listening at the table.

If I don't drink at least three or four cups of this so-called coffee, I can add caffeine headache to my growing list of jailhouse infirmities. I'm thinking I could make a killing with an exclusive on the Starbucks jailhouse franchise. I can see the headlines now—Inmate Killed in Prison Coffee Riot. Prisoners commonly kill each other over cigarettes. Imagine the mayhem potential of a Low-Fat Grande Latte. I think I'm onto something.

Tony continues to amaze me. After joining us for the breakfast blessing, he doles out his food to several of the inmates and returns to his bunk. Apparently, the Hamilton Hilton Café doesn't offer carry-out and has a strict "you-snooze, you-lose policy." Not one to waste any of the limited jailhouse resources, Tony goes through this ritual every morning. Before nominating him for sainthood, I would like to know what he might be getting in trade for his breakfasts. Clearly, the man has a heart, but he's also a pretty smooth operator. I'm bettin' there's no such thing as a free breakfast in jail.

With no Tony to talk with, it's time to make another new friend. The guy next to me looks to be around 20 years old, if you can get past the 40 years of hard living etched into his face. His eyes are only half open and he barely opens his mouth when he speaks.

"Can you really eat this stuff?" I ask.

"Ain't bad," he says.

"Pancakes better."

"No offense, but I hope I don't get a chance to try them. With any luck, I should get out of here today. How 'bout you? What are you in for?"

"Armed robbery. Yeah, I didn't do the job, but I was driving the getaway car. They caught me and let the sombitch with the money get away."

"Bummer." (Do they say that in jail?)

"Yeah, it pretty much sucks."

"How long?"

"Dunno. Couple years, maybe. Depends if the f***attorney they gave me's any good."

Lethargy oozes from this sad young man's pores. His hopeless hollow gaze seems to reflect an emptiness at the depths of his soul. I have little doubt that he'll spend most of his life in prison. Yet, something within me cannot accept this. Could I make a difference in this young man's life? Could anyone?

"So, when you do get out, what are you going to do?" I ask, hoping to offer him some encouragement.

"Might go to Colorado and live with my sister and her husband."

"Great," I'm thinking. "The mountains have a way of putting life into perspective. Now we're onto something. I wonder if he plans to support himself or just mooch off his sister."

"Colorado is beautiful country. What kind of work are you thinking of doing out there?"

"I'd like to open a tattoo parlor. There's good money in it. Not sure how to go about it though."

Well, I guess somebody's got to do it, but I can't find it within me to encourage my friend to pursue his passion for body art. How's the saying go—"Screwed and tattooed"? He'll probably never open his tattoo parlor and I should probably close my little jailhouse counseling office, lest my own depression get any worse. Futures rarely look bright through jailhouse windows, because there aren't any. I wonder if the commissary dispenses Prozac.

More than half of the inmates return to their bunks after breakfast, many sleeping in until lunch. After a morning of soap operas, resulting in a stiff neck and a bruised tailbone, I understand why napping is the preferred leisure activity in jail. But, this is one nightmare I won't be sleeping through. Besides, I'll soon be enjoying my third square jailhouse meal. I wonder what's for lunch.

Shortly after lunch, my name is called along with about a dozen other Cellblock A inmates. We're shuffled into a holding room just off the

Chapter 11

booking desk to await our arraignment hearing via "video court." Instead of schlepping all us all down to the courthouse, they bring the court to us through a video conference hook-up. Nice to see my tax dollars being used to leverage technology within the criminal justice system. I'm not sure what to expect in video court, but anything's better than more of the same in Cellblock A.

We're joined in the holding room by inmates from other cellblocks. One in particular completely dominated the conversation within these uncomfortably close quarters. He was a hulk of a man who favored Sylvester Stallone in many ways. He looked very Italian with jet black hair and a five o'clock shadow that looked to appear around noon each day. His body wasn't Rocky Balboa hard, but it was certainly solid. After listening to him, I was glad he didn't reside in Cellblock A.

He never said what he was in for, but whatever it was cost him a minimum of eight years' freedom. Somehow he had recently been out of jail, perhaps awaiting trial. He thought that would be a good time to pick up a few essentials at Wal-Mart. All was well until he "forgot" to pay for his merchandise.

"Yeah, can you believe that s**t?" he said indignantly. "They're sending me up for eight years and now I got to f***k around with some petty shoplifting charge. You know what a shoplifting charge is to me, man?" He flicks his index finger as if to shoo something away. "It's a gnat, man. A f***ing gnat. What, are you, kiddin' me? I could give a s**t."

OK, I'm really not liking jail at this point. Was this guy born a fool without a conscience or is he a product of his environment? How long does it take for the average inmate to become as callous and jaded as him? Sitting five feet from this sad state of the American male, I have no doubt that he's capable of murder. I'm just wondering if he's already proven it.

God, I wanna get out of here…fast! But, it's show time.

Showtime in the Court

The video courtroom is the size of a small classroom. There's a TV monitor at the front of the room fronted by a table with a microphone in the center. There is one chair at the table. The table is encircled by about 20 plastic chairs (thankfully, much softer than the steel stools) in a half-moon formation. One of the first to enter, I take my seat towards the far left side of the room. We are accompanied by a female deputy and another woman who appears to be a court reporter. The monitor is turned on to an empty courtroom at the other end.

"All rise," says the bailiff through the speakers. Suddenly the monitor comes to life. As the viewing field expands, we see the judge entering the courtroom. Another court reporter and a handful of people in the gallery rise to honor the judge. I nervously look around to see if we're expected to do the same. Apparently not. We remain seated as the judge explains what's about to take place. Since I'm probably the only one in the room who hasn't been there before, I was glad to get clued in.

Arraignment hearings are for the purpose of formally stating the charges against the accused, entering their plea, setting bail and a court date and determining if a court-appointed attorney is required. It's great fun, especially the attorney appointment process. How else could you learn what the indigent criminals in your county are spending on utilities and other life necessities? In three out of four cases, a court-appointed attorney was required. In every case, we had to listen to the judge extract a monthly household budget from the accused. It was painful. No doubt, I was one of the few taxpayers in good standing in the room. The irony that I was, in effect, funding the proceedings, was not lost on me. This was particularly true when it came time to set my bail.

Since the proceedings started on the right side of the room, I was one of the last to go. A case before mine involved an indigent Mexican immigrant charged with wife beating. He seemed genuinely remorseful and offered no excuse for purposely using his wife as a punching bag. His bail was set at $2,500. Now it's my turn.

"Mr. Gradley Lindemann, you have been charged with three Class A Misdemeanors involving an incident which occurred on May 20, 2001 at a soccer complex in Hamilton County. Count I is battery against Tal White. Count II is battery against Mrs. Elaine Lindemann, presumably your wife. Count III is criminal recklessness, also involving Mrs. Lindemann. How do you plead, Mr. Lindemann?"

"Not guilty, your Honor."

"Let the record show that Mr. Lindemann has entered a plea of not guilty."

"The court understands that you are represented by counsel in this matter. Is your attorney Mr. Robert Hammerle?"

"Yes he is, your Honor."

His Honor then proceeds to editorialize, something he had not done in any other case before him that day.

Chapter 11

"Given the circumstances involving your wife, I don't understand why there's not a restraining order against you," the judge rhetorically asks in his most disdainful tone which he, no doubt, reserves for the most hardened of criminals — like, me? This unjust barb was like the first flaming arrow sent across enemy lines signaling that the battle was on. Yes, the battle was on, although this closed-circuit dose of humiliation was but a mere foretaste of things to come.

"Bail is set at $5,000. Your hearing is set for October 10. Once the paperwork is complete and bail arrangements have been made, you'll be free to go. While these charges are pending, you cannot leave the state without the court's permission. Do you have any questions?"

I can't believe it. My bail is twice that of the drunken wife beater. Mine a bizarre accident. His was a weekend routine. What kind of justice is this?

"The name's Bradley, your Honor."

"What?" he asks, obviously annoyed.

"My first name is Bradley, not Gradley. They apparently misspelled my name at the jail," I say with just a slight tone of disrespect in my voice. Little did I know that this misspelling would be a true blessing in disguise.

"Is that B-R-A-D-L-E-Y?"

"Yes," I say, purposefully omitting "your Honor" from my response.

"Fine. Let the record reflect the correct spelling of Mr. Bradley Lindemann's first name. Next?"

As we're being led back to Cellblock A, a voice comes over the loudspeaker, "Deputy Duncan, do you have Mr. Lindemann with you?"

"Yes I do," says the deputy.

"There are some members of the media here. We need to know if Mr. Lindemann would be willing to make a statement to the press."

"Absolutely not," I say emphatically.

My mind races to surmise what might await me on the outside. Is my freedom about to be re-defined by the freedom of the press?

Chapter 11

Media-ocrity: Any Publicity Is Not Good Publicity

My new accountant friend strongly urged me to wear my Rocky Balboa tee shirt inside-out upon leaving the jail. No sense in giving the media any more ammo than they already had, he reasoned. Like most advice one gets from one's accountant, it's a good idea to follow it. But hey, why be any smarter on the way out than I was on the way in? Besides, I'm sure the media has long since departed in pursuit of a real story.

Thankfully, they had left just minutes before I came out. My fears of embarrassing questions like, "Hey Rocky, how do you plan to improve the accuracy of your right hook before the next match?" OR "Who ya' fightin' next anyway—Julia Roberts?" proved unfounded…for the time being.

I spotted my son, Josh, in his car waiting for me and began walking towards him. Our firstborn put us through quite a bit over the preceding 10 years. So, our current role reversal gave me some sadistic pleasure. Josh didn't see the humor, however.

"So son, how's the shoe feel on the other foot?"

"It's not funny, Dad. There's nothing funny about this whole situation."

"I know that, son, but it looks like this situation is going to last for a while. Remember, when you lose your sense of humor…you lose. Right?"

"Yeah right. I wish none of this would have happened. What were you thinking, Dad?"

What I'm thinking, but not saying, is that here's a real case of the pot calling the kettle black. After all the hell he put his mother and me through, how dare he criticize me for one very understandable lapse in judgment. But, I don't want to go there…not now.

"Well son, I admittedly wasn't thinking. Truly, what I did was an instinctive paternal reflex. I never thought about hitting him. I just automatically swung."

"Yeah, you swung all right. At least you could've hit him instead of Mom."

"Thank God I didn't. If that guy's face looked like your mother's, I'd have bigger problems than I do now. How bad is it, anyway?"

"It's bad. Real bad. She looks like she's been beaten with a baseball bat. I can't believe she didn't have any stitches."

"How do you think she's feeling towards me right now?"

"I don't know. She can't be too happy with you, but I don't think you'll have to sleep on the couch or anything."

I'm thinking the couch is a pretty big upgrade from last night's accommodations. But, surely my bride wants me by her side tonight, doesn't she? It was a freak accident. She's clear on that, isn't she?

As we pull into our neighborhood, I slouch down in the seat to avoid detection by the neighbors. Things change quickly. Two days ago I was certain most of my neighbors didn't know I existed. Now, I'm convinced they're watching my every move. Please God, please don't let there be any media types around our house. To my great relief, there aren't.

"Thanks for the ride, son. By the way, what do I owe you for the bail bond?"

"$500. You can pay me later."

"Thanks. See ya', son."

As I'm walking up the driveway, what a strange mix of emotions I'm feeling. On the one hand, I'm thrilled to be out of jail and coming home. On the other, I'm dreading both seeing my wife in her beat-up condition and what the media might do with my story. It didn't take long for my worst fears to be realized…and then some.

I sheepishly enter our bedroom to find a very groggy and gory looking wife. She's in bed, lying on her side with her back towards the door.

"Hi honey, I'm home," I say as if arriving from just another day at the office."

She slowly turns over to face me.

"Oh my God," I think to myself. "I can't believe what I've done to her face."

Josh had not exaggerated. She does look as if she's been hit right between the eyes with a bat. The proverbial "raccoon eyes" don't begin to describe her condition. Both eyes are completely encircled with bright reddish-purple rings. Her left eye is nearly swollen shut. She has multiple lacerations from where her sunglasses were shattered and then smashed into her face. Seeing my beautiful bride in this condition was bad enough. Knowing that I had inflicted it upon her was more than I could bear. I began to cry.

"Sweetheart, I am so sorry. Please forgive me. I would never purposely hurt you. Please tell me you forgive me."

She said, "I forgive you," but it's what she didn't say that drove my own pain even deeper. She didn't say, "Of course, I forgive you. It was all the other guy's fault." She didn't say, "Forgive you for what? It was my fault for getting in your way." She didn't say, "I forgive you for hitting me, but I'm having a hard time forgiving the fact that you didn't beat the crap out of the guy who started it all."

No, she just very matter-of-factly and dispassionately said she forgave me. Leaving me to wonder if she really did and if I really deserved it anyway. I fought the urge to highlight my own personal sufferings during the past 30 hours. I sensed that this would elicit very little sympathy from the true victim.

"Can I get you anything?"

"How 'bout a new face?"

"No way, I love the one you have way too much. In two weeks, you'll be as good as new."

"Sure, whatever. Did you know you were on TV?"

Her words took my breath away. "What?" I gasped in disbelief.

"Yeah, you just missed it on the five o'clock news. Mug shot and all. At least you could have smiled for the camera."

If she only knew. My mind is trying to process what this means. It's all so surreal.

"So what did they say about it?"

"Oh, of course, they got most of it wrong. They said you and Mr. White had been arguing throughout the game. They made it sound like you were angry over Caleb's ejection and decided to take it out on the first person you bumped in to. It wasn't good. You're better off not having seen it. They'll probably show it again. I talked to one of the producers on the phone this afternoon."

"You did what?" I asked incredulously. "Our attorney said not to talk to the media under any circumstances."

"I know that *now*, but the station called me before his office did."

"So, what did you tell them?"

"I told them that the newspaper account was all wrong, but that what you did was wrong as well."

Chapter 11

"Oh great, just what I needed, you convicting me in the media before a jury even gets a chance to."

With fire in her eyes now matching that which surrounded them, Elaine hits me with her first counter-punch. "Look, don't you dare come in here acting as if you're the real victim. Tal White isn't and neither are you. I am. I'm the one who went to the hospital, not you. So, if you don't like the way I'm handling this, then next time, try handling yourself a little better."

POW! Although it really wasn't, it sure felt like a below-the-belt punch. In my heart, even though it hurt badly, I knew she was fighting fair.

"You're right. I'm sorry. It's just all happening so fast and I've never been here before. I really don't know how to handle it. I do know that the last thing we need is to start tearing each other apart. So…what can I get you?"

"Just some more ice water."

"Sure you don't want a good stiff drink?"

"No, I'm taking some pain medication they gave me at the hospital. On top of the pain in my face, I have a migraine."

As I'm fetching the water, I'm thinking to myself that it actually hurts to look at my wife's face. I can't believe that one punch could inflict so much damage. Then, a really disgusting thought enters my mind—I must pack a whale of a punch, albeit misguided. Sick! I'm actually feeling a touch of backwoods machismo over the accidental conquest of my bride. Good Lord, am I really that desperate to validate my manhood? I just might be.

For years after the soccer field incident, I prayed (yes prayed) that God would put me into a situation where I could justifiably pummel someone. Anyone, so long as he deserved it and God and the law would sanction it. I'll gladly go to jail again for a righteous cause, but never again for simply being out of control. If this sounds crazy, so be it. I doubt I'm alone in praying the pummel prayer.

"Here, honey," I say, setting the glass down on the nightstand and bending over to, *very* tenderly, kiss her on the cheek. "I'll let you rest now. I need to talk to the boys."

So what does a father say to his sons when he comes home from jail? Wish you could have been there? Did you miss me? How was your school day? There's no script. This isn't Monday night television, it's my life and it's spinning out of control. I'm passing through a re-entry time warp between Cellblock A and the free world. What next? What do I do? What do I say?

I'll talk to them separately. Our youngest, Bradley, wasn't even at the soccer game, so he's probably most confused. Caleb may well be angry with me, so I need to give him some room to vent.

Before I manage to track down the boys, Emily yells from down in the basement, "Mom, Dad, quick, turn on the TV. It's on Channel 15."

I run upstairs into the master bedroom just in time to see some new footage of me in my orange jailhouse jammies sitting in video court.

"Oh my God!" I gasp. "How can they do that? How did they get a hold of that videotape? Isn't that illegal?"

Thoroughly dismayed, Elaine quickly clicks to another channel, only to find that they too were running the soccer dad story. Last night's inner-city murders were receiving no media attention, while the entire city (or so it seemed) was an eyewitness to my humiliation.

The phone rings. It's another TV news producer wanting to get our side of the story for the late night news.

"No, I'm sorry, on advice of counsel, I have no comment. I will say, however, that indeed there is another side to this story and I look forward to the day when I can tell it."

The producer continues to push. "But Mr. Lindemann, all we're after is the truth. Don't you want people to know your side of the story? As it stands, you're not lookin' too good. So tell me, did Mr. White provoke you in some way?"

Oh boy, would I love to answer that question. How I'd love to go on television and tell the whole world the whole story. Lights, action, camera...

"I'm sorry, but I have no comment. Please don't call again. Good-bye."

Stunned and speechless, I sit on the bench at the foot of our bed for what seems like an eternity. While the media castigates me, I can do nothing but grin and bear it. Bob Hammerle says that you never try a case in the media. It's a sure loser. In my case, no matter what I say or do, at the end of the day, I'm still the Neanderthal who knocked out his wife at a soccer game. Nothing else matters, says my lawyer. I'm sure he's right, but I've only been home an hour and I'm already in need of a strait jacket.

Elaine snaps me out of my stupor. "Have you seen the paper?"

"No," I say dejectedly, wondering how much more I can take.

"There are three articles about you. You should probably wait a day or two before you read them."

Wait I will. How strange, as the owner of a small business, I've always bemoaned the lack of publicity afforded me and my firm. There seems to be a direct correlation between advertising dollars spent and news copy devoted to those advertisers. Go figure. Now, I'm getting more publicity than I could ever afford to buy, but it's not exactly what I had in mind. Were I a porn king, a boxing promoter or maybe even a politician, I might see the silver lining in my media cloud. As it is, I'm trying to figure out how to continue on without ever leaving the privacy of our home.

Despite the forebodings of the night before, I awoke the following morning determined to have a "business as usual" day. After my quiet time (including home-brewed Starbucks…ahhh), I head out for the health club before going to the office. At every stoplight it feels as though all eyes are upon me. I grabbed a ball cap on the way out the door, so I'm not nearly as conspicuous as I feel. At the club, no one referenced the soccer dad caper. While drying my hair, however, I was mortified to look down on the vanity to see this morning's paper opened to one of my articles. I dress quickly and beat a hasty retreat to the office. Whew! So far, so good.

After speaking to a few of my managers about the incident, I attempt to settle into my morning routine. Among the few hundred emails awaiting me is one entitled, "Brad's In Jail." It's from an anonymous sender and includes a link to a web site carrying my story. The sender had hacked into our company server and sent the email to all employees. So much for my consternation over keeping a lid on things. Let the damage control begin.

I hastily call a meeting for all employees in our Indianapolis headquarters. Much to my attorney's chagrin, I proceed to tell them exactly what happened. I figure the risk of them telling the truth to the wrong person is less than the risk of my entire company being kept in the dark. This is then followed-up with a company-wide email from my partner. While short on details, the email offers re-assurance that I'm not the thug portrayed by the media. A tough sell, given that my mug shot spent the day on the MSNBC home page. Let's get back to work.

My Stock Market Miracle

Upon returning to my office, I receive a call from my stock broker. He's calling to report that a large open order to sell stock the company owned had just executed. I can't believe my ears. Although I had prayed daily for over a year about my fool-hearty investment in this stock (all in a single stock), I had completely forgotten about the sell order. After the stock lost two-thirds of its value, I literally begged God every day to just let me get my money back. This morning, He answered my prayers. This very tangible sign of God's love and concern for me blows me away and brings me to tears.

I envisioned God and the angel, Gabriel, looking down upon me with God saying, "Ya' know, Gabe, Brad's got an awful lot on his plate right now. What say we take that little stock problem off his hands? I think he has plenty of other things to worry about."

I'm thinking, isn't that just like God? Just when you think you can't take any more, God steps in and takes it for you. Never early. Never late. He's a just-in-time God. I'm starting to think the sun just might come up tomorrow after all.

I spend the rest of my "work day" telling my side of the story to whoever calls in. After a dozen or so accounts, I realize that I need a "Cliff Notes" version. Otherwise, I'll get little else accomplished for weeks. I try this one out on the next caller.

"Ya' know, Jim, just because a guy deserves it doesn't make it my job to give it to him." This, plus the assurance that Elaine is healing nicely and hasn't kicked me out of the house satisfies most people's curiosity. Maybe I'll actually be able to have a somewhat normal workday tomorrow.

I remain safely ensconced in my office all day until it's time to make the trek home. My sunglasses don't give me as much anonymity as I would like. Much to my chagrin, Elaine calls and asks me to pick up something to grill for dinner, since she's not up for cooking tonight.

"Sure, I'd be happy to. Does anything sound good to you? How about some nice filets?"

"Whatever, I'm not even sure I'll feel like eating, so get something you and the kids want."

She didn't sound real perky. I thought better of humoring her by saying something about putting the steak on her eyes if she didn't feel up to eating it. Unfortunately, I now have to go into the grocery store and risk being spotted by someone who knows me. Or worse, someone who doesn't know me but now recognizes me from the evening news. I feared standing in the check-out line next to some wise guy asking,

"Hey, aren't you that Rocky guy who decked his wife at the soccer game?"

"Liked that right hook, did ya'? Well, try this one on for size, bud."

And then...BAM! It's slammer time all over again.

I escape the checkout line without event. At home, Elaine's on the back deck enjoying a beautiful spring evening and a glass of our house Sauvignon Blanc. This scene sure beats the one I came home to yesterday. Could we possibly be in for a pleasant evening?

"Hi honey, how ya' feelin'?" I inquire in my most empathetic voice.

"A little better, I guess. Now, I just feel like a small truck ran over me versus an 18-wheeler. How was your day?"

"Oh, you know, just another day at the office," I deadpan. "Spent most of it telling my side of the story. The highlight was when someone sent a company-wide email entitled "Brad's In Jail."

"You're kidding?"

"Wish I was. The email contained a link to one of the news stories about the incident. Oh well, at least I didn't have to spend much time worrying about our employees finding out. Now they all know, thanks to my secret admirer."

"Can you find out who did it?"

"Probably not, but I'm not sure I want to know anyway. Whoever it is has bigger problems than I do. Anyway, I got those filets. How's your appetite?"

"I might be able to handle one, so long as you don't overcook it."

"Atta girl. I think I'll join you in the wine and the sunset before I get dinner."

The phone rings while I'm in the kitchen pouring myself a glass of wine.

"Hello."

"Yes, hello, is this Mr. Lindemann?"

"Yes it is. Who is this?"

Chapter 11

"My name is "Shelly Columbo" with Big World Productions in New York. I've spoken to your wife several times today. Is she available?"

"One moment please," I say with a very puzzled look on my face.

"Honey, there's a Shelly Columbo on the phone for you. Do you want to take it?"

"Just tell her I'll call her at home later. You and I need to talk before I talk to her again."

"Shelly, she says she'll call you at home after we've talked."

"Great. I'll look forward to her call. Thanks. Good-bye."

"OK, so what was that all about?"

"I was going to wait for you to finish you first glass of wine before getting into it, but so be it. Shelly is the producer of a new Oprah-like talk show. She found out about the incident while surfing the net for ideas and called me. After talking to me, she invited us to come on the show. Whada' ya' think?"

"I think you're crazy. What did you tell her?"

"Pretty much everything. Why not? Nothing could be worse than what the media is already saying about it. Besides, she promised me that everything I told her was strictly off the record. Wouldn't you like an all-expense paid trip to New York City?"

"Well, I hope you enjoy it, because afterwards my next all-expense paid trip could be back to the Hamilton County Jail. We can't go on national television with these charges pending against me, honey. Our attorney would go ballistic."

Her puppy dog brown eyes are now turning blue. Bad enough that I mutilated her face, now I'm denying her a once-in-a-lifetime opportunity in the limelight.

"Hammerle can't tell ME what to do. Maybe I'll just do it without you. Emily would love to go with me."

"Now wait a minute. Let's not get all crazy here. If you do this, there's no way you should do it without me. I'd have to be there to lend credibility to your statements regarding what a wonderful husband I am and how totally out-of-character my actions were. Don't you think?"

"Yeah...probably."

I can feel her reeling me in. "Just imagine it, Brad. You and me on national TV. When will we ever have another chance like this?"

Chapter 11

"Never again, I hope. It would be a great opportunity to plug my book, however. Guess I better get busy writing it, huh? This would sure provide some incentive to get it done quickly. How can we be sure they're not setting us up? Those talk shows seem to thrive on embarrassing their guests."

"I spent hours on the phone with her. She seems like a very genuine person and the show sounds like a class act. Nothing like Jerry Springer."

(Did I tell her about watching Jerry in jail?)

"She assured me that they have no desire to do anything that would embarrass us or add to your legal problems."

"Alright, I'll talk to Bob about it, but if he says we can't, then we can't. Agreed?"

"I guess, but I still don't understand how telling the truth can hurt you."

"There goes the sunset. It's grillin' time! You just stay put while I get this show on the road."

On the way to the health club the next morning, I'm trying to imagine what our attorney's going to say when I run the talk show idea past him. Actually, it doesn't take much imagination. He's going to hate it, as well he should. What was I thinking? To give Elaine even the slightest inkling of hope on this was really stupid. Now, I don't even want to talk to our attorney about it, but I promised Elaine I would. Might as well get it over with.

I call him on my cell phone, hoping to just leave a voicemail.

"Hammerle here."

"Bob. Brad Lindemann. Sorry to bother you so early, but I've got something I need to run by you...."

"Let me explain something to you one more time, Brad. Right now, in your case, there is no such thing as good publicity. The last thing you want to do is to bring any further attention to your situation. The media will lose interest. It's just a matter of time. Anything you do to remind them of it will only extend that time. And remember, at the end of the day, you're still the guy who knocked out his wife. Nothing you do is going to change that fact. Time is our friend, Brad. We just need to let this case sit until the feeding frenzy is over and forgotten. I have made it very clear to the prosecutor that I will not be happy until this whole thing just goes away. Right now, the best job I can do for you is to do *absolutely nothing*. You need to do the same. If you or your wife appears on television, you do so to your personal peril, in my opinion. Now, are there any other asinine questions I can answer for you?

"No counselor, that pretty much covers it. I had to ask, but already knew the answer. The limelight will just have to wait. Thanks Bob. Have a good day."

"Call me."

I wonder if all lawyers say "Call me" in lieu of "Good-bye." It makes sense when you think about it. Every time you call a lawyer he starts the billing meter. Good-byes, at least in theory, stop it. So, when a lawyer says "Call me" what he's really saying is, "Send money."

Unlike a lot of folks, I don't hate attorneys. I just hate living in a world that requires so many of them. My lifelong friend, S. Frank Mattox, was an attorney. In fact, he's the one who referred me to Bob Hammerle. According to Frank, Hammerle's the best criminal lawyer in town. Frank did his lawyering in New Albany, the southern Indiana river town we grew up in. Whenever I have a legal question, I just call my good friend, Frank, and he takes tells me what I need to know. Or at least he did, until he died suddenly in 2007 at a mere 51 years of age. I miss my dear friend with whom I shared some of my life's greatest adventures.

My day hasn't even begun, yet I'm already dreading going home. My battered bride won't take kindly to the news that her all-expense paid trip to New York is off. I'd rather take a beating myself than tell her. I'll rehearse my approach during my morning swim.

After countless years of counting laps, I have found my swims to be much more enjoyable and productive when I just swim for an hour and get out. Instead of being preoccupied with what lap I'm on, my mind is free to roam. I've had some of my best ideas (both of them) while in the pool. Solved many of my own and some of the world's problems while blowing bubbles. No matter how lousy I feel going in, after my swim followed by a hot steam or sauna, I always feel better.

I considered the steam room at the Five Seasons my own personal prayer closet. More often than not, I'm alone in there. For me, this room has always symbolized the pressure cooker that is my life. I enter the steam room with stress demons digging their talons into my narrow and heavily burdened shoulders. I leave, having cast those burdens upon my Heavenly Father and melted the demons' talons in the hot steam. Top it off with the closest possible shave (no mirror required) and I'm ready to seize the day. Little did I know that the day was about to seize me. Fortunately, it didn't seize me first and was pretty much business as usual…until I got home that evening.

Chapter 11

All the way home, I was trying to figure out the best way to tell Elaine that our time in the New York media spotlight would have to wait. There were no talk show guest appearances in our foreseeable future. I decided to just get it over with as soon as I got home.

"Honey, Hammerle went ballistic when I mentioned the talk show idea to him this morning."

"Really? I've never met your attorney, but I'm already sick of him."

"I hear ya'. Let's see what the evening news brings and go from there, ok?"

"Do I have a choice?" she asks.

"Not really. Thanks for understanding. Some things, however, you can't possibly understand. Like what it's like to feel as if everyone in the world is looking at you. And, what it's like to be portrayed as a wife beater. Or, what it's like to be literally attacked by the media."

"No, I suppose I don't. But, I do understand a few things that *you* apparently don't. I understand what it feels like to be hit in the face by your husband and sent to the hospital. I understand what it feels like to be too embarrassed by your looks to leave your own home. And, I understand what it's like to have a husband who's more concerned about his public image than he is about his wife."

I'm starting to think the media is going to forget about my soccer incident long before my lovely bride does. Am I missing something? It's not as though I went gunning for her. She stepped directly into harm's way. I never saw her until she lay on the ground. Isn't there just a little shared responsibility here? Looking back, I realize I really was missing something…complete ownership of the problems and pain that I had caused.

We never even chilled the wine I brought home that night. Why bother? An entire case couldn't take the edge off our raw emotions. We sit in silence for most of the evening, wondering where and when the next torpedo will hit our family. Exhausted and exasperated, we go to bed early. Sleep, if it can be found, will bring a welcome reprieve from this day of media-ocrity.

Chapter 11

Letter to Pop

May 29, 2001

Hey Pop,

Mom said under the same circumstances, you would have done the same thing. I'm not sure about that. You always seemed more under control than I've felt most of my adult life. But times were easier then, right Pop? Maybe. I'm not sure about that either. If fact, I'm confused about most things these days. Sure wish you were here to unconfuse me, Pop.

Adult life? Mine with you contained 16 years on life's shelf between two beers as bookends. Remember that illegal draft we shared just before I was married in 1976? I was neither old enough to drink nor marry, yet both worked out just fine. I've still never shared the secrets you shared with me that day. Never will. Been married to that cute little co-ed for 25 years now. I think we're going to make it, but it hasn't always been easy. Sure wish you were here to help us along the way, Pop.

About that second beer…our last one together. It was July of '91. Like always, you made the coffee that morning. That afternoon, we had a beer on the back patio. Mine went into a sick stomach and a broken heart. Yours, into a bag by your side. A few hours later, you walked me to my car and we said our last good-byes. Actually, what you said was, "See you later, son." I'm holdin' ya' to that, Pop. Sure wish you were here now though, 'cause I'm in a bit of trouble.

Remember that book you never got around to writing? Well, like I promised I would, I wrote it… for us. Sorry I sullied the family name in the process. Not the first book inspired by a jailhouse experience. Won't be the last. Do you think the end can ever justify the means? I'm not sure. Guess I'm still confused about a lot of things. I miss you, Pop. Sure wish you were here. I'll see ya' later…I'm sure…I think.

Love,

Son One

12. Take Your Marks!

I was born with fins on my feet and, figuratively speaking, water on my brain. For my first 17 years, swimming was my life. I grew up with a pool in my backyard and started swimming competitively at age seven. I routinely swam in three different age groups, often winning all three in all four strokes. Talk of Olympic promise started early and fueled what soon became my aquatic obsession. I was a swimmer. Little else mattered.

New Albany, Indiana didn't have much to offer an aspiring Olympic hopeful like me. When I turned 12, it was obvious that if my Olympic dreams were to come true, then I would have to train in the big city across the river, Louisville. My mother cheerfully made the two-hour roundtrip five days a week so I could work out with the Plantation Sea-Bees. It was during these early morning trips that I acquired my taste for coffee. I've been drinking it ever since, although I did eliminate the cream and sugar many years ago.

After five years of being *the* big fish in a small pond, I came to Plantation with some pretty unrealistic expectations. In fact, my first summer with the Sea-Bees marked the beginning of the end of my Olympic dreams. This was swimming at a whole new level and, in my heart, I wasn't sure I could measure up. But then again, I had never worked out with such intensity, so perhaps I would see some dramatic improvements. If not, I would soon become an "also swam" and I knew it.

Just before I entered high school, my family moved north to Kokomo. As luck would have it, I would be attending a brand new high school with the finest pool I had ever seen. My new swim coach had won the state championship at the cross-town high school several years earlier. If I had to move, I couldn't imagine a better situation to move into. My Olympic hopes were still alive.

That summer, I practiced twice a day and played 18 holes of golf in between. I'll never forget the first practice. I was so out of shape that I cried underwater for a miserable 90 minutes. After sweating on the golf course all day, I would often cramp up during the second practice. I started taking salt pills to compensate. By the time the summer ended, both my golf game and my swimming had improved. I was looking forward to high school.

During high school, I was always one of the best swimmers on the team, but never *the* best. My coach turned out to be the aquatic equivalent of Bobby Knight. He coached by fear and intimation, constantly reminding me of how far short I was falling from my potential.

I'll never forget walking into practice one day and seeing Coach on the bleachers. He was looking at me and shaking his head. When I asked him why, he said, "I just don't understand how you can have a body that big and strong and not make it go any faster than you do."

These harsh words from my swim coach were spoken to me during my sophomore year in high school. The Book of Proverbs says, "There is one whose harsh words are like sword thrusts." Indeed, my coach had taken the sword of his insensitive tongue and thrust it into my impressionable heart. My Olympic hopes and dreams died that day, along with a little part of me. A new journey had been forced upon me. If I am no longer first and foremost a swimmer, than who am I? If swimming is no longer my life, then what is?

My father's career once again took us northward. This time to Valparaiso, the summer before my senior year in high school. My parents would have allowed me to stay in Kokomo, so I could graduate with my class. However, I chose to move with my family. A seemingly odd choice, given that my future bride, Elaine, would stay behind in Kokomo.

Though very much in love with Elaine, I now abhorred the sport that had so defined and completely dominated my life for 10 years. By moving to a new town and a new school, I could finally move beyond my painful swimming past. In Valparaiso, I wouldn't have to explain to anyone why I wasn't swimming during my senior year. In Kokomo, I'd never be able to quit the team, so I would be forced to slosh my way through one final season. I had no intentions of swimming in college, so what was the point?

I remained in Kokomo through the summer, but moved to Valparaiso just before school started. Quite ironically, Valpo had a strong swimming program headed by one of the finest gentlemen I've ever met, Mr. Skip Bird. Coach Bird was a dwarf who stood about four feet tall, although his arms were of normal adult proportions. A brilliant man who taught English when not coaching, Skip Bird had an undersized body and an oversized heart. I'll always wonder what could have been had Mr. Bird been my high school swimming coach. As it was, I enjoyed assisting him with the swim team before my mid-term graduation in January.

Through high school, I was the academic black sheep in our family. My three sisters regularly brought home straight A's on their report cards. I, on the other hand, had the temerity to log one or two B's with equal consistency. When my swimming career ended, I became much more serious about academics. The transference of energy from the pool to the classroom was very obvious. I still longed to be the best at something, so through my college years, that something was academics.

I graduated "With Highest Distinction" from Indiana University in 1978. During my college career, I received three B's and all the rest A's. The B's came one at a time during each of my first three semesters in college — Art History, European History and Karate. It's now embarrassing to admit that the images of the three college professors who marred my perfect academic record are forever etched in my mind. I finally achieved my first perfect 4.0 GPA during my sophomore year. After that, it was straight A's all the way to my bachelor's degree. This was the first time in my life when my best seemed good enough.

Finishing the college race was particularly gratifying for me, since my life had changed dramatically halfway through. Elaine and I had gone off to IU together. She a Chi Omega. Me a Phi Psi. After two years of being the quintessential Greek couple, we got married between my sophomore and junior years. Our plan was to trade our fraternity and sorority houses in on a cozy little apartment and continue with our educations. Four months later, those plans changed forever when Elaine became pregnant with our first child — Joshua Louis.

To get ready for our new arrival, I cut back to six credit hours and took a full-time factory job. This experience probably did more to motivate me to finish college than anything else. One particularly poignant moment occurred when I cut off the tip of my finger in a sheet metal cutting machine. I remember being driven to the hospital and thinking about how cold and uncaring that machine had been towards me. The experience of having a part of my body, albeit a small one, here one moment and gone the next really shook my foundation. I couldn't wait to exchange those steel-toed work boots for a pair of wing tips.

Chapter 12

13. Business Life Lessons

The following semester I responded to an ad in the school newspaper seeking college life insurance agents. Having recently met with a veteran agent and being favorably impressed, I decided to check it out. Maybe I could get those wing tips sooner than I thought?

I quickly became fascinated with both the life insurance product and the sales process. So, with a baby on the way, I decided to leave my good paying factory job for straight commission life insurance sales. This seemingly irrational decision marked the beginning of my sales career.

I loved the life insurance business. Correction—I loved selling life insurance. Finding people to sell it to? Now that's another matter. My wife distinctly remembers listening to me making prospecting calls from the kitchen table in our one-bedroom apartment. On the best night ever, I made 50 phone calls. Talked to 25 people. Was summarily rejected by 20 of them, many simply hanging up on me. And, I got appointments with five. It was not at all unusual for this torturous ritual to yield no appointments at all. By the time it was over, Elaine was in tears and I was exhausted. Such is the life of a rookie insurance agent.

Trust Fund Baby Comes of Age

I supported our new family by selling life insurance to law students...or at least trying to. Not sure why I decided to focus on a market consisting of people with no time, money or borrowing capacity since most were saddled with student loans. There was one very memorable exception, however

William was a law student at Indiana University at Indianapolis. He came from a wealthy Chicago family and enjoyed a sizeable trust income. He wasn't haughty, despite his blue-blooded background. Somewhat unsure of himself, William was determined to stand on his own two feet, especially in the eyes of his father.

"So, William, which will it be, the $50,000 whole life or the 65-Life plan?"

"Well, I'm leaning towards the 65-Life, but I really think I need to run it by my father this weekend when I'm in Chicago."

"Really? Is your father going to be the one paying for this?"

"No, I'll be paying for it," he confidently shot back.

"Do you need his permission to take out this policy?"

"Not really. I just thought I should get his opinion."

I could sense him regressing into a well-established pattern of always seeking Dad's permission, never his forgiveness.

"So what are you going to do if his opinion disagrees with yours? Would you get the policy anyway?"

"Probably," he said with some trepidation.

"Then is there really any reason not to get it now? If you gave me a check today, the coverage would be in force as you're driving to Chicago this weekend. Wouldn't that be a good feeling, William?"

"Yeah, I suppose it would."

"Great! Would you like quarterly or annual premiums?"

With that closing question, I closed one of the most gratifying sales of my young career. To this day, few sales have equaled the satisfaction of helping William Dickinson III step out of his father's shadow and into full manhood. Come to think of it, only one other life insurance sale brought me more satisfaction than the one to young William. It was the one I made to my Uncle Bob. More on that later.

My Time At Big Blue

I've often wondered how different life would have been had I continued in the life insurance business versus joining IBM. What if my second attempt at the "DPAT" (Data Processing Aptitude Test) had once again landed me in the lower quartile versus the upper one? What a paradox. I got into IBM by the skin of my teeth, then went on to be ranked number one in my training class. I still have the gold pen and pencil set they gave me. I pull them out now and then whenever my battered ego has me feeling like a zero number one. Do we continue to derive strength and encouragement from our past successes, no matter how long ago they occurred? To date, that's certainly been my experience.

My IBM life was a good life, but it wasn't meant to be a long one. My five plus years at Big Blue gave me invaluable experience. I learned many lessons that have served me well throughout my career. One in particular stands out.

Just Passing Through Oklahoma

I left IBM in February of 1984, having spent what seemed like a lifetime in Oklahoma City during the previous six months. It was my first management job. My timing wasn't very good, however. Oklahoma was heavily dependent upon the oil business. A business which decided to go bust about the time the Lindemann family moving van rolled into OKC. It didn't take long for Elaine to start asking questions that I didn't have very good answers for.

- "Now, tell me again why we're here, 750 miles away from family and friends?"
- "Why is it that you're making less money as a manager than you did as a salesman?"
- "When are you going to stop coming home so stressed-out over work that we never talk to each other?"

I didn't know it yet, but help was on the way. It would arrive shortly after the imminent storm clouds passed.

Since times were tough in my new territory, I requested and received a $3,000 commission advance. A few weeks later, my boss called me into his office and asked for it back. He said that they had violated policy by giving it to me, so I really needed to give it back. I told him that wasn't possible, since the money was already spent. I also told him that for the first time in eight years of marriage, Elaine and I were having problems as a direct result of my work-related stress. This demand note call certainly wasn't going to help.

It was pouring down rain when I left the office that evening in my electric blue 1970 Dodge Dart. I had purchased the car from a fellow IBM manager for $400. While pondering how to break the latest bad news from the office to Elaine, my nearly vintage car sputters to a stop. Unable to restart it, I run the six blocks back to the office in a torrential downpour with neither raincoat nor umbrella. Although it was past five o'clock, the branch was abuzz with activity when I arrive, looking every bit the proverbial drowned rat. There was no mistaking it; I had hit the low point in my IBM career.

The guy who sold me the clunker helped get me started and I was once again on my way home. By now, I had entered the emotional danger zone. Beyond praying, I was literally yelling at God. My fears turned to anger. My anger added to my fears. I was drowning in a vicious cycle of self-pity, having lost all perspective on my life. Words could no longer express my intense emotions. Groans became sobs. Sobs became whimpers. Whimpers became quiet pleadings to God for grace and mercy.

As I pulled into the garage, a peace that surpasses all understanding came over me. I knew the conversation Elaine and I were about to have wouldn't be an easy one. Yet, somehow from somewhere deep within me, I also knew that it was going to be all right. Like me, Elaine would need some time to process her emotions. After that, she too would know peace in the midst of our miserable circumstances.

The following day, I received a phone call from a former IBM'er I had met the year before. Don Scott had left IBM to join a computer services company and wanted to know if I would be interested in talking to them about an opportunity. Could this be the answer to our prayers? Of course, I was interested, so we made arrangements to get together.

My wife wanted to make two things perfectly clear before I flew out for the interview. First, I could not accept a straight commission job. She was still traumatized from my life insurance days. Second, they had to buy our house from us. With these marching orders, I headed south to Memphis, my first time there. I'll always remember my phone conversation with Elaine from my hotel room late that night.

"Wow, it really sounds great, honey. What's the salary?"

"Well, there isn't a salary, but they'll pay me a draw until my commissions build up."

"Hmm, how big of them. They *will* buy our house, right?"

"Not exactly. They'll pay for the move, but we'll have to sell the house on our own."

"So what if we can't sell it?"

"We *will* sell it. You'll see. Don't worry about it"

Sell it we did, in 10 short days for more that we paid for it just six months prior. It was as if God were saying, "I'm in control. Follow me." So, we did follow Him, to our new life in Germantown, Tennessee, a beautiful Memphis bedroom community.

Chapter 13

Enter the Salad Days

Our first three years in Memphis could not have been better. Our last two could not have been worse. While we were in Oklahoma, we had to take out a second mortgage to pay off our American Express bill. After our first year in Memphis, we paid off our house and were completely debt-free. For three years, I made more money than we knew what to do with. I proved that point by making many poor investment decisions during what my partner, Don, referred to as "the last of the salad days."

Our salad days were rapidly wilting during the fall of 1986 when Elaine gave birth to our fourth child, Caleb Bradley.

Although his nickname, "C Monster," came later, baby C came into the world as a 10-pounder of monstrous proportions. How apropos that our future soccer star attempted to enter the world feet first. The resulting emergency C-Section was quite traumatizing for everyone excepting the culprit who caused it. This too was a foreshadowing of things to come. Wherever he went, Caleb would be the biggest fish in the pond and others would be expected to swim along or drown in his wake.

Entrepreneurial Terror

I wonder how many new businesses have risen from the ashes of a flamed-out career. Quite a few, no doubt. On April Fools' Day 1989, one more was added to the list. Like many before me, I entered the world of entrepreneurial terror—broke, broken and more than a little scared.

Wanting to be closer to family and friends, we moved back to Indianapolis to start our new venture—the Information Technology Division of Ambassador Financial Services, Inc. Say that a few dozen times a day for a while and you quickly realize your business needs a much shorter name. So, we soon became Ambassador Consulting until we re-branded to Ambassador Solutions at the turn of the millennium. We've been in the IT consulting business for 27 years now. Before hiring our first consultant, I would jokingly refer to myself as "an empty suit pulling an empty wagon behind me." The fact that I was a salesman, not a techie, was never in doubt.

Things were really interesting in the early days, since we couldn't afford to hire a consultant until we had work for them to do. My sales pitch went something like, "Mr. Client, if you'll commit to bringing this consultant in to do some work for you, then I'll commit to hiring him."

Employee #2

I first met "Tim" at a truck stop diner about an hour north of Indianapolis. Around 50 years old, he was overweight and out of shape, never having met a cheeseburger he didn't like. This was validated over the years. Tim never ordered anything but a cheeseburger and fries during the many meals we shared.

Although Tim was more than a little rough around the edges, he had a photographic memory and a penchant for programming like few people I'd ever met. Tim was the first passenger to climb aboard my empty wagon. I hired him on a handshake and, with that, Ambassador Consulting had its second employee.

As memorable as Tim's hiring was, his firing was even more so. He was on an assignment in Northern Indiana, so he took an apartment up there and came home on the weekends. Every Friday around three o'clock Tim would head south towards home. During that two-and-a-half-hour drive, he would consume a 12-pack of beer iced down in the passenger seat of his pick-up. That's one beer every 12 minutes while driving 70 miles per hour.

When the officer pulled him over just north of his home town, the eleven empty beer cans and the Breathalyzer results painted a pretty scary picture. Tim got busted big time. Since I couldn't find a client willing to let him work remotely from a jail cell, I was forced to let Tim go. The last words he ever spoke to me were, "Are you going to pay me my vacation?" Indeed, we did, and thus ended the first Ambassador Consulting career.

The Early Days

> *If you own a new business, it's impossible to borrow money without providing a personal guaranty. In the event of default, the lender can not only take everything you have in the business, but everything you have personally as well. This would include your home, but unfortunately, does not include your teenagers.*

Entrepreneurs who make it big tend to look back and romanticize the start-up phase of their businesses. I suppose if I ever make it big, really big, I might do the same. But frankly, from where I'm sitting, I don't get it. Starting a business is difficult at best. At worst, it can literally kill a person. If the work itself doesn't kill you, the worry will. The 24/7 burden of business ownership is impossible for non-owners to fully understand and appreciate. As to my three-legged metal desk held up by phone books, I'm not sure anybody really cares.

Three months after starting our business, I took a rare afternoon off. Yet to close our first deal, I was beyond frustration. I was starting to feel a little desperate. Easy to understand, given my lack of income and the very expensive home we had yet to sell in Memphis. I remembered what a well-known business school prof had said about entrepreneurial terror. He said that until you wake up in the middle of the night with your spine sweating, you haven't been an entrepreneur. Well, it was two o'clock in the afternoon, but I could distinctly feel my spine sweating as I was checking my voicemail.

To my astonishment, I had a message from one of my prospects saying he was ready to close the deal we had discussed the previous week. My loud "whooohooo!" was cut short by the lump in my throat. I thought of those restaurateurs who frame their first dollar. How could I memorialize our first sale? Frame the contract? Take a picture of the client and me? Every idea seemed cheesier than the one before. History was in the making and I knew it. I just didn't know what to do about it. So, I did what any self-respecting tycoon would do, I hugged my wife and took her out to dinner. Now, we're rollin'!

I'd rather be an entrepreneur than married to one. There's no doubt in my mind which duty is tougher. Elaine has filled the role beautifully. She patiently listens to my incessant whining about the state of the business. She exercises great restraint by offering advice only when it is truly sought. When she's had enough, she knocks me back in line with her favorite question, "why do you think they call it work?" As a free-spirited artist, Elaine forces me to paint at least some portion of my life outside the lines. I love her for this and so much more.

Did I mention we were broke when we started our business? Consequently, from our first day in business, we were incurring additional debt to pay the bills and buy groceries. As quickly as they had come, gone were our debt-free Salad Days in Memphis. Of the many rocks in the entrepreneur's bag, I find debt to be the most burdensome. Truly, "the borrower is a slave to the lender." This slave goes to bed every night dreaming of the day when, once again, he will owe no one anything.

If you own a new business, it's impossible to borrow money without providing a personal guaranty. In the event of default, the lender can not only take everything you have in the business, but everything you have personally as well. This would include your home, but unfortunately, does not include your teenagers.

Teenage Terror

For aspiring entrepreneurs with teenagers, I have this word of advice—*get a job!* Josh was 12-years-old when I started the company. We quickly learned that one should never combine an infant business with a pubescent child. This is particularly true if said child is the eldest of five. During our firstborn's teen years, Elaine and I were often reminded of why some mothers in the animal kingdom eat their young. It saves them both a lot of grief.

Don't get me wrong. There are some positives to raising teenagers. For example, compared to raising teenagers, running a business seems like a walk in the park. When I needed a real break, I went to the office, where it's safe...and quiet...and neat...and clean. There's something very comforting about being around people who get paid to listen to you and do what you tell them.

Option Envy

In days past, the only way to get rich in business was to put your own capital at risk by starting one. Stock options have changed all that. Nowadays, the quickest path to riches lies in joining the right company at the right time and riding the stock option express all the way to the bank. Particularly within the high-tech industry, vast amounts of wealth have been transferred to employees who never put a single dollar at risk. I've never been so fortunate.

While I realize that these employees were responsible for creating much of this wealth, it rankles me nonetheless. It seems to me that the free enterprise system should primarily reward taking risks and creating businesses versus hanging on to those who have. Stock options have created an entire Nuevo rich class of employees who make small business owners feel…small. Were the shoe on the other foot, I'm sure I'd feel differently. As it is, I guess I suffer from a mild case of option envy. But hey, I get to shave the boss every morning.

Government

I used to go to Washington DC to lobby on behalf of our industry association. After five futile years, I decided it was a waste of time. Every year we would bring the same issues before the same politicians and staff members. Every year they would feign interest, promise action and do absolutely nothing of substance. What did I get out it? An autographed picture of Newt Gingrich posing with me and my cohorts. Maybe I could donate that to a Democratic silent auction fund-raiser?

Government sure can make things difficult for business owners. The Feds in particular seem determined to maximize the liabilities associated with every employee. If I truly counted all the costs and risks of employees, I'd probably never hire another one. If you try to mitigate these risks by hiring independent contractors, then the government steps in and re-classifies them as employees, charging the business usurious back taxes and penalties. From a business owner's perspective, when it comes to employees it seems to be damned if you do, damned if you don't. Like children, if employees didn't have the ability to curse you, neither would they be able to bless you. That's why, despite their inherent liabilities, I truly love being surrounded by fired-up employees passionately pursuing a common purpose.

What Next?

Entrepreneurs constantly have to ask themselves, "What next?" Politicians, on the other hand, are led around by schedulers and handlers from stump speeches to ribbon cutting ceremonies to rubber-chicken dinners. These people predetermine what politicians do next. The politician's job lies not in knowing what to do, but rather in knowing what to say. Even at that, others are typically telling him/her what to say. Makes you wonder if what a politician truly thinks ever really matters. Personally, I doubt it.

Senators and congressman start every day with a neatly-typed 3 ½ x 8-inch schedule card. Since becoming an entrepreneur, there have been many days when I would have loved for my scheduler (the one I don't have) to simply tell me what to do.

Fortune 500 CEOs are often driven by the businesses they oversee. Entrepreneurs, by definition, drive their businesses. The entrepreneur awakens each day to the realization that "If it is to be, it is up to me." Such freedom and flexibility is what lures many into the world of entrepreneur terror. The crushing responsibilities that go along with it is what sends many back to the land of gray suits humbly asking, "Won't someone please just tell me what to do next?"

Big Business

How do big businesses get so big? This question has intrigued me since my early career days as an IBM marketing trainee. Back then, IBM trained college graduates for an entire year before putting them into the field. It began with the first two-week training class in Endicott, New York. We stayed in a beautifully-renovated mansion called The Homestead. This pristine white house stood atop a hill on a lush rolling estate. Matronly women served meals in starched black and white uniforms. Days ended with milk and cookies at 10 o'clock. I was very fortunate to start my business career with IBM at the height of their glory.

As of this writing, Sam Walton has created more wealth for

shareholders and family members than any other entrepreneur in history. Yes, surpassing Bill Gates and Steve Jobs. How'd Ole Sam do it? By executing an age-old business model to perfection—merchandizing dry goods and groceries to everyday people.

There have been some innovations at Wal-Mart, but nothing akin to Edison's light bulb or Gates' operating system. Many would-be entrepreneurs labor under the misconception that unless they can divine the new big idea, they can't enter the world of entrepreneur terror. No doubt, the late Sam Walton is smiling down upon his loyal patrons every day, saying "Attention Wal-Mart shoppers, it just isn't so." The absence of a big new idea no more assures business failure than its presence assures success. For my limited capital, give me a medium-sized, not-so-new idea with a well-thought-out execution plan. If others have tried same and failed before, so much the better.

Corporate Culture

A company's values contribute more to its success than most big new ideas. During my stint with the White Shirt Army, all IBM trainees were required to memorize the IBM Basic Beliefs:

1. Respect for the individual
2. Pursuit of excellence
3. Best possible customer service

Having committed these beliefs to memory 38 years ago, I can still recite them at gunpoint today. This is more a tribute to IBM's practice of these beliefs than to my memory capacity. As a young IBM'er, I saw the Basic Beliefs in action every day.

IBM's unique "Open Door Policy" is perhaps the best example of their "respect for the individual" belief in action. This policy grants any employee free access to any manager at any time regarding any issue. If an IBM employee has a grievance against their manager, they can take it to the CEO if they desire, without fear of reprisal.

I was once interviewed by a high-ranking IBM executive who had flown into town to investigate an Open Door matter. Apparently, one of my former managers had filed a grievance over being terminated. It came as no surprise to me that this poor manager had been fired. To my observation, he should have been. I was shocked, however, to observe firsthand the extremes to which IBM would go towards respecting an individual former employee. It made me proud to be an IBM'er.

At the other extreme, the ruthless treatment I received on the way out the door of my Memphis employer made me determined to never rob another human being of their dignity, as they had robbed me of mine. In founding my firm, I devoted as much time to the formulation of our Basic Beliefs and Core Values as I did to our business plan, perhaps more.

Bankers

Unless you're among a chosen few, if you're going to enter the world of entrepreneurial terror, then you'll be taking your favorite banker along for the ride. Entrepreneurs take money-making risks. Bankers make money avoiding those risks. Therein lies the rub. The entrepreneur-banker relationship is quintessentially one of love-hate.

Bankers are generally very nice people, though I've found a few exceptions along the way. I particularly enjoyed the time my banker gave me the "no problem" salute up to the day before a loan closing. He then walked on the deal. I guess I should be grateful to my banker for bringing my sister and me so close together. To keep the deal together, I had to borrow money from sis. Please forgive the sarcasm, but good grief, they walked the day before the closing with no plausible explanation as to why!

As if the banking house didn't already hold all the cards, then you have wild card of mergers and acquisitions. Top executives at many banks gave up running their businesses years ago. They're too busy scouring the countryside looking for other banks to buy. Pity the poor entrepreneur whose bank becomes one of them. Come renewal time, all bets are off.

Back in the summer of 1998, I naively thought it was time for a sabbatical. After 20 years in the workplace, I needed a break. My bank thought otherwise. Having sold out to a large out-of-state conglomerate, my friendly hometown bank became a cold, faceless bureaucracy. When our loans came up for renewal, it was evident that they could not have cared less about me or my business. The new terms were so untenable, we had no choice but to look elsewhere. So, instead of relaxing on the beach in Florida, my CFO and I beat the pavement in Indianapolis looking for a new banking partner. Fortunately, we found one.

When things got tight a few years ago, our banker and CFO spent the entire morning going over our bleak financial picture. This fateful day later became known as "Black Thursday" in our company, our first near-death corporate experience. We slashed expenses to the bone and, for the first time ever, had to let some people go. At one point during this most miserable day of my business career to date, I joined my banker and CFO to go over the numbers. Pretty soon all three of us were reduced to tears. I immediately knew two things. First, we were in big trouble. Second, we had the right banker helping us through it.

I must confess, watching my banker cry over our firm's situation probably took five years off my entrepreneurial lifespan. Make that seven. When you're an entrepreneur, many days are dog days. Black Thursday was certainly one of them.

Risky Faith and the Freedom to Fail

The world of entrepreneurial terror sounds pretty terrifying, doesn't it? That's because it truly is. Entrepreneurs never get over feeling like everything they've worked for could be taken away tomorrow. Why? Because it could be. Life within the ET zone is lived on the edge of a slippery slope. One misstep, and the entrepreneur plunges deep into a vast crevasse containing the shattered dreams and bankrupt accounts of those brave souls who went for broke and, like many, got just that.

Do entrepreneurs start businesses "because it's there," like mountain climbers who live to scale another peak? Is entrepreneurialism a calling of sorts, such that it must be followed, no matter what the price or risks? How else can you explain why, against all odds, otherwise intelligent people willingly subject themselves to the perils of the ET zone? To embrace such terror, they must be taking something in trade that makes it all worthwhile, even the failures.

My journey into the ET zone has been a journey of faith. While it is indeed lonely at the top, I have never been alone. God has been with me every step of the way. When I misstep, He is there to keep me from the slippery slope. At the end of my days, I want to have lived a life that was pleasing to Him. His Word tells me that "without faith it is impossible to please God." So how can I please Him? By living a life of faith in Him. It takes faith to enter the ET zone. For me, that means faith in the living God and that makes for a very exciting journey. So you ask, "Why did you start your business, Brad?" Because He is there.

Like the climber's fear of falling, the entrepreneur's fear of failing spurs him on. The true entrepreneur understands that to have a shot at success, one must have the freedom to fail. There is a sign on the gates of the ET zone which reads: *Proceed with Caution. Freedom to Fail Ahead.* Upon seeing it, many turn back, as well they should. The fear of failure obstacle is never completely overcome by the entrepreneur. He continually creates new ways over, under, around and through his many failures, yet is never immune from the fear of them. This too is as it should be.

Teddy Roosevelt knew well that the freedom to fail and the freedom to succeed were but two sides of the same coin:

> *Far better it is to dare mighty things, to win glorious triumphs even though checkered by failure, than to rank with those poor spirits who neither enjoy nor suffer much because they live in the gray twilight that knows neither victory nor defeat.*

What Entrepreneurs Do for an Encore

The book I won't write, but someone should, would be the chronicles of businesses that failed despite having been founded by an entrepreneur fresh from a fabulously successful venture. To my observation, business sequels rarely outshine the original.

There are, no doubt, a myriad of reasons as to why this is the case, but the one that stands out for me is that of timing. You know, that which has been said to be everything. Yet, despite this wisdom of the ages, most encore entrepreneurs make the mistake of believing that their previous success was due more to plan and process than to timing and good fortune (a.k.a. luck).

Let me be clear on this. Planning and process do not appear on my short list of strengths. And, most certainly, when these two are preceded by perfect timing and good luck, the combination can create the proverbial "hockey stick" curve. But, the best laid plans and processes will fail miserably if executed at the wrong time when the lucky stars are misaligned. You can take that to the bankruptcy court...as many over confident encore entrepreneurs have.

Three Things I Thought I Knew About Money

During my early years at IBM, I was constantly looking for ways to supplement our income. While my peers were single, flush with cash and driving BMWs, I was supporting a young family on one income. It wasn't enough. I fully supported Elaine's decision to be a stay-at-home mom and was willing to do whatever it took to provide for our family. That's how I found myself at an Amway meeting one evening in Indianapolis circa 1979.

The large convention hall was packed with enthusiastic entrepreneurial wannabes. Beyond the possibility of closing our income gap, I was attracted to the strong Christian and patriotic tones throughout the program. The crescendo came as one of Amway's most successful distributors took the stage. He was a very confident and charismatic speaker who whipped the crowd into a veritable frenzy. When he opened his large briefcase stuffed with bills of an undisclosed denomination, the crowd went wild. I'll never forget what he said next.

"There are three things I know about money," he boomed. "It's better to have it than not to have it. It's better to have more of it than less of it. And, it's better to have it sooner than later. Ya' know what I mean?"

Indeed, I did, or so I thought. He was talking my language…have more now! Had I known then what I've painfully learned since, I could have spared myself and my family a great deal of angst over things financial. But like many, I'm prone to learn things the hard way.

Clues were everywhere, starting with the absurd prayer I shared with the guy who had invited me to that Amway meeting. While dropping me off at our apartment afterwards, he asked me to join him in an unusual prayer…the "who wants to be a billionaire?" prayer. Apparently he did, because that's what he asked the God of the Universe to make him — a billionaire. Good grief! Of course, he was going to give most of it away and save the world. So, it was okay to ask for such a bounty from the "giver of all good things." Wasn't it? This was one of my first of many "what was I thinking?" moments relating to finances, investing and countless lame-brained, get-rich-quick schemes. All because I wanted to have more now.

Let me hasten to add that I have nothing against Amway or any of the legitimate multi-level marketing companies. Many distribute excellent products at great values, while providing their distributors with ceiling unlimited income opportunities. In fact, during the late 1990's at the height of the dot com crazy days, Amway was one of our largest clients. Our consultants played a significant role in building Amway's first business-to-consumer web site, Quixtar. All to say, Amway wasn't the problem during my early family/career building years. The problem was my misguided motives.

Stock Market

During the aforementioned Salad Days we spent in Memphis, I was an early adopter of online stock trading. After putting the kids to bed, I'd dial in to Fidelity Investments to figure out how we could have more now. Never mind that I was making more money than we knew what to do with at the time. Where we were didn't matter. All that mattered was getting further ahead. So, when my efforts to do so netted us an extra $100,000 one year, I could see my lucrative hobby one day becoming my day job.

There's a fair amount of wisdom in the old "success breeds success" adage, provided it's clear what bred success in the first place. I didn't make $100,000 in the stock market because I was using a proven formula backed by extensive research. Oh no. I made $100,000 in the stock market for one simple reason—I got lucky. Reminds me of another adage, "I'd rather be lucky than good." Best to forget you ever heard that one. I've been trying to since 1986, the year this stock market genius took financial matters into his own hands, all the while lying to his wife.

Just before my lucky year in the stock market, we had the blessed privilege of paying off our mortgage. I was 29 years old with a wife and three kids. Our Williamsburg style home was just two years old with five bedrooms and a gorgeously landscaped backyard swimming pool. We had no debt and two new vehicles in the driveway. Everyone was healthy and our oldest was only ten, so any problems we had (and I can't remember any) were miniscule in comparison to what we would face in the coming years. So, I did what I'm sure Ward Cleaver did on occasion. I created problems.

After a year of no mortgage payments, I realized that I hadn't even noticed the difference. We were making so much money that our mortgage payment had become a rounding error in the checkbook. We weren't like the hard-working blue collar couple who shed blood, sweat and tears to pay off their original 30-year mortgage by finally making payment number 360. Besides that, it seemed a shame to have all that equity in our house doing nothing to earn us even more money. Have more now, remember?

From the early days of our marriage, by mutual agreement, Elaine has had very little involvement in our finances. 40 years later, we both admit this was a terrible mistake that has caused many problems over the years. I hope to remedy this during our "transcendent years" (I hate the phrase "golden years"), but I know it will be an uphill climb. This is relevant to the rationalization process I went through in 1986 when I remortgaged our house without my wife's knowledge or consent.

"She doesn't understand finance and investing and doesn't want to. She's always left that stuff up to me, so why is this any different?" I rationalized. "I'm sure when she sees the beach house she can buy with the extra money I'm going to make in the stock market, she'll think it was a great idea."

Sure she will. I not only did what I knew she wouldn't want me to do, but when it came up later in conversation, I flat out lied about it. That was 30 years ago and remains (in my mind) my single greatest moral failure as a husband. Yes, worse than punching my wife's lights out, because that was a freak accident. Lying to her about a matter of such importance cut a piece of her heart out. Though I repented long ago, I'm still paying the consequences of that grievous sin today…and rightfully so.

"Oh what a tangled web we weave when at first we practice to deceive"

-Sir Walter Scott

Keeping Up with the Jones

Tangled web indeed. While our home equity had been laying idle, I had been watching one of my best friends get rich by trading stock in the company founded and run by his father. For the first time in my life I had some chips of my own to bring to the table. $300,000 to be exact. That money was also sitting idle waiting to be the down payment on the new home we were building on fairway number 12 of the TPC at Southwind golf course. I was sure I could double that in the market by the time the house was finished, so we would once again be mortgage free. Sure thing.

I've learned the hard way that the only thing sure about a "sure thing" is that there is no such thing. Ya' know what I mean? Investing $300,000 in a single stock might make sense for Warren Buffett, but it sure didn't make sense for Lucky Lindy from Indy back in 1986. In the wake of the bankruptcy, the local paper said my friend's father and his business partner treated their company like a "financial playground" playing very loosely with the stockholders' money. My money. At least it was my money until I lost all but $500 of it on a bankrupt company that I invested in because I was trying to keep up with the "Jones."

Note to self: $300,000 at 5 percent over 30 years equals $1.3 million.

Dream Home Nightmare

Oh how I wish the misery ended with my $300,000 loss in the stock market. But, our dream home itself became a nightmare before it was ever finished. Besides the money we'd just lost, the fortunes of my employer were rapidly reversing and my job was in jeopardy. We put our "dream home" on the market before we moved into it. With both homes on the market, we planned to live in the one that didn't sell first. That turned out to be the new one, so we did move into it, though our time there was brief. I lost my job a few months later, so we moved back to Indy to start Ambassador Solutions…broke and broken.

I should correct a misperception at this point. The Southwind house wasn't "our" dream home, it was "my" dream home. Elaine would have been perfectly content in an existing home at half the cost. It was "have more now" me who insisted upon building the house of our dreams. By then, it should have come as no surprise that in pursuit of more, I ended up with less…much less.

Once I lost my job, we couldn't qualify for a mortgage on our new home. Thanks to a very understanding banker, we were able to continue carrying the construction loan until the house was sold. Timing is everything (that I do believe) and ours could not have been worse in selling our home in Southwind. We lost over $200,000 when we sold it to the CEO of the Shoney's restaurant chain. Haven't had a Big Boy since.

If no one else needs a time-out at this point, I sure do. It's hard recalling these points of self-inflicted pain. Harder still to memorialize them for the whole world to see. So why I'm I doing this? Why in a sane and sober state of mind would I subject myself to the embarrassment and ridicule that these revelations invite? Because in so doing I hope to find some, maybe only a handful, who unlike me have the capacity to learn from others' mistakes. Helping to spare a single person one of these very costly mistakes will make the toil and the torment worth it. So please, don't do as I've done, but do learn from it.

Options and Futures and Hedge Funds

After 14 years of working for my business, by 2003 I was ready for my business to work for me. The company was on the rebound having survived its first near death corporate experience in 2001. I was more aware than ever that all of our financial eggs were in one fragile basket. Beyond that, I just wanted to broaden my horizons a bit. So, I delegated day-to-day operation of the company to a very capable chief lieutenant and began searching for a new day job.

Having joined IBM fresh out of college in 1978 and leaving only five years later, I often wondered where that career path might have taken me. No regrets, just curious as to how I might have done within a large global enterprise. I wasn't interested in going back to IBM, but I did have some preliminary meetings with several of the large companies headquartered in Indianapolis. I'll never forget what one of their managers told me. He leaned forward and lowered his voice as if about to reveal the formula for Coke.

"You do realize, Brad, that everyone in here wants to be where you are. It will be hard for them to understand why you want to be where they are."

That was a game-changing moment for me. Until then, I labored under two false premises. First, that most employers would consider me a great find in the prime of my career. Second, that I could readily adjust to life inside the big corporate world. Having owned my own business for more than half of my career at that point, I was a risky proposition for prospective employers. Fast forward 13 plus years, having turned 60, I'm virtually unemployable in the outside world. Just as well, because I really don't think I could have made the adjustment. There are simply too many "it is what it is" moments within large enterprises. Turned out my new day job wouldn't be a job at all.

Despite my miserable stock investment record to date, I was convinced that all I lacked was time and training. So, when my personal money manager came up with a "black box" approach to the market that appeared to be the financial Holy Grail, I was all ears...and eventually all in. Believe it or not, we formed a hedge fund with my partner as the man behind the curtain and me as the sales guy. Made perfect sense at the time given the "sure thing" (here's your sign) nature of the offering. There was just one problem. Our black box became a black hole. Clients lost a lot of money and I lost a few friends in the misguided 18 months I devoted to that DOA turkey.

Recall our company's Values in Action that sheds important light upon our ill-fated hedge fund venture. It states that we "Recognize weaknesses as strengths taken to extremes." Perseverance happens to be one of my strengths. Taken to an extreme, I will persevere beyond the point of reason, so it becomes a weakness. Such was the case with our hedge fund. We should have put a fork in that turkey after six months, but

I gave it another year it really didn't deserve. Looking back, I think that was the most wasteful 12 months of my career.

Still determined to find the financial Holy Grail, I set my sets on options trading. I spent an entire week in Salt Lake City alongside a professional options trader learning the ins and outs of this highly complex business. The "set it and forget it" sales pitch that lured me into the options trap proved irresistible. Once I learned the basics, I could generate a substantial income by devoting an hour per day to options trading. Not exactly. I got bored and disillusioned after losing $5,000 trading stock options. A small price to pay for another financial exorcism. And, it came with a nice bonus. Along the way, I also learned just enough about futures trading to be dangerous.

During my options training courses, one session was devoted to futures trading. It was a teaser primarily meant to entice students into signing up for more extensive futures training. For some, however, it was like holding a T-bone steak under the nose of a coonhound and telling him to "stay." As soon as the handler turns his back, the hungry hound devours the steak. Once I returned to my office and there was no instructor around saying "down boy" when the futures trading steak appeared on my screen, I couldn't resist.

Recall the fateful year I made a $100,000 in the stock market? That was nothing compared to the $5,000 I made in five minutes trading DOW futures. "Wow, maybe I really can make all the money I could ever spend in just one hour a day? This is crazy!" At least I got the crazy part right. You see, to make that $5,000 in five minutes, I put $1 million at risk. That's right, I risked a cool million dollars. Worst yet, I didn't even *have* a million dollars. What I did have was $5,000 more than I had five minutes earlier. I was hooked.

I had no idea what I was doing. But since it worked once, I figured odds were good that it would work again. I waited all of an hour or two for the DOW futures price to dip so I could reload at a lower price. Some of you savvy investors will recognize this move. It's called "trying to catch a falling knife." Little did I know how dangerous such a move could be.

As My DOW futures knife went into a free fall, my anxiety went off the charts. I couldn't believe how foolish I'd been. Barring a miracle turnaround, I stood to lose $1 million dollars and that's exactly what I deserved. After God miraculously gave me back my entire $300,000 single stock investment the day after I got out of jail, I couldn't possibly expect Him to bail me out again. Though I had no choice but to ask Him to.

Aloha Blues Christmas

Imagine sitting on a pristine beach on the island of Maui in Wailea, Hawaii. You're there on a Christmas vacation with your wife and two youngest children. The weather is idyllic. The abundant sea turtles make for great snorkeling right off your hotel beach. In a few days you'll be enjoying your favorite avocation when you go scuba diving off Molokini's back wall. Add dinner at the famed Grand Wailea Hotel and it's beginning to look a lot like one awesome Christmas. But...

Maui, we have a problem. The patriarch of this wonderful family can't enjoy a single moment of his vacation. Before departing, he made the biggest financial mistake of his life. One that could cost him dearly. With each sip of his Pina Coladas, he's feeling more and more like a real coconut. And of course, his lovely bride has no idea what's troubling him.

I was in sheer agony. The options contract was set to expire in March. It could be a very long winter. By God's amazing grace, it wasn't. Having re-entered the daily operations of my business, I was sitting in a staff meeting when I received an alert on my laptop. My order to sell the DOW futures contract had executed. The interminably long, gut wrenching saga was finally over. I fought back tears as long as I could, then excused myself from the meeting. Had I not been in my office, I would have been prostrate on the floor—exhausted, humbled and oh so grateful.

God takes vows very seriously. So should we. Vows to God should never be taken lightly. Fully appreciating that fact, I vowed to God that I would never again trade futures contracts of any kind. I documented this vow and shared it with both my wife and my CFO. Looking back, I still can't believe the position I put myself, my family and my business in. I'm truly believe that this financial life threatening situation forever cured me of my financial Holy-Grail-pursuit disease. And, it served as a poignant reminder that there is only One who is holy and fully worth pursuing.

Our Little Jewel Box on the Beach

Ours is a family of beach bums. As such, we've spent the vast majority of our vacations on a beach somewhere. More often than not, you could find us on one of the powdered sugar beaches on Florida's panhandle. One of our favorites is Seaside, Florida.

One fateful morning as we were preparing to leave Seaside after one of our many Spring Breaks there, Elaine overheard a coffee shop conversation that would alter our future vacation plans. One of the patrons was discussing a new beachside community eight miles east of Seaside called Rosemary Beach. It was being designed by the same new urbanism pioneers who had laid out Seaside about 15 years earlier. Within minutes of telling me about her new discovery, we were in the car headed to Rosemary Beach.

Not long thereafter, we became one of the first to purchase a lot at Rosemary Beach. Having witnessed the incredible success of Seaside from the sidelines, we were thrilled to enter the Rosemary Beach game early in the first quarter. As we were walking back to the sales office with our architect for our initial design planning meeting, we passed a lot that had the modest beginnings of a foundation laid down. I asked our architect, "What's this?" She said, "Oh, that's our Little Jewel Box. It's a model home and not for sale." "Not for sale?" I queried. "Everything's for sale. It's just a matter of price."

When we got back to the sales office, we saw a 3D model of the Little Jewel Box. It took our breath away. We couldn't imagine being able to design anything more beautiful than that. Within a few weeks, we had sold our lot at a tidy profit and bought the Little Jewel Box. It proved to be the best real estate investment we've ever made, though that is admittedly not saying much. We only owned it for 18 months before reluctantly selling it for nearly twice what we paid.

Believing the Little Jewel Box to have been a lavish gift from God, Elaine and I deeply regret having sold this precious gem. We didn't realize it at the time, but this also marked the beginning of the Florida real estate bubble that went on to burst around 2005. I wish I could tell you that we missed all the "fun" when things went bump in the night on our favorite beaches. But...

At the height of the Florida real estate insanity, there were over 50 new high rise condo projects under construction in Panama City Beach alone. It was sheer madness. After watching it from the sidelines since selling the Little Jewel Box, we couldn't resist the temptation to jump back into the game. Of course, we didn't know the game was already into overtime. We bought a condo in the building next door to our best friends and signed a purchase agreement for one under construction down the beach. Six months later, the market peaked. Not long thereafter the bubble burst. We eventually lost over $400,000 on the "condo from hell." But hey, at least we were still on the hook for the one under construction down the beach. That developer went bankrupt before the project was finished. You know you're in way over your head when you consider losing "only"

$45,000 to be a miracle.

So, the void created by looking our gift Jewel Box in the mouth and selling it created a giant sinkhole into which we threw nearly $500,000. Had we simply kept that which God had given us, we would own a beautiful beach house today in one of the most prestigious seaside communities in the country. Once again, the "have more now" side of me was left with less than when I started…much less.

Taxes Are Never Really Avoided

For many years after our Salad Days in Memphis (1984-89) had ended, I told people that my father had not prepared me to handle our new found wealth. Dad was a very conservative accountant who made a good living, paid his taxes and put what little was left over in the bank. That approach didn't seem to apply to the circumstances I found myself in. Add to that the fact that I somehow divined that paying more than 10 percent of my gross income in taxes was simply un-American. This goofball notion led me to make many poor investments with tax avoidance as my primary motive. I soon learned that you never really avoid paying taxes, you only defer paying them.

Of all my tax avoiding investment schemes, only one worked exactly as it was designed to do, though that turned out to be not such a good thing. It took a three-inch-thick document to describe my highly complex "wrap lease." The $1 million dollars of equipment contained therein filled an entire semi-trailer. The resulting tax deductions in the first few years were huge, worth far more than the cash I put into the deal. It seemed too good to be true and was. Eventually the tax man cometh in the form of a nasty thing called "phantom income."

Phantom income occurs when you have to report income to the IRS during a year in which you didn't actually receive any cash income. For example, if you incur $100,000 of phantom income and are in a 35 percent tax bracket, you owe $35,000 in taxes. Now, the theory of the wrap lease was that the investor would invest his tax savings in the early years, so he would have the cash to pay his tax liabilities in the latter years. Recall, taxes are never really avoided, only deferred. As you've probably guessed by now, when the tax man cometh my way, I had no cash to pay his bill. That's when I met the most creative tax accountant in the State of Indiana.

When I called my uncle for advice on what to do about my tax dilemma, he said, "I only know one man in the entire state who might be able to help you. His name is Howard Gross." When I first met Howard in 1989, I was flat broke, had a struggling new business less than a year old and six hungry mouths to feed with another one coming (unbeknownst to me) just a few months later. Oh, and I was facing an income tax bill that was twice my annual income. I left that first meeting pretty discouraged. The most creative tax accountant in the state didn't seem to have anything in his bag of tricks that would help me. I told him I'd have to declare bankruptcy if he couldn't come up with something.

During our next meeting, Howard had one of those "Ah hah" moments my uncle had known him for. "What kind of relationship do you have with your church?" he asked.

"Huh?" I said. "What does that have to do with anything?"

"Well," he said, "if we could donate the deal to your church, since they are a non-profit and not subject to taxes, they could absorb all of the phantom income. And, as an inducement to do the deal, they would receive the remaining cash payments of about $5,000. From the church's perspective, it's a nice $5,000 donation. From your perspective, it's a financial miracle worth a few hundred thousand dollars. How's that sound?"

I was speechless. It sounded like just what I needed…a miracle. No surprise that Howard's been doing my taxes ever since, as well as our company's tax and audit work for over a quarter century now. After many other failed investments primarily made for tax reasons, I came to realize that Dad had actually prepared me pretty well for my nouveau riche status. Had I simply paid my taxes during the Salad Days and put the leftovers in the bank, I'd be several million dollars ahead of where I am today.

Despite my miserable investing track record and my Dad's example, I am not suggesting that putting your money under a mattress (a.k.a. bank) is the right thing to do. I am suggesting, in fact imploring you, to check your motives for whatever investment you're considering. If you find yourself trying to catch a falling knife in the stock market…pull back. If you're convinced that you're looking at a "sure thing" …look again. If you're trying to solve a tax problem…plan ahead. If you think you're ready to own a second home in a resort area…think again. That second home could easily end up owning you.

Chapter 13

Don't Let a Second Home Own You

Since we'll never fully recover from our last second-home experience, please allow me to expand upon this painful topic before leaving it on the ash heap of failed investments. Given the glut of resort properties all around the country, buying one now makes little financial sense. If you're tempted nonetheless, consider these simple guidelines. If you can't afford a second home unless you rent it out to others most of the time, then you really can't afford a second home. If you can't spend at least three months of the year (preferably six) in your second home, then you really shouldn't own one lest it end up owning you.

There are great rental bargains to be had on resort properties of every imaginable type. Our best friends rent a luxury condo in Florida for three months during the winter for a price equal to just the annual property taxes on the unit. And, they're paying top dollar. I realize that there are intangible benefits to owning versus renting a resort property. And, it's hard to put a price tag on such benefits. Just know that a rational cost/benefit analysis of any resort property will point towards renting versus owning every time. Add to that the freedom and flexibility that renting affords those who resist the siren's call to ownership and it's an open shut case. Regardless of how our financial future unfolds, I cannot foresee a scenario in which Elaine and I will ever own another resort property. Unless of course, the current owners of The Little Jewel Box leave it to us in their will.

If I Had a Financial Do-Over

Now that my credibility as a financial advisor is completely shot, I thought it only appropriate to tell you what I would do differently if I knew then what I know now.

If I had a financial do-over, I would invest in all of the top quality cash value life insurance I could afford on every member of my family. Not real sexy. Won't make you the toast of the town at your next cocktail party. But, what consistently building a cash value life insurance portfolio over time will do is give you and yours true financial freedom at a much earlier age than most people ever attain it.

I actually believed this as a young College Agent, but I didn't have the financial means to act upon it...or so I thought. When I did come into some money, I was more interested in catching falling knives and keeping up with the Jones than in securing my family's financial future with something as seemingly mundane as permanent cash-value life insurance. Mind you, I've always been very well-insured, but the majority of my life insurance is of the term variety, so there's no investment element to it.

Consider this life insurance policy that I wish I had purchased for each of our grandchildren just after they were born. It is a *permanent equity indexed policy*, meaning that the cash values are invested in an index pegged to the stock market, much like an indexed mutual fund, such as the Vanguard Total Stock Market Index Fund. Since the actual cost of the insurance is so cheap in the early years, most of the premium goes towards the cash value investment portion of the policy. The results over time can be amazing. For a $50 per month investment in a grandchild's future, by age 70 the projected cash value is $943,615 with a $1,085,157 death benefit. And, the initial death benefit protection is $182,873.

"Why does a newborn need $182,873 worth of life insurance?" you ask. He/she doesn't...now. But later in life, they will need many times that amount of coverage. This policy is simply a way of getting an early start on a savings plan that happens to have a self-completing death benefit feature. At a long term projected rate of return of 7 percent, you virtually give up nothing for the security of knowing that the investment plan will be completed regardless of when the grandchild's life ends. To one day die a millionaire, all that grandchild would have to do is keep contributing $50 per month to this policy once ownership is assigned to him/her. But, it could be even better than that if "B-Pa" (yours truly) plans properly and arranges in his will for the policy to be paid-up upon his death.

Imagine how much brighter the financial future of coming generations could be if parents and grandparents would consistently invest modest amounts of money in quality life insurance products for their children and grandchildren? Towards this end, I would love to see 529 College Savings Plans expanded to include cash-value life insurance as an investment option. I would also love to see life insurance companies do much more to promote life insurance for newborns and infants. The Gerber Life Insurance Company has been doing this since 1967, but they promote relatively small amounts of insurance with pretty mediocre returns on their cash values. Blue chip companies like Northwestern Mutual should be doing much more to promote the incredible benefits of starting a life insurance program at the earliest possible age.

Had I done what I'm now recommending to others with regards to permanent life insurance, I would be several million dollars ahead today and, more importantly, my extended family's financial future would be far more secure than it is. Only 20 percent of my life insurance is permanent. The remaining 80 percent of term insurance will become prohibitively expensive in just a few years. Converting it to perm will likely be out of the question for the same reason. This is why I reinstated my life/health insurance license a few years ago. Someday, I just might try to more tangibly help others avoid my mistakes, by building their financial futures on the bedrock of a quality permanent life insurance program.

Chapter 14

14. The Chosen One

Throughout my personal faith journey, God has reaffirmed His love for me and mine in a myriad of ways. None more moving, however, then the way He arranged for the completion of our family with the addition of our fifth child.

In 1990 we had four children, a fledgling business less than a year old and were in the early stages of recovering from devastating financial losses in recent years. That's why when my wife started talking about adopting a "special needs" child I thought she was completely off her rocker. So much so, I assumed she'd either come back to reality or the guys in white coats would show up one day to take her away. Either way, my strategy was to wait it out. I had plenty on my plate and couldn't begin to digest anything else, much less another mouth to feed.

His given name was Samuel Alexander. His birth mother was my wife's younger sister. A few weeks after he was born, God revealed to Elaine that "Samuel" was going to be our son — a little secret she chose to keep to herself. A few weeks later, her sister called to ask for our help in finding adoptive parents for her newborn. She was at a difficult time in her life and compassionately chose the loving option of adoption. Having been very active in supporting crisis pregnancy centers and promoting adoption, I was thrilled to hear of her courageous decision. Imagine my surprise when I heard my wife say the words that would forever reshape our family tree — "we'll take him."

I nearly choked on my Hamburger Helper. Unlike when God sent an angel to Joseph in a dream to give him a "heads up" that his fiancé was pregnant with the Messiah, I was clueless in Indianapolis. After all, there were a million or so childless couples in America who would have given anything to adopt this child…this chosen one. Never mind the thousand reasons not to adopt and only one reason to adopt — because God said to. Seriously, that's the best you got? Uh ah. I'm not buying it…not yet.

If you've seen the movie War of the Roses with Michael Douglas and Kathleen Turner, you understand something of what life was like around our house in the days following Elaine's "we'll take him" bombshell. We were like two prize fighters who would step into the ring, punch each other's lights out (figuratively speaking), then retreat to our corners to rest up for the next round.

While we threw no punches, we did throw an object or two…maybe three. Pity the fool who came through that bedroom door at the wrong time. Can't recall if we fixed that before selling the house. Though we did stop short of swinging from the chandelier, beyond that it was a three day no holds barred battle of wills.

My best friend, Tim, and I ran together every weekday morning at six o'clock. It was a bitter cold February day in 1990. Our constant banter kept our minds off the cold and our aching legs. For the last three days, we had spent every minute of our run talking about one thing…my wife's insane notion of adopting her sister's son. Tim and I were in complete agreement. It would be the biggest mistake of our lives. But, Elaine was standing her ground. How would we ever resolve this, the greatest conflict of our married life?

Before heading in to shower, we stood shivering at the end of my driveway praying that my wife would come to her senses. But God had us at "Amen." All Heaven broke loose, as I looked up at Tim with tears in my eyes and said words I could not have imagined uttering until that moment. "He's my son, isn't he?" Without hesitation, Tim replied, "Yes brother, I believe he is." God had confirmed what He had revealed to Elaine two months prior.

In the blink of a tear-filled eye, God changed the hearts of two best friends, confirming His plan to change the course of Lindemann family history. His name is Bradley Louis Lindemann II, named after his father. This "chosen one" will forever serve as a poignant reminder of how God can turn our mistakes into His miracles…how He still speaks to His children today…how when two or three are gathered in His name, there He is in their midst. 26 years later, from that frigid February morning in 1990 to this very moment, I have never had a moment's doubt about our decision to adopt Bradley. He has been a wonderful blessing to our entire family who will soon be celebrating his second wedding anniversary with his high school sweetheart. God is sooooo good!

15. Life-Saving Experiences

Over the eight months from October of 2012 to early June of 2013, I had three life-saving experiences. What follows is the true accounts of all three incidents. One friend's name was changed to "John" to protect his true identity. Beyond that, I've done my best to recall exactly what happened on those fateful days. During this same timeframe, the business of life had tossed me into a raging sea without a life preserver. My hope in sharing these stories is that they might somehow provide some life-preserving encouragement for those whose seas are anything but calm.

Polihale Beach, Kauai (October 2012)

When we visited my sister and brother-in-law at their condo in Kauai, Hawaii in the fall of 2012, we explored a new beach every day. Each more beautiful than the previous one. None more beautiful, however, than Polihale Beach on the west end of the famous Na Pali cliffs. Flooding from the nearby rain forest and constantly shifting sands make this breathtaking seven-mile stretch of white sand beach difficult to reach, but well worth the effort. Such was the case on this gorgeous day.

I don't remember why our oldest daughter, Emily, called as we were getting out of the car to hit the beach. I do remember uncharacteristically cutting the conversation short. It had been a long trek. I was anxious to catch some rays before catching some epic pre-winter waves. Given my passion for sun, sand and salt, it's odd that I've never been on a surfboard. That didn't keep me from body surfing some of the best surfing spots in the world, including world famous Waimea Bay on Oahu. They won't even hold a competition there unless the waves are at least 20 feet high, about half the size of what we experienced on Polihale Beach this day.

As we settled into our beach chairs, our heads were on a swivel. To the right, we had a majestic view of the Na Pali cliffs. To the left, seven miles of the most beautiful beach imaginable with only a handful of people in sight. In front of us the turquoise Pacific glistened under the late morning sun rising behind us over the rain forest. The waves were beckoning me, but I resisted their siren call, content to be just where I was…in the moment. Such moments were all too rare for me.

Eight months before this contented moment, I was heading to a much-needed spiritual retreat at the Toth Ranch in the Colorado Rockies sponsored by Revel Ministries. It was a bright sunny day, unusually mild for late February. Our spirits were Rocky Mountain high. As the prematurely blonde designated driver, I was thoroughly enjoying the banter between the two 20-somethings in the back and my 30-something buddy riding shotgun. Then suddenly, things got quiet.

"So Mr. Brad," 20-something Jimmy said, "from your vast life experience (a nice way to call someone an old geezer), what can you tell us that could help us become the best men we can possibly be?"

I pondered Jimmy's question for quite a while. He couldn't have been more sincere and his buddy, David, seemed equally engaged. I flashbacked to Jack Palance's "One thing" discussion with Billy Crystal in the movie City Slicker. Young Jimmy was asking me, "What's the one thing?" Sensing the importance of the moment, I silently prayed, asking God to help me answer this provocative question. Then it came to me: *Wherever you are...be there.*

Wow! Talk about cutting to the chase. A mere five words, the profundity of which was lost on no one in the car that day, least of all me. Though most always physically present for my lovely bride and five wonderful children, I've been frequently mentally and emotionally absent. Choosing instead to grind on something in the painful past or fret over something in the uncertain future. Rarely choosing to truly be wherever I was. Though the world of entrepreneurial terror always comes with a high price tag, I made it more expensive than it needed to be.

How 'bout you? Do you dwell in the place Dr. Spencer Johnson refers to as "the precious present"? If it's the exception and not the rule...if you prefer grinding to grinning...if fretting is your first response...STOP! You're in the space that pastor/author Jeff Manion refers to as "The Land Between." It's the space where God will do His deepest work in your life...if you'll let Him. Don't panic. You'll be out in due time. For now, just remember one thing: Wherever you are...be there.

Back at the beach, I enjoyed watching the guy in the waves with a waterproof camera. He was standing in the water with his back to the surf, taking pictures towards the beach as the waves crashed over him. He took a real pounding, but likely got some very memorable shots. In hindsight, I wish I had thought to give him my email address so he could have sent me a few of his best ones. Though I'm not sure how he would later feel about the memories he captured that day.

I could no longer resist the waves' siren call. As is my habit, I sprang from my beach chair and ran into the surf, diving into an approaching wave then headed out to where the big boys were breaking. While the world of entrepreneurial terror had at times aged me in dog years, body surfing always brings out the kid in me. Conditions were perfect…I knew exactly where I was…and I was 100 percent there, thoroughly enjoying one of life's greatest simple pleasures. I exerted nearly as much energy in celebrating a good ride as I did in taking it, hoopin' and hollerin' like a teenager on spring break.

I didn't think anything of it when I heard the wave photographer doing some of his own hoopin' and hollerin'. No doubt, he too had answered the siren's call, now choosing to ride the subjects of his photo shoot. He was out further than me and, therefore, out of my sight most of the time, hidden behind the huge rollers. Not one to play it safe myself, I too ventured further out. It was the photographer, me and the deep blue sea. No one else was in the water. That's when I realized he wasn't hollerin' for joy, but rather crying for help…my help. "Somebody help me!"

One of the pleasant surprises I'm anticipating in Heaven is when God reveals to us the many times that He saved our lives. Sometimes directly Himself. Other times through angels. And, I think most times, through other people. Likewise, I think all of His children will come to find out that they were used by Him to save others' lives…perhaps many. How poignant those moments in eternity future will be. Equally poignant but much rarer, I believe, are the moments in eternity present when we know that either our life has been saved or when we've been used to save someone else's life. Until this day, I had experienced neither.

I cautiously approached him while desperately searching my fading memory for those life-saving lessons I'd learned over 40 years ago. The most important one was indelibly etched in my mind — never let a drowning victim make you one. When panic sets in, victims can easily take their rescuers down with them. My eyes were glued to his as I cautiously treaded water towards him.

He was listlessly bobbing up and down like a large mooring buoy. There were no signs of panic, but no signs of strength either. He was one tired guppy. I spoke calmly to him when he would come up for air. Then seemingly out of nowhere, the words he needed to hear came to me. "I'm an excellent swimmer," I said. "It's all good. Just relax and I'll get you to shore." With that, he rolled over like a Labrador retriever looking for a belly rub, allowing me to secure him in a cross chest rescue hold.

As we approached the shore, it occurred to me that my bobbing buddy might be a little embarrassed by his situation. So, when it was shallow enough for him to stand, I asked him to do so. Then I suggested that he walk the rest of the way to shore. It was hard to tell his age, so I didn't know if the woman anxiously waiting for him was his mother or his wife. Either way, I thought his manhood would fare better if he walked out under his own power. Once he was safely on shore, I went back to frolic in the waves like nothing happened. It just seemed like the right thing to do. He plopped down a few feet from the water's edge and stayed there for what seemed like an eternity. I was determined to stay in the water until he left or crashed in his beach chair. I never spoke to him or his female companion.

There was nothing heroic about what I did. It was, however, very humbling. It was humbling to think that God had used me to save someone's life. Oh sure, it could have been pure coincidence that I was right where I needed to be that morning. Someday I'll know if that's what it was or what I like to refer to as "divine coincidence." Either way, I was glad to be used for such a noble purpose.

I thought of little else the rest of the day. The "what if" questions were maddening. "What if we'd chosen a different beach that day? What if I had lingered longer on my phone conversation with Emily? What if the kid in me had stayed back at the condo and not gone body surfing? What if…what if…what if?"

No doubt, it sounds odd, but I cried myself to sleep that night. The last few years had been particularly hard. There were many days when I struggled to find reasons to go on, yet by God's grace I did. To have done so and to have gone on to experience a redemptive moment like I did that day, is humbling…very humbling. Such redemptive moments are everyday occurrences in the Kingdom of God, as I would soon learn.

Smokey Row Firehouse, Carmel Indiana (May 2013)

"John" and I had only known each other for about three years, yet we'd become fast friends. I can't really explain how that came about. We share some similar family challenges, passion for our one true avocation, some business connections and a common faith paradigm. But that doesn't fully explain the bond we formed over a relatively short period of time. Nonetheless, bonded we were.

To protect John's identity, I'll be shorter on details than a good writer should be. But you'll get the idea. John was one of the few people I knew at the time whose bag had more rocks in it than mine. It didn't surprise me that he wanted to get away from it all. But when I realized how far he wanted to get away, it shocked me.

By mid-afternoon, John's wife was in a full blown panic. She'd had no contact with him since he stormed out of the house the night before following an argument with one of his daughters. She had no idea where he was or what he was up to. Neither did anyone else…until he returned my call. Others had tried to reach him, to no avail. John chose to call me and only me. Only he could tell you why.

"Where are you, John?" I asked rather nonchalantly. "I'd rather not say," he said. "Fair enough.

What's going on? I understand you left the house in a bit of a huff last night?" This was the beginning of our two hour and 45-minute conversation. The more John talked, the more concerned I became. His suicidal references were not so subtle. His demeanor was flat-lined and detached. I didn't know if he was on something or on the downside of a nervous breakdown.

An hour into the conversation, I decided to make my way home from the office since it was getting late and Elaine would wonder where I was. In hindsight, I could have called her on the office phone while still keeping John engaged on my cell phone. As I was passing by the firehouse just around the corner from our home, it occurred to me that they might have some expertise I could use. So, I grabbed a bank deposit envelope from my glove box and scribbled out a sign:

Suicidal caller on line. I need your help. Please let me in but don't make any noise.

I rang the firehouse doorbell while holding my makeshift sign up to the window. The firemen were quick on the uptake and very accommodating. As the conversation approached the two-hour mark, my cell phone battery was about to die. They quickly came up with a charger and gave it to me. We communicated via a small grease board that we wrote messages on. It was imperative that John not perceive that I was up to anything beyond talking my friend off the ledge. Had he been the least suspicious, he would have hung up immediately.

No one knew where John was. He could have been just down the street or in another state. We had no clue. I had two basic goals in mind. First, keep him on the phone no matter what. Second, convince him to meet with me wherever he was. I was so focused upon these goals that I recall very little of what John actually said during our long conversation. He certainly said enough to validate my suicide risk concerns, though when the police officer asked me what he said to indicate that, I was embarrassingly fuzzy on details.

John was eerily calm throughout our conversation. Very monotone. No barking at the moon rants. No anger outbursts or threats to anyone other than himself. A well-read cerebral guy, he would ramble on about things famous authors had written. At times he would ask me, "Who was it that said…?" making me feel like a third place Jeopardy contestant who couldn't hang with the real Brainiacs. I'd say just enough to keep him engaged while coaxing him onto the next rabbit trail.

While John and I waxed philosophically, the firemen were able to reach his wife and let her know the situation. She didn't know where he might be or if he had a gun. The first two questions they asked her. I'm not sure what else they talked about. By this time, I was now intensely focused on goal #2—convincing John to meet with me. Since it was dinner time, I asked if he'd eaten. He said he hadn't but wasn't all that hungry. This led into a lengthy discussion about the rare opportunity for him to enjoy a nice steak dinner on ole buddy Brad. "Just the two of us. How 'bout it?"

I was exhausted by the time John agreed to meet me at a steakhouse on the north side of Indianapolis near the hotel he was holed up in. We hung up and agreed to meet there in 15 minutes. As I started to leave the firehouse, a police officer stopped me. He explained to me that legal protocol required their intervention at this point. There would be no quiet dinner shared by two friends, at least not if the police got to John before I did. So, I sped off naïvely hoping to beat the first responders at their own game.

John had parked in a remote lot behind the steak house. He was easy to spot with the two police cars hemming in his vehicle. Another friend of John's arrived just after me. We kept our distance watching to see how things unfolded. Neither of us really knew what protocol called for at this point. We slowly made our way towards John and the officers who were talking to him as he sat on the back of his SUV.

Though John's friend assured me that I'd done the right thing, at that moment I wasn't so sure. Like a surgical missile strike, John's disdainful glare painfully pierced my heart. In his mind, I had betrayed a sacred trust. I had committed an unforgiveable sin. Feelings he would reiterate to me in the days to come.

So what is the suicide risk protocol for the Carmel, Indiana police department? They cuff and stuff the "patient" and take him to a nearby psychiatric facility for a mandatory 24-hour observation period. I came to understand the sensibility of it, but struggled mightily in the heat of the moment to accept the betrayer role this policy had cast me in. But what if I had misinterpreted John's morose musings? What if he wasn't ever a true suicide risk? What if I've brought this hassle and embarrassment upon him for no reason?

This was not the first time John had suicidal thoughts. It was, however, the farthest he'd ever taken them. Suicide had been a reoccurring theme with John in recent years. Until he began meeting with a suicide support group, John continued to hold a grudge against me. He was slow to forgive me not just for betraying his trust, but also for having denied him the ultimate relief he thought suicide would bring him. John later told me he had no intention of coming out of the hotel room alive.

That was three years ago. Today, John and I are closer than ever. He's not only fully forgiven me, but thanked me for, in his words, "saving my life." Once again, my reaction to this life-saving experience has been an overwhelming sense of humility. I did nothing heroic. I simply had the privilege of being used by God to help one of His struggling children in his time of greatest need.

Since "humbling" didn't aptly describe my feelings, I turned to the Thesaurus for help. One of its synonyms is "awe-inspiring." That's better. My fateful evening with my friend, John, left me with an awe-inspiring feeling. Mind you, not for anything I did, but rather for our mighty and loving God. A Heavenly Father who does much of His work through His imperfect kids to help their siblings move closer towards His perfect plan for their lives. Truly awe-inspiring!

Backyard Pool in Carmel, Indiana (June 2013)

I awoke to hear Elaine muttering a groggy "hello" into the phone at 2:30 in the morning. Rare is good news on the other end of the line at that hour. This was the exception. At least we thought so, though it took a few minutes for the fog to clear and for us to get our facts straight…kind of.

"How much did she weigh?" asked Mimi as if our new granddaughter no longer weighed whatever the answer was. "What about her Bilirubin? Good…good."

At this point I'm coming around and asking my own questions. Basic stuff like "What's her name?" "Nesta A. Liberty Zeller," repeats Mimi. Confused, I ask, "They named her an initial? Who does that? Are you sure it's Nesta A. Liberty?" The scene is now resembling something out of the 1970's sitcom, *All in the Family*, with Edith and Archer Bunker.

"That's what she said," insists Mimi.

"Is everyone all right?" I ask.

"Yes," says Elaine as she congratulates our daughter, Ashley Kay, on the birth of her first child and tells her good night.

I go back to sleep within a few minutes still muttering to myself, "They named our granddaughter an initial, who does that?"

A few hours later B-pa's day began with a Facebook post announcing the birth of Nesta A. Liberty Zeller. "That's right FB friends, they named her an initial. What can I tell you?" Imagine our relief when a few hours and a few cups of coffee later we realized her real name—Nesta *Kay* Liberty Zeller. Turns out Mimi's (a.k.a. Elaine Kay's) hearing isn't what it used to be. Never mind that a day has rarely gone by since without her reminding Bpa that he needs to get his hearing checked. To which Archie replies, "Yeah, yeah Florence Nightengown, I'll get right on that…tomorrow."

Turns out our son-in-law, Brandon <no middle name> Zeller, was determined to double up to catch up upon the birth of his first child. Hence two middle names for our granddaughter. As to her unique first name, Nesta was the pet name given by his mother to Rastafarian legend, Bob Marley. It means "pure." How apropos, because that little initial has been nothing but pure joy to her entire large extended family since the day she was born.

Having grown up with a pool in our backyard, I was easily convinced that it would be some of the cheapest floor space our growing family would ever have. Add years of wonderful family memories made in and around our pools and it's easy to understand why we're now in our fourth home with a pool since the early 1990's. No doubt, the magnetic attraction of our current pool has something to do with the fact that all of our children and grandchildren live within a 30-minute drive to Mimi and B-Pa's backyard oasis. A few had only to walk out the backdoor to enjoy a refreshing dip.

Such was the case with Nesta Kay and her one-month old baby sister, Pele Monterey Berlyn Zeller, during the summer of 2013. You'll have to read the sequel to understand the origin of Pele's names.

When Ashley and Brandon found themselves with number two on the way, their San Diego high rent district home quickly lost its allure. Having met in the birthplace of California while attending Point Loma Nazarene University, they had many ties to the city known for its near-perfect weather. But, being near family while their own family grew proved more alluring then perpetually sunny days. Oh yeah, the rent free basement "apartment" we offered them may have factored in as well. Did I mention there's a pool in the backyard? What grandparents won't do to be close to their grandchildren.

We spent the winter of 1983/84 in Oklahoma City where I took my first management job with IBM. While visiting friends and family back home in Indianapolis, we stayed at the Holiday Inn on the North West side of town. The primary attraction was the large indoor pool with water park quality slides. This was before our first backyard pool, but our kids were already little water dogs.

Ashley Kay was two years old, the youngest of the three at the time. She loved the water and spent more time below than above the surface. Since Elaine's mom (a.k.a. Nana) hadn't seen her granddaughter in a while, she wasn't aware of just how amphibious Ashley had become. So, when she didn't come up for air after five seconds or so, it was Nana to the rescue. Despite being fully clothed in winter attire, Nana jumped in without hesitation to "rescue" our daughter. Ashley didn't understand what all the fuss was about and quickly returned to her underwater world.

Like mother like daughter. Nesta took to the water like a tadpole before her second birthday. It was our first family pool party during the early summer of 2013. It was a beautiful sunny day. Many members of our extended family were there enjoying some fun in the sun and catching up with one another. So much so, that no one was watching the pool. After going into the house to get a drink, I came out just in time to see Nesta jump off the steps and into the pool. The water was over her head. She wasn't wearing swimmies or any other floatation device. No one else noticed.

I dropped my drink, knocked over several chairs and leaped over a few startled bodies on my way into the pool. She was only under water a few seconds. But, it was the thought of what could have happened that made me temporarily insane…and a bit angry. I held my granddaughter for a long time before handing her over to her mortified mother. Then I retreated to the far side of the pool to assume the lifeguard position and process what had just happened.

Trifecta Completed

So, despite having done nothing more heroic than being at the right place at the right time, I completed the life-saving trifecta over the course of eight months. It literally could have been anyone, but it was me...once...twice...three times in eight months. A total stranger...a close friend...a grandchild.

Why? I cannot say. What I can say is that beyond the previously mentioned humility, these life-saving experiences left me feeling very grateful for having been used in such a wonderfully redemptive way.

Interesting, but "So what?" and "Who cares?" It's a fair question. I've included my life-saving stories primarily because, for me, they serve as a poignant reminder that in the game of life, we're often guilty of faulty score-keeping. That which we deem important isn't so much, while seemingly random, mundane and unrelated events wind their way towards epic climaxes. True game-changers that we never saw coming.

Though I'll likely never again see the wave photographer from Polihale Beach, I've spent many hours since our dates with destiny with buddy "John" and granddaughter, Nesta. Since talking John out of a dingy hotel room and into joining me for a steak dinner that never happened, he's talked me off a ledge or two when the business of life had me questioning my ability to go on. That little tadpole, Nesta Kay Liberty, is now a six-year-old guppy enjoying kindergarten, though she's still getting used to raising her hand to ask a question or shout out the answer to one. Precocious beyond words, she's provided her Mimi and B-Pa with some of the most wonderful laugh 'til you cry evening entertainment imaginable. We can't imagine life without her. Thankfully, we haven't had to.

Chapter 15

16. Our Good Middle Child

"We all know the stereotype: middle children are wallflowers, overshadowed by their siblings and neglected by their parents, and they turn into resentful, bitter adults. But if that is true, why are so many middle children throughout history – from Abraham Lincoln to Donald Trump and Madonna – wildly successful?

In this counterintuitive book, psychologist Catherine Salmon and journalist Katrin Schumann combine science, history and real-life stories to reveal for the first time that our perception of middle children is dead wrong.

With constructive advice on how to maximize the benefits and avoid the pitfalls of being a middle, Salmon and Schumann help middleborns, their parents and partners see how birth order can be used as a strategy for success."

– Introduction to The Secret Power of Middle Children by Catherine Salmon, Ph.D, and Katrin Schumann

Our "good middle child," as she loathes being called, is more proof that middle children truly do have secret powers. Each of her four siblings would be quick to admit that Ashley Kay was our lowest maintenance child by orders of magnitude. And no doubt, there were times during her childhood when she felt overshadowed by her siblings and neglected by her parents. She just couldn't bring herself to misbehave enough to capture as much of her parents' attention as her other siblings, both older and younger.

Thank goodness. Had Ashley attempted to compete with sibs one and two in the trauma and drama departments, I seriously doubt sibs four and five would have made it onto our family roster. So, Caleb and Bradley, you might want to give Ashley an extra hug at this afternoon's 4th of July family rib fest.

As difficult as parenting is, I've always been intrigued by the dearth of insight the Bible provides into the daily interactions between parent and child. The New Testament is nearly void of such insights (excepting Jesus, Mary and Joseph), while the insights given in the Old Testament often paint a pretty ugly picture.

Recall, King David's son, Absalom, tried to kill his father in order to assume his throne. This was the parental plight of one described as "a man after God's own heart." (1Samuel 13:14). Never mind that the very first sibling rivalry resulted in the first murder on planet Earth when Cain killed his younger brother, Abel. This, without any record of a single piece of parental advice given by the world's first parents, Adam and Eve, to their apparently wayward firstborn.

Then came Moses whose parents gave him up for adoption in order to save his life.

Fast forward to the hero of the New Testament, the Apostle Paul, and all we know of his upbringing is that he came from a well-to-do family who valued knowledge and rules more than a personal relationship with the one true God. So much so, that their son took to murdering Christians before the Messiah got a hold of him. Good grief, what's a parent to do?

The answer to that question will have to wait for yet another book that Elaine and I might well co-author. For now, we're focused on the other side of the parental coin—what's a child to do? To answer that question, we turn to the fifth commandment:

> "Honor your father and your mother, so that you may live long in the land the Lord your God is giving you" (Exodus 20:12).

This is the only commandment that comes with an explicit promise. To live long and prosper, to enjoy the benefits of God's grace towards you, every child who has ever been born is commanded by God to honor his or her parents. So, how does a child honor a parent? The same way each of us honors God. By doing that which pleases Him and not doing that which displeases Him. It's that simple and that incredibly difficult.

Back to our good middle child. When Ashley was in high school, she went to California with a girlfriend to visit her aunt. She fell in love with the land of fruits and nuts and a blonde surfer dude. Yep, just like the movies. She came home determined to find her way back to Cali country when she entered college. Having recently learned of Point Loma Nazarene University in San Diego while having lunch with our senior pastor, I told Ash if she could get into that school, I would find a way to pay for it. Note to husbands: Before making such life-changing promises to your child, you might want to float the idea by your wife.

Of course, our good middle child found her way into PLNU and my lovely bride is still looking for a way to forgive me for keeping a promise I should have never made. Except for the year she returned home to obtain her yoga instructor certification, Ashley lived in San Diego for 12 years before moving back to Indianapolis in 2012 with her husband, two-year-old daughter and pregnant with baby sister. Along the way, she honored her parents by doing what we asked her to do—graduate in four years, get married sometime thereafter and then have children after that. Check…check…check! And by the way, surfer dude broke our daughter's heart two weeks after she arrived at PLNU her freshman year. Despite this devastating setback, Ashley persevered and went on to find her true soul mate, Brandon, a few years later.

A few months after Ashley and family accepted our offer to come back home again to Indiana and set up house in our basement, Elaine had her fifth spinal surgery. This was the most invasive one of all. It involved entering the base of her neck to implant titanium stabilizing bars to support the two vertebrae fusions performed in previous surgeries. The normally long recovery period was made even longer by the infection she got in the incision. Several times a day, pregnant Nurse Ashley lovingly excised the wound with long wooden swabs, then waited on her mother hand and foot throughout the day while caring for her two-year-old. Elaine and I were both deeply touched by the way Ashley honored her mother during that very difficult time. May she live long and prosper for it.

Ashley majored in journalism at PLNU because they didn't offer a poetry major. Yes, our youngest daughter was a bit of a free spirit even before she went to the left (pardon me) west coast. Little surprise that she found her way into yoga and managed a studio on Coronado Island for many years. Since coming home, she's been constantly on me to give yoga a try. I finally did this past year and I love it. Yoga is just what my aging, inflexible body needs to supplement my usual swimming and elliptical regimes. But as much as I love my new yoga routine, I love even more seeing our daughter in her professional element. I rarely attend one of Ashley's yoga classes without someone telling me what an incredible instructor she is…and she is! I expect to do more yoga in coming years and can't imagine doing it in any class other than one led by master yogi Ashley Kay Zeller, our good middle child.

For those of you blessed to have a low maintenance child of your own, a closing word of caution is in order. These self-sufficient ones are subject to burn-out and occasional melt-downs.

Once in a rainy day Monday moon, the weight of the world they so readily place upon their shoulders becomes too much to bear. When "Sure, I can do that" turns into "I can't do it anymore," Mom and Dad may be just the safe haven they need.

But don't overplay your role. Don't grab the map and the compass and begin charting a new course for the one who takes such pride in being the captain of her ship. Just let her sail into the safe harbor of your presence and be there for her. That's usually all she needs. Once the seas are calm, she'll ask for guidance out of the harbor if she needs it. If not, you can join Roseanne Barr in saying, "If the kids are alive at the end of the day…hey, I've done my job."

Chapter 16

17. Life with My Lovely Bride

The Summer of '72

I can't tell you what I wore to work yesterday, but 44 years after first meeting my bride-to-be, I can still describe her summer of '72 bikinis in minute detail…all three of them. I could tell you more than you need to know about that blonde bombshell's blue, white and orange bikinis, but I won't.

It was Memorial Day weekend and opening day at the apartment complex pool where I was life guarding for the summer. Her parents were early house flipping pioneers, so they were living in an apartment between homes. Looking forward to a summer of poolside fun as she approached her senior year, Elaine Kay Schrader had a sassy edge to her that I found irresistible. How could we have attended the same school for two years without ever having met? Before our poolside introduction that weekend I had never laid eyes on her. I can't recall being able to take my eyes off of her for single day since.

As fate would have it, her bedroom window overlooked my lifeguard chair. Though Elaine is 15 months my senior, her mother had warned her to avoid getting involved with an older "man." I was 15 at the time and still a few months from getting my coveted driver's license. To this day, I tease her by saying I had her at "Speedos" though she recalls otherwise. She does admit, however, to catching more than an occasional glance of the svelte swimmer just beyond her curtains.

Elaine not only had a driver's license, but she had access to her dad's 1964 Ford Galaxy 500 convertible. Since my house was too far from the pool to ride my bike to work, I somehow ended up with the hottest ride to be had in Kokomo, Indiana. When she pulled up in that aqua blue ragtop, my adolescent heart would race with anticipation of spending time with her. There was one complication, however. I was going steady with someone else—"Tracy".

The turning point came while attending the 4th of July festivities at the Kokomo Country Club. Though Tracy was my date that night, I couldn't keep my eyes off Elaine. She and her rowdy classmates were on a mission to ruin our evening. Mission accomplished. A few weeks later at the end of a double date, I told Elaine I loved her for the very first time.

While stepping out of the backseat and into my driveway, I sensed I was stepping into a life that would never be the same again. I was right.

Married with Children

Ours was very nearly a case of love at first sight. We've been together ever since I officially declared it that early August evening during the summer of '72. Oddly, during all that time, the only meaningful break-up we ever had was just a few months before our wedding in June of 1976. 13 months later and one month before my 21st birthday, our first child was born—Joshua Louis Lindemann. So, we were young, still very much in love and now married with children.

Uncle Bob Cuts the Check

Recall, before graduating from college, I supported our young family by selling life insurance. But for the wise counsel of my lovely bride, the biggest sale I ever made may not have happened. That's why I'm including it at this point in her story.

It came nearly a full year after having left the insurance business to join IBM. Uncle Bob had nearly thrown my supervisor and me out of his office the year before. My supervisor, Fred Bolyard, was a great teacher with a contagious passion for the business. On this occasion, however, he stepped over the fine line between persistence and pushiness. My chances of selling Uncle Bob a large policy seemed to evaporate as quickly as we left his office that day.

Shortly thereafter, I joined IBM upon graduation and began my career in the information technology industry. During my first year at IBM, I kept Uncle Bob's file in my briefcase and with me at all times. Occasionally, I would contact him with any new ideas regarding his situation, clinging to the hope that I might still make the biggest sale of my life to him.

Uncle Bob was an engineer by trade. Nothing escaped his painstaking attention to detail. For months, I had been responding to his requests for ledger statements illustrating the various policy options he was considering. I'll never forget that fateful afternoon in the IBM bullpen when the life insurance stars finally lined up for Uncle Bob and me.

"So Brad, according to column five, the premiums paid in will equal the cash value after 10 years. Correct?"

"Yes sir, that's correct."

"And the death benefit at that point would be $550,000. Correct?"

"That's right. $50,000 more than the face value."

Silence. A full-term, nine-month pregnant pause. I'm still a rookie salesman, but I sense that I'm very close to closing this deal. A deal that will pay me more in commissions than my annual salary at IBM. I bite my tongue, knowing that anything I say could blow it. Silence is a salesman's ultimate weapon.

Finally, he speaks.

"Well, what does it take to put this in force?"

Did I hear him correctly? Is he really going to buy the policy I've been trying to sell him for over two years? My throat goes instantly dry. My heart pounds. My pulse races. I am completely unaware of what's going on in the office around me.

"All I need is a check for the first month's premium."

"OK. I'm going to be out of the office for the rest of the day. If you'll come by on Monday, I'll have the check waiting for you."

"That's great. I'll be there first thing Monday morning. Thanks Uncle Bob and have a good weekend!"

Rookie that I was, I knew enough to know that once the prospect says "yes" the salesperson should beat a hasty retreat. Decked out in my IBM blue suit and starched white shirt, I was trembling uncontrollably with tears freely flowing down my face. I could not believe my good fortune. Wait 'til Elaine hears this. I called her immediately.

"Honey, are you sitting down?"

Wanting to savor every delicious moment, I walk her back through all the details of my lengthy phone conversation with Uncle Bob.

"And then he said I could pick up the check at his office on Monday."

"Monday? That's three days from now," she said with great alarm in her voice.

"What if he changes his mind over the weekend? Worse, what if he dies? We can't take that risk. You call him back right now and tell him you'll come to wherever he is to pick up the check and close this deal."

In all the excitement, I had forgotten the most fundamental rule of selling—it's not over until the customer cuts the check. Fortunately, once I tracked down Uncle Bob and sheepishly explained my dilemma, he chuckled and arranged to meet me that afternoon. Credit my bride with an assist in closing the biggest deal of my young career. How ironic that I was no longer in the life insurance business when it happened.

Chapter 17

18. Tell Your Greatest Fear

During IBM's heyday, Big Blue often found themselves unable to meet the demand for their most popular hardware products. Such was the case with 3420 tape drives circa 1985. So much so, that the value of used drives had gone up significantly over the three years since my company had leased a string of them to one of our largest customers. That posed a dilemma when the lease came up for renewal. Customers expected renewal rates to go down, not up. Still relatively new to the company, I wasn't sure how to handle the situation, so I asked our VP of Sales.

"Why don't you just ask the customer what he thinks is fair?" suggested Jack. "Explain how IBM's production problems with the replacement product have caused the prices of used 3420's to go up since we did the lease. Then just ask him what he thinks a fair renewal rate would be." With no small amount of trepidation, I approached my customer with "our" dilemma. And, to my amazement, he suggested a price that was far more than I would have had the courage to ask him for.

So, what was going on in this exchange? I was afraid that by telling my customer what he did not want to hear I would damage our longstanding positive relationship with him. My VP's sage advice effectively put that fear right out on the table for the customer to see, then asked him to help me overcome it. At that point, his innate desire to help alleviate anyone's fears, to the extent possible, takes over. In the process, what would have otherwise been a negative situation turns into a very positive one. The customer has the dual satisfaction of having structured his own terms and alleviating his now partner's fear. On my side, by partnering with my customer I had the pleasant surprise of getting more than I could have imagined, including his complete satisfaction with the exchange.

Chapter 18

19. When It Hurts to Hug

> *"I'm still mad at you God, but still trusting that we're on the path towards your best for us. Thank you for my good health and the opportunity to worship you this morning."*

While romping through the tall cotton of the previously mentioned "salad days" during our time in Memphis (1984-89), clouds started to form over both my business and Elaine's health. Before turning 30, Elaine was told she had the spine of a 55-year-old. This marked the early stages of degenerative disc disease. Little did we know how much this dreadful condition would go on to define the quality of life that she would enjoy. Or, better stated, on far too many days, simply endure.

Like many young moms, Elaine struggled with occasional bouts of depression. Though with five children to raise, she didn't have a lot of time to waste being depressed. So, she pressed on and was an incredible mother to all five kids.

I was always quick to acknowledge who had the most difficult job between us. She took the prize, hands down. But, the emptier the nest became, the more Elaine began to struggle emotionally. Her struggle went beyond the normal mother's empty nest syndrome. It was about more than missing the kids and questioning who she was if she was no longer their full-time mother. It was about waging emotional warfare with the battles getting fiercer and the casualties more frightening with each passing day.

Getting a complete hysterectomy at age 39 didn't help matters. In fact, Elaine would tell you that was the worst decision she's ever made. I was clueless in Indianapolis at the time. All I knew was that neither of us would survive too many more flights on the PMS broom Elaine brought out for a full week every month. I couldn't spell relief fast enough. Besides, the surgeon was recommending a complete procedure to remove the risk of ovarian cancer. Seemed like a no-brainer. With four kids, who needs ovaries…right? Wrong!

Yes, those evil ovaries were turning my lovely bride into a wicked witch one week per month. But, they were also responsible for keeping her off that broom the other three weeks. Without them and the hormones they produce, life can go from an occasional living hell to a perpetual one.

When Elaine celebrated her 59th and "final" birthday, I assured her that 59 is the new 39, though her body says otherwise. Her hysterectomy 20 years ago did indeed prove to be a major turning point in her health and well-being. It's been a daily struggle since then. At one point, she averaged one surgery per year for 12 years running. Five of those were knee surgeries, the last two being total knee replacements. Five others were back surgeries (two lower, three upper) and two were for gastro-intestinal maladies. The doctors say another surgery on her upper spine is inevitable, as her condition will deteriorate to the point of restricting leg and/or arm movement, never mind the constant pain until then.

If you're reading this, it means my lovely fragile bride, no doubt reluctantly, gave me permission to write this part of her story...our story. Elaine's health has been such a dominant theme in our lives for the last two decades that excluding it would turn this non-fictional account into a novel. Doing so would also deny the many readers with similar struggles an opportunity to take something positive away from our journey through our gauntlet of pain. And selfishly, I hope the process will prove cathartic for me, while helping us through those hurtful hugging times.

In my 60 years on this planet, I can count on one hand the number of days that I've spent in any measurable amount of pain. My wife experiences more real pain in one week than I have experienced in my entire lifetime. You'll learn later why I believe it's impossible to have a perspective you've never had. Nowhere in my life is this truth more starkly apparent than in my daily struggle to empathize with Elaine's daily struggle with pain. The Neanderthal in me wants to just tell her to "play through the pain." Many days she does just that. But on many other days, it's simply not possible for her to do anything beyond simply getting through it...like today.

It's Sunday morning. As I was getting up around six, Elaine was coming back to bed, having been up most of the night with a migraine. Just before going to bed around eleven, she gave herself an injection in her hip in what apparently proved to be a futile attempt to get out in front of the worst of the pain. Not an easy thing to do when your head feels like it could explode and you have to twist your degenerated spine like a pretzel to hit the right spot. Most likely, she'd just given herself another injection, hoping to salvage some portion of her "Sabbath rest."

This pattern has repeated itself hundreds of times in recent years and is particularly common on Sundays. That's primarily why Elaine is rarely in church with me despite having schlepped five kids there nearly every Sunday for two decades. Consequently, Sundays have become my crucible. And let me hasten to add, my crucible is child's play compared to Elaine's. Nonetheless, most Sundays find me treading in a stew of emotions that have been simmering for longer than I care to remember. The first to bubble to the surface is almost always anger.

Anger…towards God on the good days (He can take it) …towards my poor pain-ridden wife on the bad days (she can't and shouldn't have to). Why am I mad at God? Anyone who's ever prayed for a sick loved one knows the answer to that question. Because He can heal her, yet refuses to, despite incessantly being asked to do so. Without question, I have prayed more times over a longer period of time for Elaine's healing than for anything else. Yet, no relief comes. The pain persists and her quality of life (and therefore ours) continues to decline. Yes, God, I'm mad at you for not healing my wife. And yet God, like Job, I say, "Though he kill me, yet I will trust in him" (Job 13:15).

Perhaps the greatest lesson learned has been to trust God even when I don't understand Him. And yes, even when I'm mad at Him. Better yet, especially when I'm mad at Him. So, just what is it that I'm trusting God for? At the highest level, I'm trusting the goodness of His heart towards me and mine. I'm trusting that His "no" or "not now" answer to my prayers for Elaine's healing somehow lead to His best for us. And, what I want more than anything is God's best, something that only He is wise enough to know what it is and how to bring it about.

Today was a "good day" with regards to how I dealt with our Sunday crucible. I was properly compassionate towards Elaine. Very gently rubbing her back and fetching the cold compress and electric back massage that she uses in an effort to relax her shoulder muscles. I can't do this for her lest I hit the wrong spot and send her through the roof. She's been told by multiple doctors that she has the tightest shoulder muscles they've ever felt due to the chronic pain emanating from her spine and head. My heart aches for my lovely bride…and for myself. I know that on this Sunday, like so many others, I will be alone and Elaine will be in pain. I'm still mad at you God, but still trusting that we're on the path towards your best for us. Thank you for my good health and the opportunity to worship you this morning.

What about the "bad days"? I am ashamed to say I've had many of them. The cause is clear and catastrophic in its consequences. I shift my anger from God to my wife. As the number of "red X" days on the calendar accumulate, my ability to cope diminishes. Coming home day after day to my soul mate who's done little more than survive, I feel cheated. I start to think of all the little things that Elaine could be doing that might help her feel better. Things like diet and exercise...acupuncture...fewer medications...or just simply playing through the pain, because "it is what it is." (She abhors that phrase.)

My anger increases every time I open the door to a cluttered closet thinking she should just buck up and get some things done around the house. Such menial labor always makes me feel better, wouldn't it help her as well? Prince Charming has left the building...enter Darth Vader.

I Believe that We Will Win

"I...I believe...I believe that we...I believe that we will...I believe that we will win. I believe that we will win! I believe that we will win!! I believe that we will win!!! USA! USA!! USA!!!"

And believe I did. In fact, believing that Team USA would beat Portugal in the second game of the 2014 World Cup was singularly sufficient to get me through another lonely Sunday, as I awaited the six o'clock kick-off.

After a cheap early goal by Portugal off a rare defensive error, Team USA dominated play. They took a 2-1 lead off a Clint Dempsey goal in the 87th minute. Then, the impossible happened. Portugal's super star striker, Cristiano Ronaldo, placed a "dime" pass onto the head of his teammate right in front of the goal for the equalizer on what was literally the last play of the game. With that, Team USA fans went from ecstasy to agony...me among them.

I watched the game at son Caleb and daughter-in-law Lena's home just five minutes due west. Elaine was supposed to join us along with other family members, but her aching head could not have taken the roars from our cheering section. I offered to stay home to keep her company, but she insisted that I go without her. Besides, enduring my war whoops would have been sufficient to land her in the ER. Just as well that she wasn't there.

When Portugal scored the tying goal, I less-than-graciously thanked Lena for her hospitality and made a beeline for the door without saying a word to anyone else. "I can't win for losing," I muttered to myself as I drove home, my mood becoming fouler by the minute. "Geez God, is it too much to ask to win one on occasion...just one?" Apparently so.

When I arrived home, I was pleased to see that Elaine was up and had actually watched the game. As we assumed our favorite position on the swing hanging from the pergola on our pool deck, I asked her a simple and sincere question, "How are you feeling?"

Sensing I was seeking something more than a perfunctory pain level update, she replied in a rather irritated manner, "What do you mean, how am I feeling?" Her instincts were correct.

"I mean how are you feeling emotionally?" I said, trying to discern how she was holding up under such physically taxing circumstances. We went downhill from there.

"I'm feeling like its Sunday night and you're acting the way you always do," Elaine said. "I don't know why you can't just let things be. Why do you have to analyze everything? Why can't we just enjoy a quiet moment around the pool? So, what about you…how are *you* feeling?"

BAM! With that, I no longer believe that we will win. In that moment, I'm convinced that nothing will ever go right in my life again. My answer to Elaine's question was as simple and sincere as my original question to her.

"I'm feeling like I don't want to talk to you," I said.

With that, the deafening sounds of silence filled the atmosphere and the real game was over before it ever really started. She apologized as we were going to bed, but it was too little too late. The one, whose mantra is "words matter," had shredded me with hers, then left me for emotionally dead as one more Sabbath comes and goes with anything but rest for our weary souls.

Team USA will live to fight another day, but I'm not so sure about myself. Thankfully, I didn't unload my emotional dump truck when Elaine asked me how I was feeling. The damage could have been irreparable. What good could come from telling my pain-ridden wife that I was losing my will to live? How ridiculous that even sounds as I write those words. Yet, in that moment, that's what I was feeling and it was by no means the first time I've felt that way. We've been inseparable for 44 years, but pain and pills have been putting a wedge between us that at times seems impossible to overcome.

And so, I do what any loving, committed Christian husband would do.

I drink.

Chapter 19

Alcohol: My Drug of Choice

I drink to kill the pain of intimacy lost and misery found. I drink to forget what was and avoid thinking about what might be. I drink to escape the raging river of sadness for a brief dip in my happy place pool. I drink because I'm weak. I drink because I'm lonely. I drink because I question my manhood. I drink because duty has drained the life out of me. I drink because most of my children rarely go to church. I drink because my business is a mere shadow of what it used to be, though I need it to be much more. I drink because I think it all depends on me. I drink because I feel like a failure. I drink because there's no fear in love, yet I'm fearful all the time. I drink to fill a void that only God can fill. I drink because I don't believe that He will win.

But He will…and so will I.

Oh yeah, I left out an important fact about my sad Sunday. I had five beers while attempting to will Team USA to victory. Worse yet, they didn't faze me. I've built up quite an alcohol tolerance over the last few years. A fact that I'm more than a little ashamed of. I'm not an alcoholic, but I rarely go a day without alcohol. Little wonder I struggle with depression, since alcohol is a depressant.

Indianapolis Colts Chaplain Ken Johnson has a saying for such behavior: "stuck on stupid." I represent that remark.

During the first few years of marriage, Elaine and I didn't drink at all. Between our faith and parenting young children, it just seemed like the thing to avoid. We had loosened up a bit by the time we moved to the high cotton fields of Memphis in 1984. There, we acquired a taste for fine wine and the daily habit that often accompanies it. Fortunately, when we moved back to Indy in 1989 to start our business, we didn't have the time or money to regularly imbibe.

After selling our beloved "Little Jewel Box" beach house in Rosemary Beach, Florida in 1999, Elaine allowed me to put some of the profit into a wine cellar in our Indianapolis home. It was a beautiful custom built cellar with an 800-bottle capacity. I loved it so much that I would occasionally just go into it to enjoy the smell of the fresh cedar and the inviting ambiance. Each time I did, those empty bins would beckon me to buy more wine.

When you have a wine cellar, you no longer buy wine by the bottle. Those bins don't get filled nearly fast enough that way. You buy it by the case. And of course, the more you buy, the more you drink. Before you know it, one bottle isn't quite enough for the two of you. I should hasten to add that the alcohol problem is 100 percent mine. Elaine has never been a big drinker and, in contrast to her lesser half, has become less so as the years have gone by.

My best friend Tim and I used to traditionally abstain from alcohol during the month of January. It was our way of checking ourselves to ensure we didn't reach the point of no return on the road to alcoholism. I took it even further a couple of years ago by abstaining for over three months. These prolonged periods of abstention, along with the fact that I never drink during the work day or to the point of blacking out, substantiate my non-alcoholic claim.

What these facts don't do, however, is justify my current level of drinking. I drink too much. It's a problem and I own it. But thus far, I have been unsuccessful in solving it.

Sidebar from The Bar (Part 1):

> In the past several months, I've reconnected serendipitously with two men whom I knew to be heavy drinkers. Prior to these chance meetings (otherwise known as divine coincidences), I would have ranked these two guys as dead last on my list of those most likely to quit drinking. One—I'll call him John—is a native Irishman weaned on Guinness beer and Irish whiskey. The other man, Ben, had been in two near-death auto accidents, both due to his blacking out behind the wheel from excessive alcohol intake. I would have expected their epitaphs to read, "He drank to whatever that was." But then things changed.
>
> Ben, the younger of these two men, comes from a family of high-functioning heavy drinkers. I knew them well. His older brother, Frank, was my best friend growing up in our hometown of New Albany, Indiana. Their mother and mine both taught English at the local high school. Frank followed in his father's footsteps and became a lawyer. Ben turned out to be the sales guy extraordinaire. Collectively, their family of four represented some of the most brilliant and talented people I've ever had the privilege of knowing. I loved them all.
>
> When Ben told me that he hadn't had a drink in over a year, I thought he was joking. When he went on to tell me about his new healthy diet and exercise regimen, I had flashbacks of the constant pranks that he and his brother used to play on one another. Surely this

was another one of those for "old times' sake." Then, when he topped it off with talk of the spiritual journey that his sobriety had set in motion, like Doubting Thomas, I had to see it to believe it.

Every Tuesday evening about two dozen men meet at the Jeffersonville, Indiana, campus of Southeast Christian Church to "Celebrate Recovery." Ben joins them along with a former classmate of mine who quit drinking around the same time. He knew his one gallon per day wine consumption habit would soon consume him if he didn't stop. So he did…cold turkey. Both say they couldn't have done it without the support of this group.

"We bury the smart ones every day," said the group leader. For the uninitiated, I'll offer some translation. Alcoholics often delude themselves into thinking that they're smart enough to manage their alcohol consumption so they avoid ending up "like that guy." Chemical addiction, however, has less to do with smarts than it does emotional pain, despair and the like. It isn't so much about the head—"smarts"—but more about the heart.

I immediately thought of Ben's entire family. Spooky smart. Perhaps too smart for their own good. And yet, there he sat with clear eyes and a full heart, fully engaged in the lively discussions around the tables. His big heart was overflowing with the new life and true joy. It was amazing to see what God was doing in Ben's life, who was now a dear friend of mine. I couldn't help but think of how brother Frank's life might have been longer and easier had he found a similar path.

A Tribute: S. Franklin Mattox

A tribute to S. Frankly Mattox

By Brad Lindemann

October 14, 2007

    S. Frank Mattox was a prominent attorney in New Albany, Indiana. He died in his sleep of an apparent heart attack on October 6, 2007. His obituary[3] appeared in the New Albany Tribune on October 9, 2007.

I first met S. Frank Mattox in the band room at Hazelwood Junior High School in New Albany, Indiana—our hometown. We were 12 years old. I last saw him at the Ocean Air Restaurant in downtown Indianapolis about a year ago. We were 50 then. So, the bookends that marked the beginning and end of our life together—from blowing our trumpets in little girls' ears to pontificating in our usual politically incorrect fashion over a fine meal, were not unlike many of the exciting chapters in between. Whenever Frank and I got together, there was always plenty of hot air to go around.

According to John Eldredge, author of the best-seller, *Wild at Heart*, the secret of a man's soul is revealed by three innate and very powerful desires for:

1. A battle to fight
2. A beauty to rescue
3. An adventure to live

Eldredge writes:

Life is not a problem to be solved; it is an adventure to be lived. That's the nature of it and has been since the beginning when God set the dangerous stage for this high-stakes drama and called the whole wild enterprise good. He rigged the world in such a way that it only works when we embrace risk as the theme of our lives." (Eldredge, 2001).

I've known few men who pursued *"adventures to live"* as passionately and successfully as did one Shrewsbury Franklin Mattox—my best friend for many years, my partner in high adventure (and the occasional petty crime). In reflecting over our friendship of four decades, I came to realize how dull life could have been, but for the always open invitation to join Frank's great adventure.

I used to introduce Frank as my co-partner in crime—my accomplice in nine of the 10 worst things I had ever done. Truth told, I thought I was giving him a much undeserved benefit of the doubt on #10. However, in reflecting upon my life with Frank, I realized that the true highlights were

---

[3] "Prominent New Albany Attorney Dies," by Eric Scott Campbell, Oct. 9, 2007. http://www.newsandtribune.com/news/local_news/prominent-new-albany-attorney-dies/article_9cc4e630-3ffe-5b8a-ab00-8f90f9c77d1a.html.

not bad things at all, but rather wonderful adventures that not only defined our friendship, but did much to define who I am as a man today.

Perhaps one day, I'll chronicle the details of my great adventures with Frank. For now, I want to pay tribute to my best friend for being there when I:

- Rode my first motorcycle.
- Cooked my first steak on an open fire.
- Shot my first goose on the coldest day of my life.
- Rode a horse faster than I ever have since.
- Became a daytime fisherman and nighttime cat burglar.
- Got the dirtiest, smelliest and most refreshed I've ever been…all in the same day.
- Did the dumbest, strangest, coolest and most dangerous things I've ever done…all on different days.
- Worked the hardest I've ever worked, then enjoyed the sweetest reward I've ever received…a cool cup of the best water I've ever tasted from a Canadian stream.

Continuing with Eldredge, God…

…rigged the world in such a way that it only works when we embrace risk as the theme of our lives, which is to say, only when we live by faith. A man just won't be happy until he's got adventure in his work, in his love and in his spiritual life.

Few who knew Frank would describe him as a "man of faith," but all who knew him know that he embraced life as a wonderful adventure to be lived to the fullest. Eldredge's writings have helped me see that Frank's unquenchable thirst for adventure was actually his way of living a life of faith…the kind of life we were all meant to live. The Bible has much to say about faith, but the distilled essence can be found in two simple verses:

Now faith is being sure of what we hope for and certain of what we do not see…And without faith it is impossible to please God (Hebrews 11:1,6).

Admittedly, I am writing this more for myself than for anyone who might read this book. It seems a much needed step in the grieving process—a process that is still getting harder, rather than easier, every day. Although we often went a year without seeing each other, whenever Frank and I did get together, it was as if time had stood still since last we met. Yet, of course it hadn't.

I wish we had spent more time being real with one another about today and less time reminiscing about yesterday. We could have done so

Chapter 19

much more to help one another through the many difficult times that we were experiencing. Looking back, I think we tended to reach out after a crisis had passed rather than in the midst of it. Perhaps this was because neither of us wanted to appear weak to the other? An apparent downside to the profound respect each had for the other.

Advice? Cherish your friends. Reach out to them in joy and in sadness…in good times and bad. Let them know you care about them even when you wonder if they care about you. Hearts are not bound by time and distance. Don't let anything come between your heart and the hearts of your friends. In this day of email, instant messaging, cell phones and text messaging there's just no excuse for losing touch with your friends. So, don't make excuses…make your friends' day by reaching out to them.

Sidebar from the Bar (Part 2):

> "Hey, how ya' doin'?" asks the guy in the lane next to me. I look over to see John, my neighbor and father to one of my son Caleb's friends. Not one for chit chat in the middle of my morning swim, I'm hoping to keep this encounter short and sweet.
>
> "Hey John, what brings you here? I don't think I've ever seen you in the pool."
>
> "That's because I'm usually here at 5:30 in the morning before work," John replies.
>
> "Really?" I say, only mildly curious as to the rest of the story.
>
> "Yeah, I had some health issues a while back, so I quit drinking and started swimming."
>
> "No kidding," I say as I quickly connect the dots between Frank's brother, Ben, and John. "How's that workin' for ya'?"
>
> "It's great. I feel better than I have in years, lost a lot of weight and don't miss the alcohol one bit."
>
> "Not one bit, huh?"
>
> "Nope. I was out with my son the other day and he couldn't believe that I haven't had a drink in six months and don't even want one."
>
> "Yeah," and I'm thinking, *I'm kinda struggling with that myself.*

> Boom! Boom! I hate it when that happens. I hate it (not really) when God makes something so perfectly clear that I would have to check my brains out to lunch and lose the claim check to ignore it. If the two guys least likely to ever quit drinking have done so *and* if I happen to find out about it despite not having seen either in several years, I think Bill Engvall would agree—here's my sign! So, I figured I should heed it.
>
> God takes vows quite seriously, so I don't make them lightly. Thus far, I've made no promises to Him or anyone else regarding my drinking. God's made it abundantly clear that He wants me drinking less. Thus far, He hasn't made it clear that He wants me to stop drinking entirely, though I did for nine days recently. Then I had some wine at a business dinner and was surprised to find how sluggish it made me. I didn't enjoy it much. Last night, I had one beer while waiting to pick up a pizza and enjoyed that quite a bit, but had no desire for any more. Right now, my only specific goal related to drinking is to once and for all break the daily habit. Once I'm confident that I've tamed that beast, I'll reevaluate and take the next step as the Lord leads.
>
> As a young IBM'er, while some of my colleagues would regularly hit the bar next to our office after work, I would be home by six o'clock for dinner with my family. This single positive habit probably did more to preserve and protect our marriage than anything I ever did. It kept me out of harm's way in more ways than one. How many marriages have been shipwrecked by otherwise faithful husbands who found themselves within earshot of the siren's tempting call when alcohol had weakened their resistance? You avoid the temptress by avoiding the places where she is. You avoid hurting those you love the most by staying out of harm's way, not by tempting fate.

Taming the Temptress

True confession. The temptress has never come calling on me. In 40 years of marriage, I have never been approached by the "loose woman" as described in Proverbs 27. Mind you, I'm clear that the man in my mirror is no Brad Pitt, but unless I've been shaving the ugliest American all these years, I'm either hopelessly obtuse or a protective force has been with me. After all, even a blind squirrel finds an acorn now and then…if he's looking for it.

Chapter 19

I haven't been. Not because I'm sanctimonious, but rather because I'm literally scared to death of the consequences:

> *With much seductive speech she persuades him; with her smooth talk she compels him. Right away he follows her, and goes like an ox to the slaughter (Proverbs 27:21-22).*

The Danger of an Unguarded Strength

When a nationally-known pastor/author publicly confessed on the radio that he had been unfaithful to his wife, I was all ears. It was April of 1989. Having just started my new IT consulting business, I was staying in a hotel on the north east side of Indianapolis. Elaine and the kids were still back in Memphis, waiting for our new home arrangements to be finalized. I will never forget that radio interview with this repentant man and his forgiving wife. One thing he said stopped me in my tracks: "An unguarded strength can become your greatest weakness."

This deeply committed Christian man was quite certain that he was fatally flawed just like every other person who's ever roamed the planet. But, there was one mistake that he was sure he would never make. He was absolutely certain that he would be faithful to the bride of his youth until the day he died. After all, as a pastor, he spent quite a bit of time counseling those who had destroyed their marriages by drinking water from someone else's cistern (Proverbs 5:15). He wasn't about to join them. And then came the temptress. With his guard down, he went "like an ox to the slaughter."

But for the grace of God, there go I…and I knew it. On that fateful day over 27 years ago, I determined to guard my strength of faithfulness to my lovely bride. The Wisdom of Solomon strongly suggests this was a pretty good call:

> *Do not let your hearts turn aside to her ways; do not stray into her paths. For many are those she has laid low, and numerous are her victims (Proverbs 27:25-26).*

So, what have I missed out on by steering clear of the temptress? Obviously, my entire family has been spared a great deal of pain and suffering. Not so obvious, is the missed opportunities that the temptress offers to validate my manhood, counterfeit though they may be. When the waters from your own cistern don't flow so freely anymore, the temptation to stray increases. After all, no one can live without water, right? Besides, when the bride of my youth doesn't seem very interested in me, could that mean that I'm simply no longer interesting…to her or anyone else? Surely that can't be? I really need to know…don't I?

No, I don't need to know that other women might find me appealing, but I sure would like to know. What man wouldn't? Having options and exercising them are two entirely different things. However, staying on the right side of the line between them is beyond risky. It's like playing a game of marital Russian roulette. The odds are strongly against a positive outcome. Even if you resist the temptation, the puffed-up ego you take home after the encounter is very likely to do damage to your marriage. Having tempted fate to the marital breaking point, how will you react the next time your wife says, "Not tonight, honey, I have a headache"?

The One Question Your Wife Can't Answer

This is tough territory for any man to be in. The key to marital survival within it lies in finding validation outside of the marriage relationship, but not by any means through a relationship with another woman. Rather, validation comes through a relationship with a man, preferably one's father.

Again, Wild at Heart author John Eldredge writes extensively on the importance of men being validated first by their fathers (or father figures), then by God Himself. If this does not occur, most men will spend the rest of their lives trying to get their validity question answered by the women in their lives ("Do I have what it takes?"). Eldredge refers to this as "taking the question to Eve."

So, let's unpack this notion of "taking the question to Eve" just a bit. It's the morning after the Fall. Adam and Eve are sipping coffee and discussing the prior day's events. After her first cup, Eve kicks off the conversation with a real zinger.

"Adam, how could you just sit there and let me do such a stupid thing?"

"Really Eve…really? You're blaming me for your inability to stay away from the one thing that Papa had forbid us from having? I can't believe you're saying this."

"Oh yeah, well you might recall that *we* are created in His image. Not you…not me…*we!* That means *we* are in this thing together, buster. That means when you see me about to do something really stupid, you're supposed to stop me. It's your job."

"My job, huh? And just what is your job? What is it about being a help mate that you don't understand? I'll tell you what your job isn't. It's not to destroy the planet by being unable to control yourself. You just had to have it, didn't you? What's the harm in one little bite, you said? Well, now ya' know."

"Oh, I know all right. I know that when I need you the most, you won't be there."

"No, no. I'll be there. But what I won't be is your scapegoat. I won't let you blame me for your mistakes."

"So that's why you sat there like a stooge, because you didn't want Papa to blame you. How's that working for you? I'm just not sure about us any more, Adam. On second thought, I'm just not sure about you."

"What are you getting at, Eve?"

"What I'm getting at, Adam, is that I'm not sure you have what it takes to be my husband."

"I'm not sure anyone ever will, Eve."

Not a pretty picture. Taking the question to Eve never is. She was clearly telling Adam that she needed him. Adam's response effectively told Eve that he needed her, perhaps even more than she needed him. I wish every man alive could hear and understand what I'm about to say. God designed women with an innate desire to be loved, first and foremost. It is very unnerving to a woman when her man seems to need her more than he loves her, as Adam seemed to on that fateful day in the Garden of Eden.

Had love prevailed in the Garden, Adam would have done whatever it took to rescue his beauty from the unfolding disaster. But since his need for her approval, her validation of him as a man, was greater than his love for her, he froze like a deer in the headlights. And then, all hell quite literally broke loose.

It's no coincidence that the first words out of the momentarily repentant wife-beater's lips are often, "I need you" just after saying, "I didn't mean to hurt you." From the beginning of time, taking the question to Eve has had dire consequences. Nowhere is it more painfully obvious than when a husband chooses to treat his wife as his personal punching bag.

My purpose here is primarily to point out the pitfalls of men seeking validation from the women in their lives. In *Wild at Heart* and *Fathered by*

God, John Eldredge masterfully explains how the road to true validation ultimately leads men to the throne of God. Rather than further unpacking that here, I want to encourage men (and their wives) to read both of these life-changing books, starting with *Wild at Heart*. I would also encourage my female readers to give these books as gifts to the men in their lives. Most will thank you profusely. Some will look longingly into your eyes, as Jack Nicholson did to Helen Hunt in the movie "As Good as it Gets" and say, "You make me wanna be a better man."

I know what you're thinking. Why am I dwelling on this male validation issue? Sounds like a personal problem, right? Oh, it's certainly that, but it's also a pervasive problem in American culture. The problem of misplaced or completely missing male validation is epidemic in our society. And it starts at a very young age.

This past week in the quiet community next to ours, two 18-year-old young men were fighting over a girl. Both had just graduated from their neighboring high schools. One was pronounced dead at the scene, having been stabbed six times by the other. The knife was purchased a few days earlier and purportedly kept in the attacker's glove box for personal protection. One young man's life is over as it was just beginning. Another will almost certainly spend the rest of his in prison. The families of both have been devastated, forever changed…why? Because both of these young men sought to be validated by a young woman. How tragic.

There is a way that appears to be right, but in the end it leads to death (Proverbs 14:12).

Love and Respect

Elaine's mounting health problems in recent years have forced me to look elsewhere for validation. But wait, you say, why were you looking to your wife for validation in the first place? Great question. So glad you've been paying attention. It's because like Adam in his moment of truth, I am a flawed man living in a fallen world and I can't help but look to my wife for a substantial portion of my validation. The truth is if Elaine doesn't think I have what it takes, then what others think matters little. That's why God wired Eve and Elaine's circuitry in a manner conducive to following His mandate for wives to respect their husbands (Ephesians 5:33), a mandate, by the way, that is preceded by an even stronger one for husbands to love their wives.

Chapter 19

Husbands, love your wives, just as Christ loved the church and gave himself up for her (Ephesians 5:25).

After ruminating upon the above verse for months, the message seemed clear enough. When it came to how God would have me love my wife, there were no limits — even to the point of giving my life for her. Got it. Now what? How does that verse apply to my life when I come in the door at six o'clock after a hard day's work? Even more to the point, how does it apply when there's no one there to greet me, because she's been in bed all day with a migraine? Fortunately, that was not the case on this night. We were alone at the dinner table when the subject of this verse entered the conversation.

"What's wrong?" she asked. "Why are you so down?"

"I've been asking God to show me how to love you as Christ loved the church, but I don't seem to be making any progress. It's not a question of loving you. Of course I do. The question is how to love you as you need me to…as God would have me to."

"Isn't there another place in the Bible that says you need to love yourself first before you can love anyone else? It seems to me that you don't love yourself, Brad."

BAM! She could have knocked me over with a feather in that moment. As He'd done so many times over the years, God used Elaine to communicate truth that I couldn't receive any other way. Here's one of the many similar passages she was referring to:

'…You shall love your neighbor as yourself.' There is no other commandment greater than these" (Mark 12:31).

So, if self-love is the guideline for loving my neighbor (or my wife), if I don't love myself I will find it very difficult to truly love anyone else…even God. Yet, I'm commanded to love God with my entire being and to demonstrate His love towards others. How can I resolve this dilemma? The answer is found in another Bible passage that we included in our wedding ceremony:

"We love because he first loved us" (1 John 4:19).

To love anyone the way God intended requires that we first understand how much He loves us. If I'm lacking a healthy self-love, then I'm lacking a full understanding and appreciation of God's love for me. This explains why I find myself muttering "I'm sorry" to my Heavenly Father when I've disappointed myself and, therefore, feel like I've disappointed Him. He's not the least surprised by whatever it was that I did and His love is unconditional. There is nothing I can ever do that would separate me from God's love (Romans 8:37-39). The same is true of everyone reading this book.

So, how can I love my wife the way God loves me—fully, unconditionally and sacrificially? By understanding, accepting, and living in light of the reality that the God of the universe has chosen to love me—fully, unconditionally, and sacrificially. It's that simple and that difficult. Why difficult? Because no one truly feels worthy of such a perfect love. Rightfully so. We are not worthy. There's only One who is and that's why He had to pay the terrible price He did. His name is Jesus…the worthy one.

Nice theory, huh? The real test comes on Monday morning. Or in our case, far too often on Sunday morning, as happened just a few hours ago. After a pleasant Saturday evening of reading and watching a movie, Elaine awoke early this morning with a terrible migraine. As she has so many times before, she cried out in pain from the master bath, asking for my assistance. She'd already given herself the usual injection in her hip. Crying in pain on the edge of the bed while holding a cotton ball on her hip to stop the bleeding, she asked me to get her a pain pill, cold pack for her head and some fresh water. And the beat goes on…

This morning, I handled it better than many times in the past. I gently held her and told her it just wasn't fair. I'm ashamed to admit how often I've reacted to my wife's pain in anger. Not at her, though there have been times when I simply couldn't handle the truth of her pain. I'd wonder if it was psychosomatic, some kind of an escape mechanism. But mostly, my anger has been directed towards God. Why won't you heal her, Lord? Why are you allowing her to suffer so? We've been through so much; can't you give us a break?

Nothing. No healing. No words of hope or encouragement.

Silence.

Pain in the Neck

While accompanying Tim on the second half of the John Muir Trail, I had constant neck "stingers" and spine compression pain. So much so, I had to stop every five minutes over our 12-day hike to bend over and rotate my head 360° to get some very temporary relief. The correlation to Elaine's neck and spine problems was not lost on me. So, every time I stopped for what came to be known as a "stinger break," I would pray for Elaine's healing. After a few hundred such prayers, I felt impressed by the Spirit of God to stop. It was as if He was saying, "I've got this. You can stop now." So I did.

This morning, after settling Elaine back into bed, I reminded God that He told me He had this. Elaine's pain was His problem, not mine. When was He going to do something about it? Was her constant pain and the medications required to cope with it really something she was to "count all joy" (James 1:2)? Besides, she's on so many medications, she's not herself…not even close on many days. "Do something God! Please do something," I whimpered.

It's now quarter to ten. In a few minutes, I'll take a shower and head off to church…alone, as I've done so many times in recent years. When I return, Elaine will almost certainly still be in bed. On "migraine days" she usually doesn't get up until late afternoon or early evening. Sabbath rest? Hardly. On most such days, my despondency grows as another lonely weekend fades to black. By the time I go to bed on Sunday night, I'm deeply depressed and wondering if I'll have the strength to face another week. So far, by God's grace, I have…as has Elaine.

Weather isn't the only cause of Elaine's brutal migraines, but major fronts moving in and out of the area can cause excruciating pressure in her head. Such was the case this week. Though it's mid-August in central Indiana, we've been having fall-like weather. This, following the coldest month of July ever recorded. So much for global warming. Given the severity and prolonged nature of the pain, we went looking for a new form of relief.

Having read about "trigger point massage therapy," Elaine was encouraged to find a masseur who specialized in it just 10 minutes from our home. If it triggered some relief, the $200 sessions would be a bargain. She made an appointment for the following morning. Here's the text message she sent me afterwards:

> *"The most awful pain I have ever experienced without sedation. I feel like every muscle in my upper body was plucked out. I'm shaking. And yes it is supposed to be that painful."*

Here's an excerpt from the follow-up email the masseur sent her:

> *"You left with improved range of motion but you did look as if you were in shock. That is not unusual but it will dissipate quickly."*

If trigger-point massage is how my lovely bride spells "relief," then there's apparently none in sight. Granted, it's only been 48 hours since her time on the torture table. But, barring a miraculous recovery this weekend, she's more apt to run the Boston Marathon on her twin titanium knees than to subject herself to another massage treatment. And yes, we've tried acupuncture with similar results.

What do you do when it hurts to hug and there's no relief in sight? Before providing what I feel certain will be less than satisfying answers to this very challenging question, I offer as a backdrop this quote from A.W. Tozer. (Tozer, 1955):

> *"It is doubtful whether God can bless a man greatly until He has hurt him deeply."* – A.W. Tozer

I know. No waiting required for the thunderous applause to die down. Few people want to hear Tozer's "no pain, no gain" theology. Fewer still will embrace the notion that a loving God would not only allow pain into their lives, but actually purposely inflict it as a prerequisite to His blessings. And yet, the Bible is chalked full of such accounts, the lengthy Book of Job being chief among them. My own life experiences strongly suggest that Tozer is spot on with this hard truth. Like most, on my many pain-filled days I cry out to God, "Say it isn't so!" His response? Silence.

The title of this chapter, "When It Hurts to Hug" came from a Toastmasters speech I gave a few years ago. The closing slide showed a man being embraced by a huge tiger with the caption reading – "Hug even when it hurts, because it hurts more not to." The simple point being that chronic pain sufferers and their loved ones must resist the temptation to pull away from one another. While doing so may provide some temporary relief, such separation over time will only add to everyone's pain. Admittedly, the speech was primarily a therapeutic exercise for me. As I have for many years, I was merely seeking one more way of coping with Elaine's chronic pain and the devastating impact it's had on our quality of life.

When The Painful Path Has a Terminal End

I want to speak briefly to those (and their loved ones) who not only suffer from chronic pain, but live with the daily dread that their painful path may have a fatal end. I truly feel your pain. Helplessly standing by as my father succumbed to colon cancer when he was only 60 years old was painful beyond words. Having been down that path, I would never equate our current situation to yours. We are very conscious of and thankful for the fact that Elaine's condition is not terminal. Though I must admit to having times when I thought it might be easier to cope with if it were. Let me explain.

Someone dying of a terminal disease has a clear, albeit horrible, answer to the basic question, "Why am I in pain?" Because you're dying. The answer for someone suffering from chronic pain with no end in sight is a bit more complicated, or so it seems from this co-sufferer's perspective. I'm not saying this makes sense. I'm merely admitting to having had such thoughts and supposing that I'm not alone.

Take empathy and sympathy for example. Recall my confession to having very little of either for Elaine on some days. Why? Because I can neither feel her pain nor do anything about it. Were she suffering pain unto death, however, I suspect my empathy and sympathy buckets would be overflowing, though still unable to feel or fix her pain problem. Please forgive me if these words are upsetting to anyone dealing with a terminal disease situation. God forbid that I add to your pain. I just want to give those in situations similar to my own as much coping help as possible. Sometimes it helps just knowing that others have felt and thought similar things.

I mentioned the Old Testament Book of Job earlier. I've logged quite a few hours in that book over the years while trying to gain some much-needed perspective on the trial du jour. During one such time many years ago, I was studying the last chapter which states that after Job's trials were over, God restored everything he had lost twofold. So, after losing 7,000 sheep, Job received 14,000. After losing 3,000 camels, he received 6,000, and so on. But, when it came to the 10 children who had perished at Satan's hand, God gave him only 10 more, not a two-fold 20. The apparent discrepancy troubled me. After all, doesn't God value people above animals and things?

I was still ruminating upon this troubling truth while attending a Steve Green concert at our church in Memphis circa 1987. As I'm thinking to myself, "Why didn't you give Job 20 new children, Lord?" the answer came as clearly as the notes from the song being sung. "I didn't need to replace the 10 children Job lost, because he was reunited with them in Heaven when he died. So Job will enjoy the company of his 20 children for all eternity, twofold what he had before his trials began."

Whoa! As God is my witness (and He was), my spine tingled. I got goose bumps all over my body. The entire sanctuary took on a mystical glow. The God of the universe had just "spoken" to me. No, I did not hear His voice, but the message and its source were perfectly clear. I never understood just why the answer to that question mattered so much to me. Once I had it, all that really mattered was that God had spoken...to me! Why? Because I asked Him to. I will be forever grateful to have experienced what Francis Schaeffer so poignantly describes in his book, *He Is There and He Is Not Silent*.

In The Meantime

Yesterday, I started listening to a new sermon series called "In the Meantime" by Andy Stanley of North Point Community Church in Atlanta.[4] Within it, Andy attempts to answer the seemingly unanswerable question—"What do you do when there's nothing that you can do?" He speaks directly and powerfully to those who find themselves between the proverbial rock and a hard place with no way out. During such times, most people, regardless of their faith paradigm, usually get around to asking themselves this question: "Where is God?"

Where is God when your hopes and dreams lie dashed to pieces on the kitchen floor? Where is God when that condition has become chronic and increasingly debilitating? Where is God when trust is broken between you and the most important person in your life? Where is God when the addiction has a choke hold on you or a loved one and talk of a lasting recovery seems like a cruel joke? Where in the @#$! is God when...???

Why do we wonder where God is when life has spun out of control and left us bleeding in a ditch by the road? Stanley says it's because we mistakenly believe that God is either absent, apathetic or angry with us. He's either not there, doesn't care or is on a mission to punish us for some grievous sin we've committed. Believing this about God, we draw some very bad conclusions about ourselves—I'll never be happy again *and* nothing good can come from this. These destructive false beliefs will become self-fulfilling prophecies if not countered by the real truth about God's intimate role in our lives.

Stanley goes on to unpack this truth by recounting the New

---

[4] In The Meantime is a six-part sermon series by Pastor Andy Stanley, North Point Community Church in Atlanta, Georgia, August 17, 2014. http://MeantimeSeries.org.

Testament stories about two of Jesus' closest friends, John the Baptist and Lazarus. About John the Baptist, Jesus said, "among those born of women there is no one greater than John" (Luke 7:28).

As to Lazarus, his sisters sent word of their brother's illness to Jesus with this simple message: "Lord, the one you love is sick" (John 11:3).

Jesus cared deeply for both of these men, yet he was notably missing in action during their times of greatest need. John the Baptist was imprisoned and eventually beheaded. Lazarus's illness proved to be terminal.[5]

At this point, it might be helpful to briefly circle back to the Book of Job. Though satisfied with God's amazing answer to my question regarding Job's children, I remained deeply troubled for decades over why God allowed all hell to quite literally break loose in Job's life in the first place. Mind you, this is the guy about whom God said, "There is no one on Earth like him; he is blameless and upright, a man who fears God and shuns evil" (Job 1:8).

Really? Then what kind of a crazy meritocracy is God running up there? Job's reward for being valedictorian of his class was to become Satan's whipping boy and have everything he valued in life taken away from him. The sign-up line for that course is pretty short. Just what was God up to?

Clearly from the story, we know God was fully present, intimately involved and not the least bit angry with his servant, Job. And yet, when Satan came knocking to ask if Job could come out to play, God effectively opened the door and tossed his favorite son to the wolves. Or so it seemed. Was God stroking His ego at Job's expense by having Job prove his loyalty to God just to win a bet with His arch enemy? Surely not. Surely there's something much more redemptive than that going on here. Surely there's a satisfying answer to the question that's been handed down through three millennia, "Why did God allow Satan to pummel Job?" I've come to my own conclusion, though admittedly, it might not be a satisfying one to many.

I believe God allowed Satan to pummel Job for two primary reasons. First, because it was good for him. Second, because it would be good for

---

[5] For the rest of the story, I highly commend Andy Stanley's August 17, 2014 podcast entitled, "In the Meantime: The New Normal."

multitudes of God following truth seekers throughout the ages. In saying that Job's trials were good for him, I'm not by any means suggesting that his suffering was worth it because God gave him twice what he started with when it was over. Not at all. Job had plenty to start with and didn't need to go to hell and back to double-down. That part of the transaction, in my opinion, was just a loving Father doting on his son. After all, who really needs 14,000 sheep? Job probably could have squeaked by on the 7,000 he started with. No, I think his real reward was much richer than that.

Comfort and Character Make Strange Bedfellows

One of my early spiritual mentors once told me that while we spend most of our time trying to order our circumstances to maximize our comfort, God spends His time ordering those same circumstances to mold our character. In God's economy, character is priceless, while comfort is dirt cheap. Comfort and character do not abide one another. Character simply cannot be built by remote control from a La-Z-Boy.

But you say, "Job had unimpeachable character before his trials began." Indeed, he did, but that does not negate my point regarding Job's trials being primarily about building his character. As good as Job was, he was a mere man and fatally flawed in comparison to a holy God. This was powerfully pointed out by God and acknowledged by Job towards the end of the story:

> *Then the Lord spoke to Job out of the storm. He said, "Who is this that obscures my plans with words without knowledge? Brace yourself like a man; I will question you, and you shall answer me" (Job 38:1-3).*

My second point is that Job's trials were also good for all God-following truth-seekers throughout the ages. Trials and tribulations will either draw a person to God or push them away from Him. Throughout such ordeals, we often experience the equivalent of a spiritual tug-o-war during which we are pushed towards and pulled away from God with the ups and downs of the daily battles. When the smoke clears, we're left either closer to or further from God. Job's story tells us that no matter how hard fought the battle or how great the casualties, when it's over our new beachhead should be closer to Him.

Job's story reminds me of what Pastor Randy Pope of Perimeter

Church in Atlanta once said, "Faith isn't truly faith until it's the only thing you're holding onto." Job clung to his faith in God throughout his ordeal. In the end, faith was the only thing he was holding onto. This, despite a wife who thought he'd be better off cursing God and dying (Job 2:9).

Just yesterday, I met with a friend—I'll call him Bill—who finds himself in a situation very similar to Job's. When Bill's employer lost a major contract a few years ago, he lost his job along with hundreds of others. He hasn't had steady employment since. At 60 years old, his odds of getting a job comparable to the one he lost are very low. He's lost nearly on everything, including his younger wife who "didn't sign up for this." Having married late, John has a young son with serious health issues requiring constant and costly care. My heart aches for this modern day Job holding on for dear life to his faith in God.

John is at a critical juncture in his time of trial. Survival could well depend upon what Andy Stanley describes in his sermon, A Purpose and a Promise (Part 2 of the "In the Meantime" series). Stanley says that sometimes the only way forward is to embrace your current circumstances as having come from the hands of your loving Heavenly Father. Sometimes the only way forward is to stop trying to get out of your circumstances and start trying to find what God wants to impart to you within them. Getting to that point may be the hardest thing you ever do. Once there, however, you can know "the peace that surpasses all understanding" (Philippians 4:7).

From Job to John the Baptist to Lazarus to the Apostle Paul to Jesus Himself, one Bible story after another is penned in the red ink of adversity. Time and time again, serious God followers find themselves in serious trouble. Circumstances so bleak that only a miracle can save them. And yet, time and time again these God followers see a higher purpose and cling to a precious promise that transcends their circumstances and shows them the way forward. As Andy Stanley points out, the way forward may lead to the ultimate sacrifice, as it did with John the Baptist and even Jesus. But come what may, the God follower knows that he is never alone. His Heavenly Father is ever present, intensely interested and overflowing with grace towards His children.

Chapter 19

20. Hope Floats from the Bottom Up

Our oldest daughter, Emily, is bipolar. Like many so afflicted, Emily has been prone to self-medication since she was a young teen. Consequently, she's been in and out of countless rehab and recovery facilities spanning two decades now. Of all the challenges our large family has faced over the years, none has been greater than that of coping with Emily's self-destructive disease and its related addictions. If you've walked a similar road or (God forbid) are about to, I hope you find some solace and encouragement in Emily's story. Told with her permission.

I knew it was a dangerous prayer, but we were desperate for some relief. As Christmas 2012 was approaching, the telltale signs that Emily was using again were everywhere. She was living in squalor. Dirty dishes throughout the house. Dirty clothes piled so high on the floor you couldn't open the door to the laundry room. The garage had become one giant dumpster into which she threw trash and whatever else she didn't know what to do with. It was disgusting…and heart-breaking.

"Lord, I don't know how much more we can take. I want to help Emily, but I fear that I'm enabling her. What can I do to help? It seems I need three things. First, I need to know the truth about her. Is she using or is she suffering from her bipolarism, possibly not taking her meds correctly? Second, I need the wisdom to know what to do in light of the truth. Third, I need the courage to do whatever that is. Amen."

She was supposedly moving out of her house in a few days, yet she'd done nothing to prepare for it. I knew better than to do it for her, but I had to do something to help. So, I did what I often do at home when feeling desperate and unable to move the boulders in life's path…I cleaned out her garage. Through tears, I separated the trash from the things worth saving. I swept up the garbage and the broken glass. With the rest of the house still looking like a bomb went off in it, my efforts were more symbolic than substantive. The man in me had to take some action. The father in me had to somehow let my precious daughter know that I still loved her, that I was still there for her, though thoroughly disgusted by the state she was in.

Emily was a ticking time bomb. My heart skipped a beat whenever her number came up on my cell phone. She rarely called with good news. She frequently called asking for money, as addicts are wont to do. This call was different. It came on New Year's Day afternoon 2013.

"I can't do this anymore," she said.

"What do you mean, Emily?"

"I'm sick. I need to go to the hospital. I'm scared, Dad"

I remembered my dangerous prayer for truth, wisdom and courage. "Is this the truth we needed to know, Lord?" Having been down this road so many times before, I knew what was making her sick and why she was so afraid. I told her to pack a bag and I'd be there within the hour. Within that hour I was hoping to find the strength to handle the truth. Happy New Year!

The check-in process at the Psych Pavilion is laborious on an average day. On New Year's Day, its pure torture. It took hours to get Emily evaluated and admitted. Zoned out on Xanax, her drug of choice, Emily couldn't keep her eyes open. Fearing she'd fall out of her chair and hurt herself, I sat next to her and put my arms around her. As I caressed her hair, memories from the 20-year trail of tears we'd traveled flooded my mind. My broken heart was still bursting with love for my broken daughter.

A few years earlier, desperate for relief from her bipolar disorder, Emily underwent Electroconvulsive Therapy (ECT). This entails inducing a seizure by sending an electric current through the scalp to the brain while the patient is asleep under general anesthesia. When it works, the seizure can have a calming effect upon the brain waves causing the patient's manic-depressive mood swings. ECT is the psychological equivalent of a "hail Mary" pass in football. When all else fails, slap jumper cables on your brain and hope for the best.

While her husband stayed home with their two daughters, I would pick Emily up at five o'clock in the morning to go to her ECT sessions. She'd stumble out the door in her pajamas, robe and slippers and off we'd go to jumpstart a seizure. While Emily's brain was being scrambled, I'd order up some scrambled eggs at a nearby restaurant and try not to think about what she was going through. It was awful. So much so, the fact that Emily was willing to go through it had my wife and me convinced that her root problem was mental illness, not drug addiction. Over time, we came to realize that the two are so inextricably linked both need to be treated as if each was the primary problem. We'll never know if Emily's six ECT sessions were helpful, though she did experience some relief in the ensuing months. Not enough, however, to ever subject her to that barbaric treatment again.

Ever smiling, Emily was a beautiful, bouncy, pigtailed, blonde little girl. She was incredibly strong and athletic. An accomplished gymnast in her early years, she transitioned into a competition cheerleader on her high

Chapter 20

school's state champion team. Emily briefly took up judo when she was a senior in high school. Her coach told her she could be a national champion if she set her mind to it. Unfortunately, her mind was on other far less healthy things by that time. Though very intelligent, Emily couldn't stay focused on her studies. We weren't sure she was going to graduate from high school until commencement night. It only got worse from there.

We were on our way to our 25th wedding anniversary dinner when Emily called. It was June of 2001, just two weeks after the bizarre soccer field incident that landed me in jail. Emily would be celebrating her 21st birthday in just a few days. She spoke the words we had feared hearing since early adolescence.

"I'm pregnant," she said. With that matter-of-fact pronouncement, Emily exponentially raised the stakes in her game of life. She went on to marry the father, her high school sweetheart. They had two beautiful daughters, but their marriage couldn't carry the baggage brought into the relationship, so they eventually divorced. Emily remarried a few years later and gave us our first and thus far, only, grandson.

Addiction experts will tell you that there's little hope for the addict until she hits rock bottom. For the addict, hope floats from the bottom up. While still in the Psych Pavilion in January of 2013, Emily insisted on describing what "rock bottom" looked like for her on New Year's Eve before calling me the following day. She thought it was important for me to understand how bad things had gotten. Emily did all she could to prepare me for the hardest truth I've ever heard. But, nothing could have fully prepared me. I wept bitterly upon hearing how dangerous a desperate addict can be when their entire world revolves around the next fix. Even now, the memory of that moment brings me to tears and reopens wounds that I suppose will never fully heal this side of eternity.

Yet, hope does indeed float from the bottom up. After her release from the Psych Pavilion, Emily went into a halfway house program and landed a great job that she excelled in. For the first time in her life, she held a job for more than a year while celebrating one year of sobriety on January 1, 2014. She also went for that entire year with no financial assistance from her parents, another first.

As much as I'd like to offer a "happily ever after" ending to Emily's story, I can't…not yet anyway. She relapsed early in 2014 and has been back on the road to recovery since. Clean and sober, Emily is looking for a new job and we're looking with renewed hope for the end of our trail of tears. Hope that, once again, is floating from the bottom up.

Fast forward to Black Friday 2014. I'm up early in pursuit of my self-imposed deadline of having this manuscript in my editor's hands by Christmas (a deadline I missed by a mile). I don't really feel like writing this morning, despite having a wonderful Thanksgiving gathering at our home yesterday. The joy of watching Elaine singing and dancing with our children and grandchildren was somewhat muted by the absence of one faction of our extended family. Emily chose to stay home with her family of five for all too familiar reasons. She was mad at the world, especially her parents, who finally refused to give her the money she's been asking for every other week since losing her job too many months ago.

When bipolar people get hurt and angry, they can viciously turn on those closest to them. They're capable of saying anything and at their worst, doing just about anything. They're truly scary to be around. The emotional scars of their tirades left with their targets linger long after their own memories of what they said or did have completely faded. When they do remember, they usually justify their behavior by how their targets made them feel at the time. More often than not, what they're hurt and angry over stems from the desperate tough love efforts of friends and family members who sincerely want to help them, but in so doing must also consider the needs of their own family members. Such was the case this time around with our precious daughter.

Most bipolar people can live reasonably normal productive lives once they land upon the right combination of medications to stabilize their wild mood swings. That's the good news. The bad news is that the process of finding the optimal med regime can take years. And, once found, if that regime is not followed consistently, Dr. Jekyll can become Mr. Hyde within a few days. The rub lies in the fact that even when properly medicated, it's very difficult for a bipolar person to maintain the discipline of taking their meds as prescribed. Sometimes they simply forget to take them. Other times, a particularly strong manic cycle overwhelms their meds. Falsely believing they don't need their meds anymore, they just stop taking them. Or, at the other extreme, a particularly strong depressive cycle kicks in, perhaps triggered by some life event like losing a job. This sends them into a downward spiral that causes them to stop taking their meds, sometimes turning to dangerous self-medicating alternatives. That's when the risk of suicide is at its highest.

These vicious cycles are utterly exhausting to everyone within the bipolar person's sphere of influence. A sphere that, sadly, tends to shrink over time as friends and family members distance themselves from "the troubled one." That's why I told Emily's husband a few days ago that even if she changed her mind about joining us, it would be best for them to have their own Thanksgiving gathering. That's why I took the second turkey we had ordered for the occasion and left it on their back porch Wednesday afternoon without talking to my daughter. After all, she had made it clear that she didn't want to see us and, at that point, the feeling was mutual. Sad but true. That's why when I hugged Elaine as we were finalizing preparations for our feast, surrounded by four of our five extended family units, she said, "I just wish I didn't feel so sad." I knew the feeling all too well. It feels like a rock in the pit of your stomach, making it impossible to fully digest the goodness of life.

At this point, the foreman of the jury of reader opinion is crying "foul." Emily's sad tale risks failing the "So what?" and "Who cares?" test. Somebody call the "wambulance" and let's move on. Right? If your life's journey has by-passed the ups and downs of the bipolar trail, you may be struggling to find the point of her story. On the other hand, if you've lived a similar tragic tale, you may be struggling to find any comfort or hope within this one. You know all too well what it's like to dread seeing your troubled loved one's number on your phone. It's almost never good news and the timing usually couldn't be worse. I quite literally feel your pain and want to help you find relief. Like you, our family desperately needs to find solace in the present and hope for the future.

I must confess that writing the preceding paragraphs about the sad hole in our Thanksgiving story has me feeling quite depressed. Our bipolar battle has been raging for over 20 years now. Our 34-year-old daughter's rent is due in three days and they don't have it. We paid half of it last month along with hundreds of dollars in uninsured prescription expenses. Her family could be homeless within weeks and we could be faced with the moral dilemma of either allowing them to move in with us or into a homeless shelter. That rock in the pit of my stomach is getting bigger by the minute. If we get through this day without receiving another desperate plea for money, I'll be quite surprised…and worried. Worried that she's given up. Worried that she just can't face another day. Worried that the next number I see on my phone will be her husband's. Worried for good reason….

…because Elaine and I will never forget the call she received from Emily telling us that her best friend, Stacy, had just committed suicide. Another of her closest friends found Stacy hanging in her garage with her 10-year-old daughter playing in the backyard. It was a horrific scene, as the friend desperately tried to cut the rope per the instructions of the first responder on the phone. It was too late. 31-year-old Stacy was gone. Leaving her daughter to grow up without her mother and her parents to go to their graves wondering if they really did all they could do to save her from herself. So yeah, we worry about Stacy's best friend and constantly wonder if we're doing all we can to save her from herself. It's truly maddening.

Emily's never out of our consciousness. I hang on every positive sign as if life depended upon it (because it does) and I too often see downturns in her mood and circumstances as the beginning of the end. The madness of it all came through loud and clear in a text I received from her a week or so ago—"Bank account went down to $1,800 in the red back in September." At that point, I paused to compose myself before continuing. This was obviously just another "same s@#t different day" plea for money. I must further confess that I was driving while reading her text.

She went on to say, "Today it's finally caught up and at 25 whole dollars. I can't believe we did it. It sure feels good though." I nearly ran off the road. Proving once again that those who text and drive are truly stuck on stupid.

"Let me read that again. Surely she's not saying what I think she's saying." But she was. Once again, I needed to compose myself. This time because I was elated over this rare piece of positive news from our daughter. I called her just to be sure. And then something equally rare occurred...she answered my call. Bipolar people are masters at dodging calls they don't want to receive, which is most of them. But, they get hoppin' mad when someone returns the favor. Hearing Emily's perky voice on the other end of the line made for a perfect end to an otherwise mundane Monday. I couldn't wait to get home and share the good news with Elaine.

As hope continues to float up into our precious daughter's life, I'm pleased to report that Emily has a new job that she loves and is doing well overall. As of August of 2016, her faith is stronger than ever and she's been clean and sober for over 18 months. She and her husband still struggle to make ends meet, but they're making it. About a month ago Emily shared a wonderful story about how God provided for them in answer to her prayer.

With no money and no food to feed her six-year-old son when he got home from school, she prayed that God would provide. In doing so, she realized that all she needed was 10 dollars. Then, she looked at her bank account on her phone and noticed that she'd been charged twice at a nearby store for something she bought recently. She went to the store, had the clerk check their records and walked out with a 10-dollar bill and a million-dollar smile. Bottoms up!

One last update before closing out Emily's very hopeful story. Later this morning I'll be picking her up from the hospital after being admitted three days ago with acute pancreatitis. I'll never forget those literally gut-wrenching hours in the ER waiting for the pain meds to take the edge off my daughter's excruciating pain. I've never witnessed anyone in so much pain. It was such an awful helpless feeling. But, as Emily tossed and turned in every direction, futilely trying to find a position that would bring some relief, she repeatedly cried out for help. "Please God, help me...Jesus, please take this pain away...PLEASE!" My eyes filled with bittersweet tears. Bitter from my child's pain...sweet from where she was choosing to take it...to her God...to her Savior. Thank you, Jesus!

Chapter 20

21. Wisdom from Above...and Below

When You Lose Your Sense of Humor...You Lose

We were about an hour into a five-hour drive home from our first and only family union. The memories couldn't fade fast enough. We'd just spent a tortuous weekend trapped with four children and countless relatives on two huge houseboats sitting in the cove of a large lake in Tennessee. As cousin Gordy looked upon the huddled masses from his ski boat, he declared in a thick southern accent, "Ya'll look like a buncha piss ants on a jelly roll." Indeed, we did. Haven't had a jelly roll since.

Let's just say my lovely bride wasn't quite herself that weekend. Probably had something to do with my 18-month old namesake running around the slippery decks like a drunken sailor. And of course, I was the designated lifeguard. When Bradley fell in the water between the two boats, our family's SOS signal went off loud and clear. Then...the dreaded silent treatment.

As I was mulling over ways to break the silence without admitting fault (it's a guy thing), three ducks come flying out of nowhere straight across our windshield. The third one in formation didn't quite make it. A loud thud was followed by a flurry of feathers, a few sticking in our wipers. My wife and I looked at each other with wild-eyed astonishment and then laughed until we cried.

The silence had been broken. The weekend was a bust, but our marriage had been saved by a poor unsuspecting duck who never knew what hit him. Some 24 years later, I quack up whenever I think of this story. One of many poignant reminders that when you lose your sense of humor...you lose.

You Can't Teach Pigs to Sing. They Never Learn and It Annoys the Pigs.

Most sales training curricula teaches students how to surface their prospects' objections with good probing open-ended questions. Logic being that you can't overcome an objection without knowing what it is. The pig-singing axiom suggests that some objections can't be overcome, no matter how hard you try. In fact, the harder you try to overcome them, the stronger the objection becomes. The annoyed prospect assumes the opposing position and nothing short of dynamite is likely to move them. In such cases, its best to set that objection aside and move on to the next one.

To illustrate, let's enter everyone's favorite selling venue—the new car showroom. The buyer seems to like everything about the car except its color. He walked in determined to buy the fire engine red sports car his mid-life crisis was screaming for. But, his favorite model doesn't come in red. What's a savvy salesperson to do? Trying to convince the buyer that red really isn't his favorite color would be a waste of time and it would annoy the "pig." A far better approach is to set the color objection aside, then focus on the many positive features of the car. Besides, isn't black the new red anyway?

You Can't Have a Perspective You've Never Had

At this stage of my life, it's safe to assume I'll never see the world from the top of Mount Everest. Though I do anticipate looking down upon the world's highest peak in my next life and perhaps even climbing it. In this life, I will never have the perspective of those chosen few who have stood on the top of the world. Though I have personally met one of them.

It was during that spiritual retreat in Colorado in the winter of 2012. Tom was in my small group of guys who started to peel back the onion of our lives by sharing our personal stories. He was a young gentle soul in his late twenties. Lean and wiry, he seemed to calculate his every move like a predator stalking his prey. As the youngest among us, Tom seemed painfully shy and slow to warm up to the notion of bearing his soul to complete strangers from all over the country. But once he did, the rest of our stories paled by comparison.

Though he never described himself as such, young Tom was a mountain climber. He worked for an outdoor adventure ministry that helped people along in their spiritual journeys by exposing them to some of God's best handiwork. Climbing mountains was both Tom's vocation and avocation. And he was very good at it.

This soft-spoken mountaineer held us spellbound recounting the time that he led a small group of climbers up one of the famed Seven Summits in Argentina. At 22,837 feet, Aconcagua is the highest mountain in the Western and Southern Hemispheres. Depending upon the chosen route, it can be a relatively easy climb when compared to other peaks of similar height. However, as with any technical climb, weather is often the game-changer. As it was during Tom's expedition.

Having taken one of the more challenging routes, Tom's team had several harrowing close calls before reaching the Aconcagua summit. Their relief was short-lived, however, as a massive snow storm blew in, leaving them no choice but to hunker down and wait for it to pass. It was still snowing in the morning. Visibility was near zero. A descent was impossible under such conditions. Fully exposed on the summit, they laid in their tents contemplating their dangerously decreasing odds of survival with each passing hour. Again, they had no choice but to ride out the storm for another night.

With the morning came the realization that they could not survive another night on the summit. They had to attempt a descent regardless of the weather conditions. Looking at the sky, they saw little hope on the horizon. Feeling desperate, they gathered everyone under a single tarp to pray for divine intervention. Every member of that party knew that only a miracle could save them. They prayed fervently for the storm to pass and the sky to clear. They pulled the tarp back, as prepared as they would ever be to begin their death-defying descent.

Imagine their joy when they looked up to see the clouds parting with a ray of hope shining through. God had indeed answered their prayers. Their descent was nonetheless still quite challenging, with several more near-death experiences. But, every member of Tom's team made it down safely. As he finished his story, our small group of guys let out a collective sigh of relief. Having read many high mountain adventure stories, I was particularly taken with Tom's.

As our small group time was winding down, I attempted to engage Tom in further mountaineering conversation. He was reticent to talk about himself though, because he saw God as the main character in his story. Then I overheard him say something to the one person in the group whom he already knew.

"Did you say Everest," I asked, thinking I surely misunderstood.

"Yes," Tom said very matter-of-factly.

"You climbed Mount Everest?" I gasped with my eyes wide open in astonishment.

"Yeah," he calmly said as if that feat was on every 20-somethings bucket list.

I was beyond stunned. "Did you summit?"

"Yep." That's it? Yep? Seriously? The dude climbed Mount Everest before he was 30 years old and when it came time to tell his story, he left that part out? No way! Rest assured, if I had ever made it to the Everest summit the world would soon grow weary of my triumphant tale. Such humility in such a young man is, well…humbling. Young Tom, my hero, gave me quite a history lesson that day. He understands better than most that history is first and foremost His story. That's why he chose to tell how God calmed the storm and miraculously delivered his team from the Aconcagua summit.

I did manage to get some tidbits from the Everest climb out of my humble friend, albeit reluctantly. Turns out they had perfect weather on their summit day. So much so, that he and his climbing partner decided to go ahead of their main party. When they returned to camp, fellow climbers greeted them with consoling remarks, assuming they had failed in their summit attempt. Knowing when they had departed, they thought it impossible to have returned from the Summit so quickly. They were wrong. Tom and his partner did the final summit trek as fast as anyone ever has. Amazing!

Towards the end of the retreat, like a groupie at a rock concert, I asked my new hero to autograph the tee shirt I was wearing. That sounds pretty silly, I know. But how many people do you know who have climbed Mount Everest? I only know one and doubt I'll ever meet another. If I do, I suspect he'll be a bit fuller of himself than my humble hero. It was Tom's humility that I found so irresistible. I suspect his Heavenly Father does as well.

Tom has a perspective from the top of the world that I'll never have. The only way to see what he saw is to go where he went. Not gonna happen. And, like most spectacular sights, pictures just can't do Everest justice. That's why I say it's impossible to have a perspective you've never had. Try as we may to walk in someone else's moccasins, until we've navigated the same trail in our own boots, we can't fully appreciate another's perspective.

Elaine and I didn't appreciate what it was like to have financial margin until we had it during our "salad days" in Memphis. And once we had that perspective, we were shocked at how quickly we lost our previous "too much month at the end of the money" perspective. For many years, we've supported several overseas ministries caring for disadvantaged children in under developed nations. Yet, I didn't fully appreciate their life-changing impact until spending time with some of those kids in South Africa during a short term mission trip. Seeing truly is believing. Having stood atop Mount Whitney, Pacer and I have a perspective of those who've climbed Mount Everest that can only be attained from half the height. That's right...only half. As breath-taking as Whitney is, we can only imagine what it's like to be twice that high atop Everest. But, our imagination coupled with our real-life experiences will get Pacer and Buster closer to the ultimate summit than those whose perspectives are limited to the foothills.

So, why is it important to understand that you can't have a perspective you've never had? Accepting this truism will make you less judgmental and more understanding. It should also spur you on in your lifelong learning journey. The more you learn, the more perspective you gain and the more fulfilling life becomes. Though you can never have the exact same perspective as someone else, as your horizons expand, so will your ability to relate to those previously beyond them. It never ceases to amaze me how two people can look at exactly the same set of circumstances, yet see them very differently. Why? Because it's impossible to have a perspective you've never had.

Good Thing or Bad thing? God Only Knows.

Actions have consequences. Teaching this immutable truth to their children from the earliest possible age is chief among every parent's many responsibilities. Hot stoves burn fingers. Pulled puppy dog tails can cause painful bites. Failure to look both ways when you cross the street can be catastrophic. This endless list put the "terrible" in "terrible twos." As those toddlers turn into moms and dads themselves, however, it becomes increasingly difficult to judge the rightness of their actions by the resulting consequences. Let me explain.

Parents of temperamental teens often find themselves seemingly on the wrong side of right following a battle of wills with their former little angels. In meting out the appropriate punishment, parents understandably fear how their children might react. When teens overreact, as they're wont to do, parents then begin to question if they did the right thing. While staring into the wild eyes of a their little darling now frothing at the mouth and spewing forth expletives at the speed of light, mom and dad start to wonder if the consequences are worth it. But, a child's inappropriate reaction does not make a parent's action wrong. Many times, you simply cannot judge the rightness of an action by the resulting consequences.

What about when seemingly bad things happen to no fault of the apparent victim? Judging something to be either good or bad is much harder than it sounds. So, you're sick and can't go to work today? Is it a good thing or a bad thing? If your boss just found out the night before that his wife is leaving him, it may be a good thing. After repeated absences from a prolonged illness, you lose your job. Good or bad? If the stress of that job was making you sick and the job of your dreams awaits you, it's probably a good thing. Had we not spent what seemed like a lifetime in Oklahoma City in six miserable months, I could have easily passed up the opportunity of a lifetime. But for the present misery, the unimaginably bright future may have never become our reality. What felt like a very bad thing at the time, turned our family in a very good, life-changing direction.

Stories of grateful cancer survivors giving thanks not only for their healing, but for the disease itself, have become almost commonplace. How is this possible? Many such survivors will tell you that the ultimate "bad thing" soon became a poorly disguised blessing. As they learned to live in the moment and to appreciate the joy of being surrounded by those who love them, they learned to love life itself. Sometimes for the very first time. If cancer gives us pause to ask the good thing/bad thing question, then so should just about anything that happens in life. Don't you think?

God's Best!

George H.W. Bush, the 41st President of the United States, always closed his prolific letters with his now famous "All the best" phrase, the appropriate title of his memoirs published in 2013. It had a warm and endearing ring to it, so many adopted this closing as their own. I considered doing the same before something I like much better came to mind some years ago. It emanates from the line of thinking that we're currently on regarding the limits of human reasoning to judge current circumstances. While I certainly want the best for all, I rarely know what that is. There's only One who does. Ergo…God's best…to you!

What's better than God's best? Absolutely nothing…say it again! There is nothing better in the entire universe than the best from the God who created it. Taking it further, does God ever give anything or anyone less than His best? Never. But, He will not force His will upon our free will. So, if you feel like you're experiencing less than God's best for your life, one of two things is true. Either you are, but can't see it as such, *or* you're not, because you're choosing something less than His best for you. The former can be cleared up by a change in perspective. The latter requires a change in position. It's your move.

Whoa! Where are you going? I seem to be losing some of you. Be honest. Given your current life circumstances, the preceding paragraph reads painfully shallow and simple-minded. Right? Before tossing this book in the recycle bin, take a deep breath and consider the possibility that what you desperately need to know at times is the last thing you want to hear.

"But what about the cancer?" you ask.

"What about the dark cloud of bankruptcy hanging over my head?"

"Where can I find God's best when dealing with a rebellious teenager bent on self-destruction?"

"If this is God's best for my life, then maybe I'd be better off without Him in it."

I hear you loud and clear…and so does He. A qualifier is in order. This side of Heaven, God's best is not *the* best. It's as good as it gets in a fallen world temporarily ruled by a fallen angel. His name is Satan and he's as real as the vein in your head that's threatening to pop about now.

"So what are saying, Brad, that Satan has God's hands tied?"

No, but for God having Satan's hands tied he would have destroyed Earth a long time ago. Like the ocean tides, Satan is temporarily permitted by God to operate within certain boundaries until Christ returns to reign over the Earth for 1,000 years and Satan is cast into the pit (Revelation 20:1-3).

As to why God allowed sin to enter into the world in the first place, that's more theology than this book can bear. But, insight into that deep subject begins with understanding that the thing God desires above all things is the one thing that even He cannot will into existence — the requited love of his children. Love that is coerced from one's lover is not love at all. That's why it's possible to describe the one true God in one simple word — love (1 John 4:8b). God is love. And, true love must emanate from the pure heart and free will of one's lover. If we had no choice but to love God, then we couldn't truly love Him. So, when Eve chose the forbidden fruit and Adam chose to be silent, together they were choosing to pursue other lovers. And that is when all hell broke loose on planet Earth.

Are You Running Towards or Away from Something?

Months before my ruthless firing in the spring of 1989, I started looking for another job. Though written in French, the writing on the wall of our Memphis headquarters was easily interpreted. I knew I was a marked man and that my company was in big trouble. Broke and broken, I was looking for shelter and a fresh start for me and my family. I found both in an Indianapolis-based leasing company owned and operated by like-minded Christian men. Our courtship provided triage for my bruised ego and wounded heart. Was it really possible to run a business with a people first philosophy to the glory of God? I would soon find out, but not before fielding a curve ball out of far left field.

The long-awaited decision had been made. We were moving back to Indianapolis to start a new IT consulting division for that small leasing company. After six years away from our Hoosier home, Elaine was thrilled to be moving back. I too looked forward to reconnecting with family and friends, but my primary focus was upon the new business I was about to start. While my new employer would provide support services and modest financial support, it was up to me to figure out how to start a brand new line of business. The thought of it both energized and terrorized me.

The curve ball from left field was thrown by the senior pastor at our large church in Memphis. Pastor Jimmy had somehow inherited responsibility for a small, troubled Christian college in the area. He was looking for someone to run it. Someone like me. When Jimmy and his entourage showed up at our front door, I was more than a bit confused. But, when your highest spiritual authority with skin on comes calling…you listen. Besides, I was still looking for the silver platter that my head had been handed to me on just a few weeks prior. To become president of a college at the tender age of 32 was pretty heady stuff. And, to have the backing of one of the largest churches in Memphis sounded much more secure than the unchartered territory that awaited me back home again in Indiana. Just when I thought the decision waters had cleared, my mind was once again as muddy as the mighty Mississippi just a few miles to the west.

I'll never forget what my second highest skin-clad spiritual authority had to say when I posed the dilemma to him. Since we first met in the spring of 1975, Tom had been my "go to guy" whenever I was facing a tough decision. He never let me down. This time was no exception. After I laid out the pros and cons of the two very different career paths before me,

Tom asked me a question that I'll never forget. "Brad, I see your dilemma. You have two very attractive, yet very different options before you. In choosing one over the other, I would encourage you to ask yourself this question—am I running towards or away from something?"

Tom had wisely discerned that my primary attraction to the college choice was the additional security it seemed to offer. I wasn't particularly passionate about post-secondary Christian education. But, I was very passionate about starting and eventually owning my own business, though admittedly losing sleep at the prospects of entering the world of entrepreneurial terror. Tom helped me to see that if I ran away from it, I could be running for the rest of my life. With that, I ran towards my greatest fear and haven't looked back.

What about you? What are you running from? A broken relationship that's easier to ignore than to endure the pain of repairing it? A destructive habit that's sapping the life out of you? An unconfessed sin that you can't get past? Whatever it is that you're running from, consider a change of direction. Consider turning around and moving towards that which scares the daylights out of you. Consider facing your fears.

Unlike the physical world, in the emotional and spiritual realms, scary objects shrink in size the closer you get to them. Because "There is no fear in love, but perfect love casts out all fear" (1 John 4:18). Recall, our one-word definition of God—love. If we substitute "God" for "love" in the previous passage, we see that "There is no fear in <God>, but perfect <God> casts out all fear. The reason fears shrink as we face them is because God is facing them with us.

On the flipside, consider what passions you feel prompted to run towards? In my case, back in 1989 I was prompted to run towards owning my own business. Looking back, I probably should have been running faster away from the toxic environment my employer's workplace had become. The gold rush was over before the acquisition took place, much to the chagrin of our new owner. Then greed took over. I was never privy to the details, but it was pretty clear that the good ole boys of Memphis had sold the Frenchman and his Euro banker buddies a pig in a poke. With each passing miserable day, he and his minions were in an increasingly foul mood over it. But I digress...

For me, owning my own business was more about keeping my fate out of the hands of others than it was about putting it in my own. I really didn't want full responsibility for my future, but I was sure fed up with the alternative. As a Christian, I've never believed that my family's destiny was solely mine to determine. There are many passages in the Bible supporting this view. This is one of my favorites:

> *"For I know the plans I have for you, declares the Lord, plans for welfare and not for evil, to give you a future and a hope" (Jeremiah 29:17).*

Back to you. Consider the possibility that the above passage is not only true, but it could be true of you and yours today. Then, for the sake of illustration, let's oversimplify your complicated life. Let's pretend for a moment that you're in one of three states of being. You're either running towards something, running away from something or just plain stuck, not knowing which way to run. So, your first task is to determine which state of being you're in. Simple enough, right? Or maybe not so simple.

I'm not the first to suggest that your journey to "there" cannot be taken until you've determined where "here" is. If you doubt this basic principle, then try putting where you were into your GPS in an effort to get where you want to be. You can't get there from *there*...only from *here*. Perhaps it would help to acknowledge that your complicated life allows for multiple states of being simultaneously. Within our simple three-state construct, you could be running away from something, towards something and stuck on something all at the same time. Getting closer to home are we? Let's take a closer look.

Again, we're being purposely simplistic to make a few basic points. What do you run towards? Comfort. What do you run from? Pain. What are you stuck in? Discomfort. What gets you unstuck? When discomfort turns to pain, you will run away from it and towards comfort. Keep this in mind as you answer the following questions. There will likely be multiple answers to all three:

- What am I running from?
- What am I running towards?
- Where am I stuck?

You might be saying, "I'm stuck all right. Stuck trying to answer these silly questions. Help!" I hear ya'. More importantly, God hears you. He's the only one in the universe who knows you better than you know yourself. He talks about it all the time, but never more poignantly then within my favorite Psalm:

> *"O Lord, you have searched me and known me! You know when I sit down and when I rise up; you discern my thoughts from afar. You search out my path and my lying down and are acquainted with all my ways. Even before a word is on my tongue, behold, O Lord, you know it altogether. You hem me in, behind and before, and lay your hand upon me. Such knowledge is too wonderful for me; it is high; I cannot attain it. Where shall I go from your Spirit? Or where shall I flee from your presence? If I ascend to Heaven, you are there! If I make my bed in Sheol, you are there! If I take the wings of the morning and dwell in the*

uttermost parts of the sea, even there your hand shall lead me, and your right hand shall hold me. If I say, "Surely the darkness shall cover me, and the light about me be night," even the darkness is not dark to you; the night is bright as the day, for darkness is as light with you. For you formed my inward parts; you knitted me together in my mother's womb. I praise you, for I am fearfully and wonderfully made. Wonderful are your works; my soul knows it very well. My frame was not hidden from you, when I was being made in secret, intricately woven in the depths of the Earth. Your eyes saw my unformed substance; in your book were written, every one of them, the days that were formed for me, when as yet there was none of them. How precious to me are your thoughts, O God! How vast is the sum of them! If I would count them, they are more than the sand. I awake, and I am still with you. Oh that you would slay the wicked, O God! O men of blood, depart from me! They speak against you with malicious intent; your enemies take your name in vain. Do I not hate those who hate you, O Lord? And do I not loathe those who rise up against you? I hate them with complete hatred; I count them my enemies. Search me, O God, and know my heart! Try me and know my thoughts! And see if there be any grievous way in me, and lead me in the way everlasting!" (Psalm 139).

Recall what Dr. Tim Gardner said, "the cry of every human heart is to know and be known and to love and be loved." To fully know and fully love is to fully live. The exchange of such knowledge and love between God the Father and His children is as good as it gets this side of Heaven. If you doubt it, then please read Psalms 139 again. But this time, before you do, ask God to speak to you through the words of the Psalm and His spirit about the depths of His knowledge of and love for you. Then, ask Him to help you answer the three questions above.

Living a Life of Divine Coincidence

While chatting with the head lifeguard at my fitness club last week, I discovered that we were headed in opposite directions over the upcoming weekend, but for similar sad reasons. We were both headed to funeral services for relatives who had recently committed suicide. She to Michigan. Me to Tennessee. "Coach," as I call her, went on to tell me the club had lost a young lifeguard to suicide just last year. Imagine that. In the course of a few minutes, our conversation surfaced three tragic cases of suicide within the past year. I was too dumb struck to even mention the fact that our daughter's best friend also took her life just two years previous.

Sidebar: Suicide.

There seems to be a growing sense of hopelessness in our country that is increasingly leading some to despair and the desperate decision to end it all. According to the Centers for Disease Control and Prevention, "More people now die of suicide than in car accidents. In 2010 there were 33,687 deaths from motor vehicle crashes and 38,364 suicides." Closer to home, the suicide rate amongst male baby boomers (currently in their 50s) is increasing faster than any other group.

The Great Recession of 2008 was, no doubt, a key factor in this, as many primary breadwinners found themselves unable to support their families. However, whatever the current causes of stress might be, the ultimate cause of suicide is hopelessness. No way out…and no reason to go on.

In contrast, the good news of the Gospel is that God's children are never without hope:

"Blessed be the God and Father of our Lord Jesus Christ! According to his great mercy, he has caused us to be born again to a living hope through the resurrection of Jesus Christ from the dead…. In this you rejoice, though now for a little while, if necessary, you have been grieved by various trials. Though you do not now see him, you believe in him and rejoice with joy that is inexpressible and filled with glory, obtaining the outcome of your faith, the salvation of your souls" (1 Peter 1:3-9).

Before leaving this suicide sidebar, I should mention that some forms of depression have little to do with one's circumstances and everything to do with bio-chemical deficiencies within the brain. As the pastor noted during my relative's funeral service just yesterday, victims of such depression literally cannot process the many positive suggestions of their well-meaning friends and family members. All they see is black and all they hear is bleak. The suicide of "the world's funniest man," Robin Williams, brought international attention to this tragic problem.

Redemption in the Making

Back to living a life of divine coincidence. While on my way home from the funeral service in Tennessee, Elaine sent a text asking me to pick up a couple of things at the local Meijer store. It wasn't an unusual request, as I've picked up these same two items many times. On a bad day, I've been known to have a bad attitude about both of them.

Item #1 was Elaine's favorite low calorie snack, Edy's Coconut Water with Pineapple fruit bars. Item #2 was the "puppy pads" that we go through faster than you can yell "don't pee on that rug." As a breeder of long coat Chihuahuas, Elaine once gave me a key fob that reads, "it's a dog's world...adjust." Some days I adjust better than others.

There's nothing quite like a funeral to positively adjust one's attitude. Particularly if the deceased died young and at his own hand. So, when I entered the Meijer store last night, I wasn't sweating the small stuff. It didn't really bother me, as it sometimes did, that the fruit bars and puppy pads were at opposite ends of the large store. I just grabbed the last two packages of pads they had and headed to the frozen novelty section. On the way, I looked up to see a young woman in a wheelchair approaching me. "Is that who I think it is?" I thought. When I saw who was pushing her wheelchair, I knew that it was.

Lana is the only daughter of my former employee, Diana, now pushing her wheelchair. "Lana, why are you in that wheelchair?" I gingerly asked. She explained that she'd been partially paralyzed for nearly a year after contracting a virus resulting in paraplegia while home visiting her parents. Lana was a brilliant and brave young woman whom I last knew to be attending medical school. It didn't surprise me in the least to learn that her condition had interrupted her surgical residency at a New York City hospital. Nor was I surprised to hear her describe her condition as a mere "bump in the road." She's a special young lady, the pride and joy of her immigrant parents.

Diana and Ardy arrived in the United States over 22 years ago with Lana in arms, one suitcase in hand and $300 in their pockets. Theirs is truly a great American immigrant success story. Born, raised and educated in the former Soviet Union, Diana and Ardy came to America seeking the best life possible for themselves and their precious daughter. When not working, their world revolved around Lana. She rarely disappointed them, while following her parents' example of hard work and even harder studying. Like all parents and children, they disagreed on some things. But since Lana's early teenage years, on one thing they were all three in perfect agreement—Lana was born to be a doctor.

After saying a few encouraging words to Lana, I made eye contact with her mother for the first time since a very awkward meeting on the street about five New Year's Eves ago. Despite being one of my most valuable long term employees, Diana and I had parted ways about a year prior to our New Year's Eve encounter. It was a less than amicable, very painful parting, one that I've rethought many times. To this day, I'm not sure I handled it correctly. I am sure that Diana and Ardy would say I didn't. At least that's what I took from her refusal to speak and his refusal to shake my hand when we met on the street that night. I've thought many times about extending an olive branch to them. But, I wasn't sure how I'd react if they turned a cold shoulder again. I certainly didn't want to make matters worse. After looking into Diana's eyes last night, I now know that I have no choice in the matter. The olive branch will be extended. Hopefully, in God's perfect way and timing.

"You're looking well" said Dr. Lana. "Why thank you. As is your mother, as always," I said while looking into Diana's eyes for the first time in five years. Gone was the usual fire. Her eyes appeared sad and weary. Her face gaunt. Etched with stress lines that seemed to run deeper than the inevitable lines of age. I was pleased to see her smile. Warmly, not forced. At least it seemed so. A natural born hugger, I fought the temptation to hug either of them. In our former life together, this would have come quite naturally. Not now…at least not yet.

What are the odds of my "chance" meet up with Diana and Lana in the Meijer store last night? "Pure coincidence," you say? "No way!" I say. There's unfinished business to be done between Diana and me. Business so important that the God of the Universe arranged for us to meet under circumstances that would cause each of us to lower our guard and begin to slowly move towards reconciliation. How awesome is that? How awesome is it to be so well known and so much loved by God that He's more concerned about healing our broken relationships than we are?

Fast forward to July 1, 2016. I couldn't go back to sleep after getting up at 3 AM to use the restroom, so I decided to get up and do some final editing before finally submitting this manuscript to the publisher…finally! As divine coincidence would have it, I'll be picking up Diana in a few hours to escort her to a job interview that I've arranged. It's a wonderful opportunity for her to reenter the workforce after being out of it for 18 months caring for Lana. If this job is God's best for her, then I'm confident she'll get it. If not, I'm confident she'll find the one that is, with or without my help. Come what may on the job front, I'll be forever grateful for the redemption of my relationship with Diana, Ardy and Lana. As Diana often says, "how cool is that?"

Chapter 21

Handicaps or Stepping Stones?

Hopefully, Lana's "bump in the road" is only a temporary handicap. But, should it become permanent, I'm confident that it will only serve as a stepping stone to a level of achievement that she could not have otherwise obtained. I've long believed that "handicaps" are often times unique advantages to the so-called handicapped. We don't have to look far to find inspiring examples of this.

Following a disease that left her deaf and blind before she was two years old, Helen Keller went on to be the first deaf-blind person to receive a Bachelor of Arts degree. Albert Einstein, the famous mathematician and physicist, had a learning disability and did not speak until he was three years old. He found math and writing difficult at school, but went on to become one of the best-known scientists of all time winning the Nobel Prize for Physics in 1921. Beethoven composed some of his finest pieces after losing most of his hearing following a bout with tinnitus at the age of 20. The list of such handicapped over achievers is virtually endless. So, it should come as no surprise that the only American president to ever serve more than two terms, the beloved Franklin D. Roosevelt, did so from a wheelchair.

There's a very fine line between a loser's limp and a winner's leap. As sad as I found the sight of Lana in that wheelchair, I found the determined look in her eyes and the feisty confidence in her voice to be awe-inspiring. I have little doubt that, with or without a wheelchair, Lana will one day be a renowned surgeon. One in whose capable hands I would entrust any member of my own family. I don't merely believe in Lana, however. I believe that good doctors are God's gift to a sick and hurting world. Great surgeons are an even greater gift. That's why it's imperative for Lana to get past her "bump in the road" and on to fulfilling her destiny. On to realizing God's best for her life, which will in turn help many others to realize His best for themselves.

The Curse of Too Much Capital

Thanks to the Frenchman who bought my Memphis employer, I learned early in my career what venture capitalists have always known. Too much capital can kill a business faster than too little. When my previous employer was acquired in 1987, we operated for the next two years as if capital was an inexhaustible resource. Our new CEO had European bankers throwing money at him and he loved spending it lavishly. One of the first signs that our lack of fiscal restraint would eventually catch up with us was the printing of a huge full color coffee table book showing pictures of our sprawling global empire. There was nothing of true business value in this book that likely cost $50 per copy. It was the ultimate puff piece, symbolizing the hubris of our leader.

Too much capital helped me make one of the more foolish business decisions I've ever made. One that eventually cost me my job. As the Salad Days were wilting in Memphis, we found ourselves trying to double up to catch up with some of the leaders in the computer leasing and brokerage industry. Chief among them was Comdisco, a Chicago-based company that effectively controlled the after-market for IBM mainframe computers. While they were wisely pulling back from a shaky market poised for a decline, we were determined to be real player. Did I mention that hubris is contagious?

So, we decided to join the mainframe trading big leagues just as the smart money was walking off the field. When the value of a box we sold dropped sharply before the buyer had paid for it, he reneged on the deal. As the youngest senior officer of the company, I had authorized the purchase that resulted in a $500,000 loss for the firm.

Though I lost my job over it, I learned several valuable lessons from this painful experience. Such as, never go to war with the French as your ally. Just kiddin'. I'd gladly share a foxhole with a Frenchman. He'd be a pretty easy target at such close range.

Now that's funny. Or, as they say in gay Paree…Maintenant que ce drôle.

All right, I'm over it…really. Lesson one, of course, is that too much capital will kill a company faster than too little will. It did, in fact, eventually destroy my former employer. Lesson two is that just because you can, doesn't mean you should. Timing's everything in life and in business. You may have a great idea whose time has either not come or has passed. Knowing the difference can make all the difference in the world.

Chapter 21

Chapter 21

22. Courage

Survival is Success

During the depths of the Great Recession, as Murph's stellar career at Cisco was winding down, mine seemed to be swirling down the drain. It was an unusually balmy St. Patrick's Day in Indianapolis. We were enjoying a late afternoon beer on the outside terrace of a restaurant within Indy's tony north side shopping district. After listening to me whine about the poor state of the economy and our business, Murphy chimed in.

"Brother," he said, "there's no doubt in my mind that survival is success during times like these. The Ciscos of the world will be fine, but there will be lots of small to medium-sized businesses that don't survive this recession. Do whatever you have to do to make sure yours isn't one of them." Truer words were never spoken.

We were already hunkered down in our foxholes, coming out occasionally to complete the disassembling of the business we'd worked so hard to build from 2005-2008. By the end of 2011, we'd come full circle. It took three years to build and another three years to dismantle. With our strategic plan on the ash heap of history, our company was a mere shadow of its former self. But, we survived while embracing Murph's notion that to do so was to succeed. There were many days when I faced that dumbest American in the mirror and said repeat after me, "Survival is success…survival is success…survival is success." And it was…for a time.

Overstaying My Foxhole Welcome

Many brave soldiers owe their lives to the protection provided by their foxholes and the fellow soldiers they shared them with. But, every soldier knows that foxholes only provide temporary sanctuary. Linger too long and you become a fish in a barrel at the mercy of your enemy. Looking back, I can't help but wonder if the remnants of our "A-Team" lingered too long in our foxholes. Did we overstay our welcome in survival mode? I think we probably did. But, more important than the timing of our return to the business of building our business is the reason for its delay.

As the leader, I was frozen by fear. Too scared to stick my head up to figure out when and how to get us out of the foxhole and back onto the battlefield. Like Maverick in the movie Top Gun, I had a confidence problem.

After five long years of declining revenues, it was clear that we couldn't save our way to prosperity. We had to grow our way back. Easier said than done. With very little dry powder left in our ammo supply, there was no room for error. One misfire could be our last. Looking out over the still smoldering battlefield, there was no easy way out. Nothing was obvious…absolutely nothing. Each morning gave rise to the strategy du jour, only to be discarded by sunset. "That'll never work…we can't afford that…so and so is already doing that…maybe we should try this…."

By the end of most days, I was mentally exhausted and completely demoralized by my seeming inability to formulate a winning battle plan. Like a good soldier, I didn't want to die in my foxhole. I just didn't know how to get the h#*l out of it.

Speaking of hell….

One of the most unnerving passages in the Bible describes the line forming around the gates of hell (also known as the "lake of fire") following the formation of the new Heaven and the new Earth:

> *"The one who conquers will have this heritage, and I will be his God and he will be my son. But as for the cowardly, the faithless, the detestable, as for murderers, the sexually immoral, sorcerers, idolaters, and all liars, their portion will be in the lake that burns with fire and sulfur, which is the second death" (Revelation 21:7,8).*

Notice who is at the front of the line—the cowardly and faithless. Since the two are inextricably linked, they're likely holding hands.

What makes us cowardly? Lack of faith. And, what's the great dividing line between Heaven and hell? Faith.

Does this mean that Heaven is the ultimate "home of the brave" and the timid need not apply? Hardly. What it means is that a supernatural by-product of faith in Christ is the courage to bravely face life's battles, knowing that the war has already been won. Ergo, lack of courage is no more and no less than a lack of faith, without which it is impossible to please God:

> *And without faith it is impossible to please him, for whoever would draw near to God must believe that he exists and that he rewards those who seek him (Hebrews 11:6).*

Chapter 22

Back to the foxhole. Every month for the past six years, my dear friend and CFO, Tom, and I have finished our review of the monthly financial statements in prayer. We begin by thanking God for his past provision and end by asking Him to prosper the work of our hands in the future. By the time we're done, I'm usually shaking my head and pulling my hair. Amazed at how well God provides by so little apparent means, but apoplectic over how poorly I'm doing at expanding those means. Month after month, year after year, we get enough to keep going but not enough to see how we can possibly go very far. And so, a severe case of corporate near-sightedness sets in and we lose the ability to see anything beyond the end of the month…or beyond a few feet from our foxhole.

Veterans of the Vietnam War know how difficult it is to fight an enemy you cannot see. One of our brave A-Team veterans will never forget seeing the whites of his enemy's eyes just before plunging his bayonet into his chest. Neither soldier saw it coming from that dark jungle. Only one lived to tell the story. Thankfully, the stakes aren't nearly so high within the corporate jungle. But, the fear of making a company-ending move can be nearly as intense. In both scenarios, at some point those on the frontlines ask themselves a critical question—*what's the worst that can happen?*

With our limited corporate resources, a move in the wrong direction could put us out of business. That's the worst that could happen. So, how bad would that be? When I started the business at age 32, the option of failing wasn't nearly as scary as it is today given the aforementioned small market for 60-year-old white American males who've been in business for themselves for over 27 years. Just as well, since Elaine recently reaffirmed what I've known for many years—I really can't work for anyone else. So, the worst that can happen is we lose everything.

Son One Chooses New Battlefield

Our firstborn, Joshua, came into my office in the late winter of 2013 to announce that his wife was pregnant with their second child. This, nearly 17 years after the birth of their firstborn, Zoe Elizabeth (a.k.a. Princess Z). According to John Lennon, "Life is what happens to you while you're busy making other plans." Josh represented that remark that day. He truly seemed to be in a state of shock.

Having married young and parented well, Josh had long looked forward to the day when the weight of the parenting world would be lifted from his shoulders. Then, he and wife Brooke would be free to pursue life on their terms. Or more accurately…Josh's terms.

For years, Josh stubbornly refused to consider having another child, a desire that never left Brooke's heart. Instead, he often talked about moving to Mexico and becoming a scuba dive master once Zoe was emancipated. When he really wanted to get my goat, he'd wax eloquently about his future life on the road in a big rig with his biggest daily decision concerning what rest area to bed down in. Think Mel Gibson in Braveheart shouting "Freedom!" just before losing his head. The realization that his child-rearing years had just doubled rocked Josh's world to the core. And, the after-shocks would soon be felt within our company.

Josh was the only recruiter left aboard the good ship Ambassador in 2013. By his own admission, his heart was never fully in it, but he was a quick study and very disciplined in his approach to the recruiting process. Good thing, because in 2009 we found ourselves with three recruiters, while only needing one. Had she not moved to New York the previous year to be with her new husband, Josh's mentor, Kristin, would have been the last recruiter standing on deck back then. But, I couldn't see having our only recruiter working remotely. So, Kristin was out along with another recruiter we had hired just days before the market came to an abrupt halt.

"If you go down with the ship, I'm going down with you." Josh reiterated this commitment to me several times during the worst of the recessionary storms. I was very deeply touched by the love and loyalty behind it. But, knowing that he and his family would go down with the ship, should that be our fate, only added ballast to my already overburdened heart. The weight of it all was crushing at times.

Josh wasn't alone in his commitment to staying aboard even when the future looked bleak. Though some crew members later changed their minds, every member of our core team signed the following letter on February 12, 2010 acknowledging the risks inherent in remaining aboard and reiterating their commitment to doing just that. I had forgotten that Josh edited his version of the "re-up" statement he signed, replacing the first line with one from the song, I Won't Back Down, by Tom Petty & The Heartbreakers:

February 12, 2010

Dear Brad:

I am resigning from Ambassador Solutions effective at 5 pm on Friday, February 12. Per our meeting yesterday, I understand that I will receive a severance package to include my salary through March 31 and any bonuses or commissions due me through February 28. Full current benefits will be extended through March 31, including medical insurance.

In exchange for this severance package, I agree to aggressively seek a new job and to begin my new employment as soon as my new employer will allow me to. Should that be before March 31, I will notify Ambassador Solutions, then all salary and benefits will be discontinued as of my first day of new employment. I will do everything within my power to find a new job and will do nothing in an effort to "double dip" by being paid by both Ambassador and my new employer.

I appreciate all that Ambassador has done for me and wish the company and everyone within it the very best.

Sincerely,

Josh Lindemann

Recruiter

Sorry Brad, but you're going to have to fire me to get rid of me. "You can stand me up at the gates of hell, but I won't back down." This company and my job are worth fighting for. I'm going to give it all I've got until we turn this thing around. I understand that by turning down this severance offer, I risk losing my job and any future severance benefits, as they will not likely be available.

_____ *Date: 2/12/10*

Josh Lindemann

All 10 members of our Leadership Team, including myself, signed up to "re-up" that day. I knew at the time that some, if not most, of those commitments were more form than substance. I hadn't exactly made leaving an irresistibly attractive option. We didn't have the resources for that. Only two of those 10 employees remain with the firm today — myself and Tom.

Tom is my ever-faithful and indispensable Chief Financial Officer…and so much more. As a former pastor, Tom has the strongest faith of anyone I've been privileged to know. As a result, he's the also the most even-keeled person I've ever known. When the ship is taking on water, Tom's the perfect first mate. Nothing rattles him. He just picks up the bucket with a smile and starts bailing. God has used Tom mightily in my life and the life of our firm. We've spent many hours praying together. Some tearfully, though I don't recall Tom ever being the one in tears. Tom's a rock standing upon *the* rock. He helps keep my life on solid ground and I love him for it.

You're probably wondering what happened to Josh. Did he end up backing down from the gates of hell after all? Much to the contrary. He stormed them. About the time Olive Elizabeth Lindemann came into the world on August 24, 2013 (my birthday), Josh decided that he too needed to get out of the foxhole and back onto the battlefield. But, his would be a different battlefield this time around. His next battles would be fought on the soccer field (a.k.a. pitch), as he took a "now or never" approach to pursuing his soccer coaching dreams.

Josh understands "the beautiful game" at a level that is incomprehensible to mere mortals, especially his father. But, having played soccer for 30 years and coached it for nearly 20, he truly has a gift. One that I've long encouraged him to cultivate to the fullest.

Towards that end, we embarked on a great adventure during the summer of 2010. We went to South Africa to watch Team USA compete in the World Cup, the biggest sporting event on the planet. Neither of us will ever forget being in the stands when Landon Donovan scored the winning goal in stoppage time against Algeria in game three. This, to win the group and go forward to meet the Black Stars of Ghana in the next round. It was a surreal moment as we hugged perfect strangers decked out in red, white and blue while crying as if we'd each just won the lottery.

It took great courage for Josh to leave a comfortable position in his Dad's company to pursue a dream that many would say was unattainable, given his delayed start. The fact that he stepped out so boldly at the same time his parenting responsibilities were doubling told me the move and the timing of it were perfect. You heard me right…*perfect*. Our firstborn prepared his whole life for the crack that still remained in the door of opportunity and he was determined to blow it wide open.

Josh properly saw baby Olive as the inspiration she truly was, not the impediment he could have made her out to be. A year into it, he's re-upped his fatherhood contract, landed a paid coaching position with the premier club in the area and is fast making his mark. Josh has the ability to coach soccer at the highest possible level.

I truly believe that we both could make it to at least one more World Cup. He walking the sidelines looking dapper in a Euro cut suit. Me in the stands crying like I'd just won the lottery, hugging perfect strangers and telling them all, "That's my son the coach down there!"

Chapter 22

Alone in My Foxhole

With Josh gone, I found myself alone in my foxhole contemplating my next move without him there to watch my back. It was unnerving, but I knew in my heart that both of us would soon be in a better place. My first order of business was figuring out how to fill the hole that Josh left behind. His recruiting assistant had a heart of gold and the work ethic of a mule, but very little experience and some health concerns. We needed more help in this critical function, but couldn't really afford a seasoned recruiter.

In April of 2014, we hired a young lady with a few years of industrial sales experience who had enjoyed a summer internship in a hospital HR department assisting with the recruiting function. When she saw our posting on the internet, she jumped at the opportunity. Six weeks later we had a rare opportunity to hire an industry veteran with deep experience in all three of our main business functions—sales, recruiting and technical services. I've learned over the years that when your plan doesn't call for hiring a great person when they become available, it's time to change the plan. And I'm sure glad we did. Six months later both new hires have made tremendous progress, while our revised budget has managed to stay in the black.

All true, but also true that we've took some hits that tested our mettle going into the fourth quarter of 2014. Our largest client had a hiring/contracting freeze, while our two most lucrative contracts both terminated on the same day—Halloween. That's pretty scary stuff!

And of course, all this as we're about to pull the trigger on completely redesigning our long-in-the-tooth web site—a move I've been working towards all year. It's very tempting to kick the web site can further down the road, but it's too late to jump back into my foxhole. I'm back on the battlefield and retreat is not an option. General Douglas MacArthur understood why:

It is fatal to enter a war without the will to win it.

Fast forward another six months, both of our new hires walked into my office on the same day, independent of one another, and resigned. Like a mortar shell landing in a foxhole, I didn't see either one coming. Though I did know in my heart that it was probably for the best in both cases. Hopefully…God's best.

On Taking Chance(s)

Just last night, I was poignantly reminded of how tame my so-called battles are when compared to those fought by the brave men and women of our armed forces. By divine coincidence, Elaine and I closed-out our Black Friday by watching the movie, Taking Chance. It's a true story of Marine Lt. Colonel Michael Strobl (Kevin Bacon) escorting the body of fallen fellow Marine, PFC Chance Phelps, back to his hometown in Wyoming. 2,000 people attended the funeral of this fallen hero, twice as many as lived in the town itself. We were deeply moved by the painstaking attention to detail and honor afforded this good soldier at every point along his journey home. It was a life-changing experience for Lt. Colonel Strobl. So much so that the journal he kept of his experiences became the basis of the movie.

It was highly unusual for a senior officer to escort the remains of a non-officer like PFC Phelps. It's interesting to note that Strobl volunteered for the mission under false pretenses. Phelps' last residence was listed as a town in Colorado, Strobl's hometown. But, Phelps was actually from Dubois, Wyoming and that's where his final journey would end. Having opted out of combat duty some years ago, Strobl had been struggling with his safe life behind a desk, while his fellow Marines were putting their lives on the line in Iraq. Escorting PFC Phelps seemed like the least he could do to honor those whom he had come to see as the "real Marines." That's why he chose to sleep next to Phelps' casket in the airport cargo bay the night before the final leg of his journey. That's what real Marines do for real Marines.

The title of the film is packed with meaning. Taking Chance(s) was something Lt. Colonel Strobl stopped doing early in his military career. At least that's the way he saw it. As he explained to a fellow Marine who had served in the Korean War, "I just got used to seeing my wife and kids at night."

The sage veteran respectfully chastised the Lt. Colonel for implying that he was somehow less of a soldier for also wanting to be a good husband and father. The movie ends as he returns home to his family having taken Chance home to his. No macho move volunteering for combat duty. Just hugs, kisses and a home cooked meal for a real Marine who had completed a very important mission.

Incoming...Take Cover!

Incoming! Incoming! Incoming! Take cover!

It's 10:08 Saturday morning. I'm headed into the sauna having just finished my swim. An all-too-familiar text hits my phone: "Where are you?" This from my wife who is no doubt still in bed. For some of you younger bucks, that question might be a veiled proposition on a lazy weekend morning. But, not for this ole buck. I've seen this one way too many times to confuse a call to duty with an invitation to a dalliance.

"In the sauna," I reply matter-of-factly, bracing for the rest of the story. It wasn't long in coming.

"I dropped my glasses and reached over the edge of bed," came the reply text message. "I literally became wedged and really stuck. It pulled on my neck and to get out I had to twist my neck, crush my forehead on bottom of bed and twist my back causing me to jam my hip into table. I know it sounds funny but it wasn't. I was really stuck. It hurt so badly. My neck is totally jacked."

I kid you not, that gal has taken more falls than Humpty Dumpty on his worst day. This one was fairly mild in comparison to some, although with three fused vertebrae at the base of her neck, all such falls come with well above-average risks. For that reason and the Ground Hog Day nature of such occurrences, I wasn't laughing...though maybe I should have been.

As we were falling asleep the night before, I realized that Elaine hadn't mentioned having a headache all day. That's highly unusual. I asked her about it. She said she started the day with a mild one, but had been headache-free most of the day. Had I not already been half asleep, I would have jumped out of bed and commenced doing the happy dance. But, when this morning started with the calamity described above, I was anything but happy. Was it too much to ask for Elaine to have two relatively pain-free days in a row? "Really God...really? Why do you allow my wife to be pummeled day in and day out? Isn't it your job to protect her? Why are you allowing her to suffer so much?"

It's okay. You really don't have to put the book down and walk away, fearing a lightning strike. God can handle our tough questions. Even the misguided ones launched in the heat of a battle we feel we're losing. Especially then. Don't be afraid to hit Him with your best shot. My buddy, Kurt, did just that a few years ago.

Recall, Kurt is the one credited with inspiring the "Live Ammo Living" concept. He tells a story about taking a jeep ride through southern

Indiana during one of the lowest points in his life. On the verge of losing everything, Kurt felt he had nothing to lose by getting down and dirty with Jesus in his jeep that day.

In language that would make a sailor blush, Kurt poured his heart out to God. Primal screams erupted from the depths of his weary soul. It was a no holds barred slugfest between a desperate man who had come to the end of himself and the God of the Universe who's only Son lived and died for moments like these. God took Kurt's best shots that day without returning a single counter-punch. Shortly thereafter, Kurt's life took a dramatic turn for the better. He's quick to tell anyone who'll listen that the turnaround came when he got real and raw while jeepin' with Jesus in the rolling hills of Southern Indiana. And that, my friends, is why we call it Live Ammo Living.

Pass the Pill Bottle

Back to Calamity 'Laine. It seems a double dose of my own medicine might be just what the doctor ordered. Let's start with a perspective pill.

We've already talked about my belief that "it's impossible to have a perspective you've never had." Meaning, if you haven't "*been* there and *done* that," it's very difficult to *be* there and *see* that from the vantage point of those who have. Something else I've learned about perspective over the years is:

Like eyeglasses, once lost, perspective can be very difficult to find.

Over the past decade, my lovely bride's health challenges have often left me challenged to maintain a healthy and helpful perspective on our life together and life in general. On those mornings when Elaine shuffles into our bathroom, barely able to walk from her neck and back pain with that miserable migraine glaze in her eyes, while helping her administer the injection in hopes of finding some relief, I fight the urge to crawl back into bed with her and just give up. Quit. While lying there, I'd dream of donning my hiking boots, hitting a trail to anywhere but here and never looking back. But wait, I think I see something under the bed….

Like Elaine groping in the dark for the glasses she dropped from her night stand, I often find myself desperately groping for a perspective lost when pain is all that can be found. But by God's grace, I always manage to find it. Sometimes while the pain persists. Other times not until it's subsided. It's really up to me. I can choose to wallow in self-pity or I can choose to search every inch of our bedroom floor until I find my lost perspective. Sometimes I become so exhausted in my search, I have to take a break from it. While I'm on break, God often breaks through. "I found it! I found my lost perspective!"

Just when I was about to quit looking for it, there it was.

Side Bar: Take the Funny Pill

> Elaine has a relatively new pair of beautiful turquoise and black designer glasses. She really looks cute in them. Since she's on her iPhone constantly, I don't understand why she ever takes them off. But, she constantly does and, of course, is constantly losing them…as in *every day*.
>
> On good days, we laugh about the daily ritual of searching for her lost glasses. On bad days, I find myself wondering if I have enough Hilton Honors points to get a free room at the hotel down the street. For the love of 20/20 hindsight, honey, keep your beautiful glasses on your beautiful face!
>
> Seriously. Thanks. I needed that.
>
> Now, where was I?
>
> Oh yeah, I was about to wash that perspective pill down with a half-full glass of water. Ahh, that's better. Now I can see what a blessing Elaine's headache-free Black Friday was. A blessing that cannot be taken away by the black and blue Saturday that followed.
>
> But wait, there's another easy pill to swallow.
>
> Who doesn't want to take a funny pill? Remember what I said a few chapters ago—"When you lose your sense of humor…you lose"? When I got Elaine's latest text, I had a choice to make. I could either choose to let it ruin my day (and hers) or I could choose to focus on the blessings of yesterday and the humor within the crisis du jour. So, grab your funny pill, raise your half-full glasses and have yourself a box of jiggles weekend. Jiggles is what you get when Jesus makes you giggle.
>
> Some of you are scratching your head wondering how we got from stories of courage in battle to downing funny pills and getting a case of the jiggles. Here's how those dots connect, at least for me.
>
> A shrewd enemy attacks his adversaries at their most vulnerable

and weakest points. As the head of a rather large family, I am most vulnerable to attacks upon my wife and kids. Nothing takes me out more effectively than anything that blows up in any of their lives. I truly believe I can handle the same direct hit myself better than I can handle watching a loved one take it. Add to this my annoying tendency to project a negative incident into a negative future, and you begin to understand why this battle plan works so effectively against me.

Just a few hours ago, it nearly caused me to write-off this weekend as a lost cause, while setting the stage for a major case of post-holiday Monday morning blahs. Turns out, Elaine is up and about. We'll soon be headed out to a craft fair featuring our daughter-in-law's very hip, happenin' and cool leather goods followed by early church and dinner out. BAM! Take that you evil doers!

Side Bar: IBFL is a HIStory book

I just realized that this book is not only about what being in business for life has taught me about the business of life. It's all that and two bags of chips. This is not merely a history book, as most memoirs are. This is a history-in-the-making book, because I have a secret co-author who's determined to weave His story into it. As such, it's also a change-the-world, future-in-the-making book, because that same co-author, to coin Colin Powell's favorite phrase, is the greatest "force multiplier" the world has ever known. Wow! How cool is that?

Courage in Action: One Good Soldier's Amazing Story

It seems fitting to end this chapter with a true story about courage as told by the most courageous man I've ever known. I'm honored to call him "friend." Though I've read this account many times, I've never gotten through it without a lump in my throat and a tear in my eye. I have no military experience, but have tremendous respect for all those who have served our country. One of my most prized possessions is an American flag that flew over the Marine camp where my soldier friend was stationed during his second tour of duty. You'll be stunned to learn how it came about.

The story you're about to read reminds me of something General Colin Powell said while speaking at a leadership conference a few years ago. The General's favorite question to ask a veteran upon meeting him is, "Were you a good soldier?"

He explained that vets tire of the well-meaning "thank you for your service" comments. They're more interested in genuine recognition and respect. Most want/need to talk about their experiences, because without knowing something of their personal stories, attempts to recognize and respect them ring hollow. Powell's simple question is an invitation for vets to tell their story. Stories like this one, as told by my humble friend who insists that the only true heroes contained herein are the ones who never came home.

Journal Entry, 2009

Oceanside, California

The afternoon was spent washing uniforms and other clothing, calling my wife to wish her a happy Mother's Day and generally getting myself ready to report aboard my U. S. Marine Corps infantry battalion at Camp Pendleton tomorrow morning. I spent the early evening catching up on some emails with family and friends and then I drove alone down to a small fish house overlooking San Diego Bay for a celebration of sorts. I had been there once before many years ago. I will explain what I was celebrating later.

The following story I have never told to another living soul before now. I am recounting it now so my family will know my real reason for volunteering for this mission to save young Marines and soldiers from being killed by IEDs (Improvised Explosive Devices).

Let me go back in time. The year was 1967 and I was a U.S. Marine stationed in Vietnam. Some of my fellow Marines were heading out on a mission. I went to where they were loading up the truck so I could tell my buddies to watch their backs and to crack a few jokes before they left. They loaded up and then climbed aboard. I told them I couldn't go with them because I had to stay in camp. In true Marine Corps fashion, they all gave me the "one-fingered-salute." Then they drove out the front gate.

I busied myself with my assigned duties for the next hour or so until another Marine ran up to me and asked me if our guys had just left our camp in a truck. I said they had and he spoke words to me that I will never forget. He said, "Their truck hit a mine buried in the road. They're all dead." I just stood there. I couldn't and wouldn't believe it. I told him he must be wrong. They had just left. It had to be somebody else. He told me he thought the truck belonged to our battalion because he heard it had our markings on the doors. I remember walking to the motor pool where they brought in damaged vehicles. I sat on a sandbag by myself and waited. It wasn't long before a flatbed truck and trailer drove into the motor pool with what was left of a damaged truck resting on the trailer. I walked up to the damaged truck and saw our battalion markings on the doors.

I sat down again on the sandbag and stared at the damage to the truck and my heart sank. I don't have words to express how I felt. I guess I would say now that all people have defining moments in their lives that change their core being. You are just never the same as you were and you will never be what you would have otherwise been. That moment in time stood still for me and it seared my soul forever. My buddies, my fellow Marines, the guys I ate with, slept with and had laughed with had vanished from my life and from the face of the Earth forever. I have never forgotten their names or their smiles or the sparkle in their eyes.

Now I will finish my story about the celebration dinner overlooking San Diego Bay and you will understand. The time was the summer of 1966 and the place was Marine Corps Base Camp Pendleton, California. A bunch of young Marines were getting ready to ship out to Vietnam. One evening it was decided that we would treat ourselves to one last great meal before we left. We drove down to a fish house overlooking San Diego Bay and got a table outside. I can't remember what any of us ate but I can remember lots of laughs, arms around each other's necks, punches in the shoulders to see who could 'really take it like a Marine' and just a great time of fun and fellowship for a bunch of innocent, young guys getting ready to go off to war. We all made a promise to each other that night. We would all return to that same place when we came back from Vietnam, to have dinner and to celebrate coming back home. We couldn't admit it then, even to ourselves, because we were tough Marines but what we would really be celebrating was our love for each other as brothers-in-arms.

Tonight, some 43 years later, I was alone at the table outside on the deck overlooking the bay at that same restaurant. The evening was cool so no one else was eating outside and I was glad it worked out that way. The waitress had looked at me rather strangely when I requested a table outside because it was so cool. I ate a great meal and afterwards I asked the waitress to bring me a brandy. I sipped it as I looked out at the sea that we all had sailed across in 1966 to meet our destinies. I remembered that celebration and the promise we all had made. I raised my glass and toasted those brave, young heroes, my fellow Marines, six pieces of my heart that were torn out so many years ago. I was the only one to make it back and it was my duty to them to keep the promise.

To my family, all of whom I love more than I can tell you, now you know why I had to accept this mission to go to Iraq with the Marine Corps. I will use my skills to seek out insurgents and terrorists who plant hidden explosive devices that kill young Marines and soldiers and I will do my part to try and stop them. I have made a silent promise to this group of young Marines to do all I can to help save their lives and to see them return back home to their families. God willing, I will keep that promise too.

Journal Entry, 2010

Camp Pendleton, California

Today I arrived back at Camp Pendleton with the rest of my battalion after our deployment to Iraq. We left the United States with over 1,000 Marines and Naval personnel in our battalion. We returned with everyone who deployed. Second promise kept.

Real Life...Real Courage

Most of us will never be called to demonstrate courage on a real battlefield. We'll never have to watch our every step for fear that a hidden IED might send us into an early eternity. We'll never look into the eyes of our enemy, just before plunging a bayonet into his chest. We'll never escort the remains of a fallen soldier back to a grieving family, forever changed by their loss.

No, for most of us, life's calls for courage will come in the form of too much month at the end of the money. Or, too little time at the end of the chemo. Or perhaps, too little too late at the end of the relationship. Whatever your current battle may be, when the odds of victory seem stacked against you, the call for courage comes. When it does, know that it comes from the Courageous One. The One who has all the courage you'll ever need and He died giving it to you:

> *I have said this to you, so that in me you may have peace. In the world you face persecution. But take courage; I have conquered the world!" (John 16:33).*

23. I'm Failing and I Can't Get Up

Few things will change a person more profoundly than the experience of standing in the unemployment line over a long period of time. I've met with many such people over the years and had the privilege of providing some with their first job in many months...sometimes years. Given the demographics of the IT industry, most of the unemployed people I've encountered have been men. As such, most were the primary breadwinners in their families. It's been my painful privilege to walk with many of these men down the humble highway of unemployment. Given my own brief time in the unemployment line, I have a great deal of compassion and empathy towards anyone who's out of work and usually go out of my way to help them find it. Unfortunately, I can't help them all.

I never met our former employee, "Greg." He worked out of our Denver office. Greg was very accomplished within a unique skillset that our largest client desperately needed. So, we were surprised when his contract was terminated early. Greg was devastated. Unable to find another job over the following 18 months, Greg took his life on New Year's Eve. The news of his passing cut me to the core. I grieved the loss of the employee I never met and vowed to redouble my efforts to do all I could to help every unemployed person whom God brought into my life.

That's when I first wrote my "Message to the Unemployed" and published it on our web site. Updating that message has become a New Year's tradition for me. One that brings me back to center no matter what else is going on at the time. I've received some very kind responses from people who have read this message and been deeply touched by it. I take no credit whatsoever. It's a message that emanates from the heart of God. I've just been privileged to be the messenger:

Message to the Unemployed

January 3, 2014

From our President/CEO/Founder: Brad Lindemann

As we approach our 25th anniversary on April 1, 2014, I'm once again thinking about the many unemployed professionals I've met with over the years. If you're currently among them, it really doesn't matter what the rate of unemployment is. For you it's 100 percent and that's a tough situation to be in. Economists may have called it a recession, but if you lost your job in the midst of it, for you it was a depression. That's why I offer these words of encouragement…for you.

As with any advice, you should always consider the source. If the one telling you how to live your life has never walked in your shoes, proceed with caution. Such is not the case here. I was ruthlessly fired by my previous employer and have survived two near death corporate experiences over the last 25 years. 2009 was far and away the most difficult year of my life, both personally and professionally. I clung for dear life to the words of encouragement that I'm about to give you…and it worked! God showed up for me and He will show up for you.

Do not lose hope. THERE IS ALWAYS HOPE. I know. You've heard it all. I'm sure you haven't been wanting for career advice from well-meaning family members, friends and former associates. No matter what they say, what you hear them saying is, "Get a job!" It hurts at the core of your being. As you click-through another unemployed day on your Outlook calendar, with it goes another shred of your ever-shrinking self-esteem. If you've been the primary breadwinner in your family, the mounting financial pressure seems unbearable at times.

So, how can anyone bear the burden of unemployment? The truth is no one can…alone. The truth is people were not designed to bear such burdens alone. The truth is, God alone can and will bear your burdens (job-wise or otherwise), so that you don't have to bear them alone. YOU ARE NEVER ALONE.

The God of the universe is with you. Your reading this message is no accident. Read on, to hear what God Himself has to say…to you:

"Cast all your anxiety on him because he cares for you" (1 Peter 5:7).

This short passage is so very relevant to your current situation. Please don't discount it. Right now, God is saying, "I care about you more than you can possibly imagine." Right now, to you, God is saying, "I know what you're going through. It hurts me to watch you suffer. Please let me help you."

Right now, God really is saying to YOU, "Give me the burdens that you can no longer bear. I want you to literally throw them at me, so you can stop worrying about them."

Chapter 23

I don't know you, but I do know that GOD LOVES YOU...with or without a job. I do know that if your circumstances seem impossible, then it's time to turn them over to the God who makes all things possible. I do know that if you're feeling like a failure, then it's time to turn to the One who will never fail you nor forsake you. I do know that if you're lacking bread for the table, then it's time to turn to Him who is the bread of life.

Only you know if it's time to turn to God. Is it? If it is, then the Ambassador Prayer Team would be honored to take your requests before Him. Just let us know how we can best pray for you.

Could Ambassador be the answer to your job prayers? It's possible, but we don't want to build false hopes. If you're a seasoned IT professional, please make sure we have your up-to-date information in our data base. If we can help you, we will.

My friend, there is always hope...you are never alone...God loves you. May you and yours know God's presence, peace and providence — both now and forevermore!

God's best,

Brad Lindemann, President/CEO/Co-Founder
Ambassador Solutions

Double Torpedoes Broadside

Having just reread this message, I'm reminded of one of the lowest points in my career. Second only to the day I stepped into the unemployment line. Elaine and I were in our quaint hotel room on the beach in Jamaica. We had just married off child #4 in an intimate destination wedding ceremony two days before. I was checking my email and preparing to re-enter "the matrix" the following day. Without warning, our little wedding party boat took a torpedo broadside. It came out of nowhere and landed in my inbox. I couldn't believe what I was reading.

A subcontractor at our largest client had gone rogue and was in the process of stealing hundreds of thousands of dollars of business from us. The email detailed his intentions and set forth his baseless legal case for the severe damage he was determined to inflict. I sat stunned and speechless for what seemed like an eternity. Then I was overcome by an overwhelming weariness rendering me unable to move. Extreme exhaustion…utter despair. I truly doubted my ability to go one step further into the world of entrepreneurial terror that had defined me for the past 23 years.

With tears in my eyes, I turned to Elaine looking and feeling like a refugee still dazed by the attack that sent his family packing. "I am just so tired. I can't do this anymore. It's too hard. I have to find some relief…somehow…some way…someone." Elaine knew I wasn't looking to her for answers in that moment. Her words were few, but her empathy was strong. She gave me the space I needed to process what had just happened.

As I cried out to God, He gave me just what I needed in that moment…and so much more. This is the powerful passage that He led me to:

> *Come to me, all you that are weary and are carrying heavy burdens, and I will give you rest. Take my yoke upon you, and learn from me; for I am gentle and humble in heart, and you will find rest for your souls. For my yoke is easy, and my burden is light (Matthew 11:28-30).*

The Yoke's On You

I could write an entire book on what God has taught me from this powerful passage since that defining moment in Jamaica. Perhaps one day I will. For now, however, I want to focus on the yoke analogy that Jesus is using here. He's saying that walking through tough times with Him is similar to the way a young ox is trained to plow. He's yoked to an older, experienced ox that does two very important things. First, he shoulders most of the burden of the yoke, because he's bigger and stronger. Secondly, he teaches the young ox how to plow by simply dragging him along for the ride. Wherever Senior goes, Junior has little choice but to follow. So, from Junior's perspective, the yoke is easy and the burden is light. But, he's still learning some very important things along the way.

I don't know about you, but my first reaction when disaster strikes is not to ask, "What can I learn from this situation?" My first reaction is to run for the nearest exit. The only thing I'm interested in learning is how to get the heck out of Dodge. Still trackin'? So, where's Jesus coming from with His seemingly terrible timing on this teachable moment notion?

Perhaps He knows something about both the student and the subject matter during such times.

What's the first thing a teacher needs to know when trying to teach students a new lesson? More than the students. Then, what does the teacher need from the students? Their attention. Preferably their undivided attention. Nothing accelerates the learning process more than the elimination of everything that distracts from it. And, nothing eliminates distractions better than a good crisis. Knowing His students better than they know themselves, Jesus, the greatest teacher who ever lived, never wants to see a good crisis go to waste. He wants to help us learn all we can from it. Once we do, it's every student's favorite part of the day…rest time.

The Rest Is Never Easy

You know…rest. No, it's not a foreign word, but it is unfamiliar territory for the average American today. Perhaps a little synonymic stroll is in order? I challenge your hyperactive mind, body, soul and spirit to take a refreshing pause and consider these synonyms for the word "rest," courtesy of Theraurus.com:

1. break
2. breather
3. breathing
4. calm
5. calmness
6. cessation
7. coffee break
8. comfort
9. composure
10. cutoff
11. downtime
12. doze
13. dreaminess
14. ease
15. forty winks
16. halt
17. holiday
18. hush
19. idleness
20. interlude
21. intermission
22. interval
23. leisure
24. letup
25. lull
26. motionlessness
27. nap
28. pause
29. peace
30. quiescence
31. quiet
32. quietude
33. recess
34. recreation
35. refreshment
36. relaxation
37. relief
38. repose
39. respite
40. siesta
41. silence
42. sleep
43. slumber
44. somnolence
45. standstill
46. stay
47. stillness
48. stop
49. tranquility
50. time off
51. vacation

Doesn't exactly describe your typical day, does it? If you cheated and didn't read every word, please either do so now or go sit in the corner until you're ready to. Seriously, true rest is harder to come by than a winning lottery ticket.

So, go read every word and then come back. Don't worry, I'll be here when you're done.

Okay.

God understands that much better than we do. He also understands how critically important rest is to our health and well-being. That's why He added His own synonym to the list above…*chill-laxin'*.

Okay, so I made that part up, but I do dig that phrase and can't wait to experience the Heavenly version of it. For now, I guess *quietude* will have to do.

So, let me get this straight. The best time to crack the books is when disaster strikes. Then, once we turn in our homework, we get to take a nap.

Got it...I think.

It seems a bit counter-intuitive and one thing still bugs me. Whilst I'm learning and napping, who's cleaning up after the disaster? Oh yeah, I forgot to mention that "First Responder" is among God's many titles. It sort of goes with His one true Master of the Universe territory. While you're gunnin' for the honor role in between naps, He's repairing that big hole the torpedo ripped into your wedding party boat...so to speak.

Back to the matrix. That rogue subcontractor couldn't act alone. Our client had to help him. Boom! Boom! Make that two torpedoes broadside. The stage was set for the most confrontational meeting I've ever had with a customer. What they had set in motion was both legally and morally wrong. The damage to our company would be devastating. I couldn't just step aside and allow it to happen. Nor could we afford a protracted legal battle. Somehow...some way...someone had to show up. And He did!

"What you're doing is wrong," I told the C-level executives of our largest client. The contract we were operating under came out of our client's massive legal department. For second tier vendors like us, it was a "take it or leave it" proposition. That's why I merely scanned it before signing. It essentially said the client could do whatever they wanted to do. That included cutting us out of the middle and going straight to our employees and subcontractors. "Your contract may allow you to do what you're about to do, but that doesn't make it right. And, my contract with our subcontractor clearly does not allow him to go directly to our client." At that point, one of the executives said, "That's not our problem. The sub is working on mission critical work that only they can do and they're refusing to do it through you. We have no choice but to work directly with them."

I took a deep breath, looked both gentlemen straight in the eye and said, "Then you're leaving me no choice. If you proceed, I will get an injunction against the subcontractor and legally prevent him from working for you."

They were not happy and I was not blinking. With that, I knowingly put a highly valued client relationship at risk. I did so also knowing that the value of the relationship would be seriously diminished should they follow through on their intentions. What they didn't know is that there was an invisible fourth party in the room that day...and He had my back.

While one executive stubbornly held his indefensible position, the other said, "So, what would you propose?" Though school was still in session, I could feel a nap coming on. I stood up and started scrawling out a compromise on the whiteboard. Within a few minutes, we had agreed in principle to an approach that compensated us for allowing them to deal directly with our subcontractor. We didn't come out "whole" but it was a whole lot better than where we were headed. Nap time!

That was four years ago. Countless disasters since have frequently found me back in Matthew 11:28-30.

On one such morning, I had enjoyed a particularly sweet time with the Lord while ruminating upon this rich passage. It was well with my soul as I drove east heading to my fitness center for a workout. There was a beautiful sunrise that morning. While admiring it, I was stunned to see the clouds forming a near perfect cross just above the rising sun. It looked as though the cross was emanating directly from the sun. I stopped twice in an effort to capture the surreal scene on my phone camera.

It wasn't just a beautiful sight. To me, it was a wink from the watchful eye of my Heavenly Father, as if to say, "Thanks for spending time with me this morning. It was just as sweet for me as it was for you. Now, go take on the day." That's why today, one of my most prized possessions hangs prominently in our office is a beautiful framed picture of "my" sunrise with my favorite passage inscribed below it. Every time I look at it, I swear He's winking at me ;-)

Chapter 24

24. It's a Dog World...Adjust!

Second only to our children, our pets have defined life within the Lindemann household since our wedding day on June 12, 1976. Come to think of it, the pets came before the kids and are sure to linger long after them. Though not exclusively, our primary pet of choice has been of the canine variety. About 10 years ago, the resident queen of the canines (a.k.a. lovely bride) decided to fulfill a childhood dream and kick the dog thing up a notch by becoming a breeder (though that word is anathema on the dog show circuit). A few years later, apparently feeling a need to memorialize the furry truth that life as we once knew it had now forever changed, she gave me the previously mentioned key fob that reads, "It's a dog's world...adjust." And yes, I've been adjusting ever since.

Don't get me wrong, I love dogs. I really do. But, I'd be lying to say I've loved all of the dozens of dogs that we've owned over the years. Yes...dozens. In fact, as a "small time" breeder, Queen Canine has occasionally housed a full dozen at one time. Did I say it was a dog's world? And oh, did I also mention that we live in a fairly typical upper middle class suburban neighborhood on slightly less than a one-acre lot without a fence? Not exactly the kennel-in-the-country setting you envision when you think about dog breeders. In fairness, I do appreciate my lovely bride choosing a toy breed to roam our vast estate –long coat Chihuahuas.

By the way, do you actually ever think about dog breeders? Unless you are one, you probably don't. I know I never did. Talk about a rare breed. Those "dog people" as we call them are...oh, I don't know...dog crazy. Yes, that's it. They're just plain dog crazy and there's apparently no turning back. Hence the admonition to their friends and loved ones...adjust!

Signs of my ever-increasing need to adjust to our dog world came early and often in our married days. Though we didn't have two nickels to rub together, we did have a dog and a cat within the first few months of marriage. I must admit they were a relatively inexpensive form of entertainment, especially once the dog chewed the holes in our couch. They really enjoyed chasing one another over, under, around and through our couch as we rolled on the floor laughing. I was not laughing, however, when that same dog chewed up the carpet in front of the apartment door. Although I supposed I'm indebted to him for providing me the opportunity to learn how to lay linoleum to avoid losing our damage deposit upon moving.

Not long thereafter, Elaine showed up at our apartment with a stray dog she'd gone to the other side of town to pick up from what had to be the world's greatest salesman. It was the mangiest mutt I have ever seen. The ugliest, smelliest, poor excuse for a dog imaginable. Think giant sewer rat. This time Elaine was going to have to do the adjusting. Thankfully, she was quick to admit she'd made a huge mistake. So, we did what any self-respecting dog lovers would have done. We drove him right back to the west side and dumped him around the corner from the world's greatest salesman.

Adjustment made! We laughed the whole way home.

Sidebar: Ashtray change

> Regarding the previously mentioned two nickels we didn't have to rub together: One day during our first year of marriage, we found them along with a quarter or two hiding in our car's ashtray. It was all the money we had in the world at the time. Unlike the widow in the Bible who gave her last two cents to the church, we spent our last pennies on a single order of fries at Steak and Shake and washed 'em down with two glasses of water. Best fries we ever tasted.
>
> Back to the dogs. Frankly, I'm a bit embarrassed by how much I actually could write on this subject if I really set my mind to it. But, as I admitted up front, it may be a dog's world, but I'm still adjusting. So, I'll save much for the canine chronicles that Elaine and I probably should co-author one day. So as not to spoil that book launch, for now we'll just touch upon a few more highs and lows from our dog days. But before we do…

Sidebar: Giddy Up!

> Elaine's love of animals is not limited to dogs. She grew up loving animals of all kinds, including horses. She dreamed of having her own horse one day. That day came during our time in Germantown, Tennessee, one of the premier equestrian communities in the country. It was a thrill to watch her ride that beautiful thoroughbred in the local hunter/jumper competitions.

As for me, I loved being around the stable and the horses, but was content to leave the riding to my brave bride. I was more than a bit unnerved the one time I did ride her horse, particularly when he took me over a jump. It was a small jump for a horse, but one giant leap for a stable hand. To this day, I'm awestruck with how confidently Elaine used to ride that horse and so grateful she got to fulfill her childhood dream of doing so.

Speaking of dogs, you'll hear about my all-time favorite momentarily, but a close second has to be Puccini, our Italian Greyhound. He was a beautiful black-white mixed color, fast as greased lightning and the ultimate snuggle hound. The latter quality being the reason why this breed was a favorite among royalty in the days before central heat.

Remember the rock band Three Dog Night? Well, the origin of that name harkens back to the days when the royals would gauge how cold the nights were by how many dogs they had to sleep with to keep warm. A three-dog night was a particularly cold one. From the bed to the beach, we loved watching Puccini dart around the beach like an oversized fire fly on crack. Truth is, we loved everything about Puccini except one…his penchant for peeing on the carpet. Back to the breeder he went.

Remember the movie *As Good As It Gets* with Jack Nicholson and Helen Hunt? Verdell, the dog in the movie, was a little known breed called Brussels Griffon. I loved the movie and, of course, Elaine loved the dog. Wasn't long before we had one just like it. And not long after that, little Annie disappeared one morning when I let her out unaccompanied to do her business. A coyote likely snatched her. Since it was my fault, I adjusted and bought another one. Like most sequels, Annie's stand-in never measured up to the original, though her name, Raisin, was one of the best ever.

Raisin's time with us ran out not long after the batteries in her invisible fence collar ran out of juice. With nothing to stop her, she frolicked onto the sidewalk and proceeded to take a bite out of the passing neighbor lady's backside. When the none-too-happy victim came to our door, Elaine invited her in for aid and comfort, which she refused. Her reaction was mild, however, compared to her hotheaded husband who later came storming up our driveway demanding Raisin's rabies shot history. I would have gladly obliged, but took umbrage to his opening question—"When are you going to fry that bitch?"

Fortunately for him, he was referring to the dog and not my wife.

Chapter 24

Nonetheless, I told him to get off our property and never come back. I may have also said something about where he could put the vet records once I provided them to him. Not sure. I may have just dreamed about that afterwards.

Elaine's never forgotten her "Griff," precious Annie. When it comes to dogs, she truly was as good as it gets. It will be interesting to see if Griff number three, Bentley, will be able to finally take her place. Guess you'll have to read the sequel to find out. You already know the title — "It's a Dog's World…Adjust."

True confession: I really like Bentley, but don't tell my wife.

Many believe Weimaraners to be the most beautiful dogs in the world. We happen to agree. The breed has grown dramatically in popularity since 1989 when artist/photographer William Wegman began using "Weimies" as subjects in his work. The breed is known to be a bit high strung and highly protective of their owners. We found that out the hard way.

Our first Weimie was a male named Willy. He was banished from our dog Heaven home after attacking the neighbor girl and ripping the sweatshirt off her back. Fortunately, he didn't bite her. Learning that females were a bit calmer than males, we replaced Willy with Belle. She too was not long for our dog world after tearing a serious gash in another neighbor girl's foot as she went dashing across our front yard. Different neighborhood…different girl…same outcome. Beautiful though they may be, I'm sorry to say Weimaraners have no place in our dog future. We've made the necessary and appropriate adjustments.

So what does all this dog world adjusting have to do with the real business of life? Does it merely make for good stories and less discretionary spending in the family budget or is there something more to it?

Before the past pain-riddled decade, our canine friends had done for us what they've been doing for dog lovers the world over since the first puppy was born. They've reminded us that "simple pleasures are the best" as the Campbell's Soup folks did a few decades back. They've loved us unconditionally and been our best friends when it seemed as though we had none. And on some days, they have quite literally given us a reason to get out of bed.

Elaine and I have a longstanding understanding regarding "our" dogs. She is their primary care-giver. I'm happy to fill in on those occasions when she isn't home or is in too much pain to get out of bed. But, those are rare exceptions and that's just how she wants it…as do I.

Here's why. But for her dog duties, Elaine could all too easily choose to remain in bed. After all, when it hurts to hug it also hurts to do just about anything.

There's much wisdom in the old adage, "we do what we have to do." Elaine has to get up every day to care for her furry friends. And that's a good thing. That's also why I thank God that our life together has gone to the dogs and our otherwise empty nest is lined with fur.

Sidebar: Dog House Days

That last line makes me sound like a much more loving and understanding husband then I truly am, at least on some days. Some days, I wouldn't mind obliging my estranged neighbor buddy by just frying the friggin' fuzz balls.

Figuratively speaking, of course.

Those are my anti-dog days. Those days find me in a dog house of my own making, pondering the meaning of life and surviving on a Milk-Bone diet.

Finally, I'd like you introduce you to my favorite dog of all time. His name was Kona, because he was the color of our favorite coffee and warmed our hearts with his presence. He had some good years left in him when he died from pancreatitis complications caused by his insistence upon getting into our kitchen trash can, despite the dog-proof locks on it. I'll never forget lying on the vet's floor with Kona, Elaine, Caleb and Bradley as we put our beloved chocolate Lab to sleep. We were all sobbing. That was over seven years ago and memories of my favorite dog still bring tears to my eyes and a lump to my throat. He'll always have a special place in my heart, as the following eulogy suggests.

Kona Goes to Head of Class

I wrote the following piece primarily as a way of coping with my own personal grief. Then it occurred to me that others might somehow benefit from my therapeutic musings. After all, I'm probably not alone in my tendency to put my head in dark places while being too pre-occupied to stop and smell the dog food. It helped me to write it. I hope it helps some who read it.

Our beloved chocolate lab, Kona, was put to sleep on Wednesday evening, July 8, 2009 around 5:10 pm. His penchant for raiding the kitchen trash gave him a "garbage gut" that led to an acute case of pancreatitis from which he could not recover. Despite the child protective locks, crafty Kona found his way into the trash whenever we'd forget to take it out before going to bed. When I awoke last Thursday morning to yet another mess on the kitchen floor, I thought nothing of it. The following morning, our normally ravenously hungry hound refused to eat and I knew something was wrong. As it turned out, something was fatally wrong with our family's best friend.

Kona was more than just a furry friend. He was a gifted teacher. He taught me lessons that I'll never forget, though I was often too self-absorbed to learn them while school was in session. I guess that's why he so often repeated the lesson about keeping my head out of my butt.

"From that vantage point," he would bark, "the only person you can see is…you, and it's not pretty." He made this point many a morning while standing patiently by my chair, nudging my hand with his nose and quietly grunting. I'm just now realizing what he was saying: "If you'd just scratch me behind the ears, whatever it is you're currently grinding on won't seem nearly so overwhelming. Ahh yes, that's it…now how 'bout the other ear? Whad I tell ya'?"

Loyalty? Kona wrote the book. Every morning he would hear me get up and go to the bathroom. By the time I was out, he had left the comfort of his leather sofa (a.k.a. Kona's bed) and plopped down in front of our bedroom door to await his early rising master.

Then the feeding ritual would begin. He'd do his duty whilst I fetched the morning paper. By the time I returned to the garage, he would be jumping up and down, barking loudly and frothing at the mouth. Breakfast is served. I was usually just finishing my first cup of coffee when he'd appear at the back door scratching to be let back in. The timing was important to me, because I could let Kona in and fetch my second cup of coffee while only getting up once. I was efficient. Kona was loyal. Loyalty trumps efficiency every time.

Simple pleasures. For Kona, life was a steady stream of simple pleasures. He was even named after one of our favorite simple pleasures — a hot cup of Hawaiian Kona coffee. Cup in one hand and dog ear in the other…now that's truly the best part of waking up.

During our 10 wonderful years with Kona, he shared our home with many other little furry friends. He loved playing with his barking buddies. They would show their appreciation by helping him maintain a fastidious personal grooming program. They say a clean dog is a happy dog and Kona was always a very happy dog. I suppose that's why he was so kind to his many attendants. They had some canine quid pro quo thing going on…"I'll scratch your back (or whatever) if you'll scratch mine…a little lower…no higher…no left…now right…that's it…that's it…Ahhhhhh…thanks. Arf!"

Love. Oh God, how we loved that dog. Though love means never having to say you're sorry, I can't help myself. Kona, I'm sorry for the walks we could have taken, but didn't. I'm sorry for the swims we could have swum, but didn't. I'm sorry for the sticks you could have fetched, but couldn't, because I was too busy to throw them. I'm sorry for all the times when my self-absorbed efficiency blinded me to your undying loyalty. I'm sorry for the many simple pleasures I missed while worrying about things that invariably missed me and mine. I'm sorry that I took your love for granted; while you lived to unconditionally love everyone in your path.

Kona, I'm sorry that you had to die to get me to pay attention in school. But, now that you have my undivided attention, I hope you can teach me in death what I stubbornly refused to learn in life. So, whenever you look down from that big leather couch in the sky and see me with my head up my butt, please bark loud and long until I take my eyes off myself and focus upon the things that really matter. Things like loyalty, simple pleasures and love…and paying attention in school. You will be forever missed, our faithful and furry friend. We love you, Kona!

Chapter 24

25. 'Til Debt Do Us Part

For me, talking about debt is more painful than a root canal with no anesthesia. Or, for those of you with an unusually high pain tolerance, it's more unpleasant than that annual ritual when my doctor speaks those dreaded words: "drop your pants and bend over. I'll try to make it quick."

Ugh! That's really not the kind of Live Ammo I had in mind when I set about to write this book. It's no accident that the dreaded topic of debt is one of the last that I've chosen to write about. I absolutely hate debt…and I'm not alone.

To set the stage, we need to briefly go back to those Salad Days in Memphis. Imagine yourself in my shoes…or pool. It's a beautiful summer Saturday in 1985. You're floating in your new, gorgeously landscaped backyard pool, keeping a watchful eye out for the three kids splashing around you. Your lovely bride is reading a magazine in the hammock. The yard has been meticulously manicured by your lawn care company and the two new vehicles in the driveway are sparkling inside and out, though you didn't lift a finger along the way. You recently paid off the mortgage on your five bedroom Willamsburg style home.

You owe no one anything. And you, my friend, are feeling like "a man in full. A "master of the universe." A "king of the world."

One more thing…you're 29 years old.

For those old enough to remember, that pool scene might take you back to the old Lipton Tea commercials. The ones depicting a very hot and thirsty man drinking a tall glass of Lipton iced tea, then falling backwards into a swimming pool while letting out a long and very satisfied sounding, thirst quenching, "Ahhhhhh." I remember thinking at the time, "it doesn't get any better than this." And you know what? I was right. But it sure could get a whole lot worse…and it soon did. There was a myriad of reasons why, but chief among them was my insanely foolish choice to once again become a slave to the lender.

As you already know, after being mortgage-free for a little more than a year, I made the ill-fated and despicably deceitful decision to remortgage our Germantown, Tennessee home. 30 years later, we still have a mortgage and it's three times the size of the one we paid off in 1985.

The unnecessary interest paid over those three decades is easily calculable. The pain and suffering caused by having incurred it is not.

God forgave me before I even committed this sin. It took Elaine quite a while, but she eventually did. But I can't honestly say that I've fully forgiven myself. Painful reminders cut me to the quick daily like glass shards preventing a wound from healing.

Sidebar: Do as I Say Not as I've Done

You've probably realized by now that most of my financial advice centers on what *not* to do with your money. For the other side of the coin (pun intended), I commend Dave Ramsey to your attention. Check him out at DaveRamsey.com. Heed his wise counsel and financial freedom could well be yours one day.

Back to the slavery that indebtedness brings. Nothing enslaves consumers more quickly than the bane of the American economy — credit card debt. It's been many years since we had any credit card debt, but don't give us too much credit. Like many Americans, we've chosen the lesser evil of home equity debt instead. Thankfully, interest rates have been at historic lows during the time of indentured servitude to our home equity line of credit. Hopefully, we'll get it paid off before the inevitable and significant rise in interest rates comes.

As to traditional credit cards, just say "no." We've been American Express members since 1978 for one very simple reason…we have to pay the full balance every month. Even then, we receive constant enticements from AMEX to roll our monthly balance into an account that would allow us to carry the balance forward. Never have and never will.

So why use the card at all? Frequent flyer miles, of course. Another bane of our economy, but one I appreciate every time we fly free which is virtually every time we fly. That said, no rewards program can possibly justify carrying credit card balances. So, if that's the excuse you're using for doing so, lose it along with those balances. If you don't, you'll be losing far more over time.

We've gone to great extremes over the years to avoid car loans. We got an early lesson in this by answering the siren's call to buy a brand new fire engine red Ford Granada in 1978 after I graduated from college. Ford was offering special financing to recent college grads. Why not? Surely we could handle the payments with my $14,500 starting salary at IBM and only three mouths to feed.

Not!

> We sold that beauty six payments in and drove a car we borrowed from my in-laws for a while.
>
> A few years later, we once again stepped into the car loan trap again. This time with a stripped down Chevrolet Citation. I don't think it had a single option on it, but it was new. That lasted for about a year, then we sold it to buy a 1968 Chevy Nova. With a heinous Martian green amateur paint job, it was nothing like the blue collar muscle cars I had grown up admiring. But, it was paid for and that was all that mattered. At least until I took three of my customers to lunch.
>
> We rode together in my lunar landing module to a lunch spot in downtown Indy. Ever the transparent one, I explained to them why I didn't drive a BMW like most of my contemporaries. They seemed to respect my frugality. While driving them back to their office, I rounded a corner and heard a horrible screeching sound.
>
> "What was that?" asked one of my passengers. One of the guys in the back said, "I think it was the tire rubbing the wheel well underneath me. At least that's what it felt like."
>
> When we rounded the next corner, his diagnosis was confirmed. They all had a pretty good laugh at my expense that day. But at dinner that evening, one topic Elaine and I did not need to discuss was how to make our next car payment. I'll take momentary embarrassment over years of enslavement every time.

The 10/10/80 Financial Freedom Formula

Since receiving their first allowance, every one of our five children has heard me talked about the 10/10/80 financial freedom formula dozens, perhaps hundreds, of times. It's Finance 101 at its most basic level, but if followed from early adulthood, this formula will set most people financially free by the time they're 40 years old. Do the following with every dollar you earn and you'll avoid much of the financial pain that many have come to accept as a way of life:

- **Give** the first 10 percent of your income back to the One who gave it to you
- **Save** the second 10 percent of your income
- **Live** on the remaining 80 percent of your income

"Yeah right" you say.

To which I say, "Yeah, it *is* right."

"Impossible" you say.

For most, it will be impossible to fully apply this formula from the get-go. After all, you didn't get into the financial shape you're in overnight and you won't get out of it overnight either. I like the "journey of generosity" concept that we talk about all the time at our church. Our pastors challenge the congregation to begin a journey of generosity from wherever their giving level is by incrementally increasing the percentage over time until the desired percentage is obtained. For example, if you're only giving two percent of your income today, increase that by one percent per year for eight years until you've reached the 10 percent goal.

How can you give to God if you don't even go to church? Financial matters aside, I would encourage you to sincerely seek God. If you do, He'll eventually lead you to a community of like-minded believers with whom you can grow in your faith.

You may find them within the context of a traditional church or you may not. But when you do find them, one of the telltale signs of their authenticity will be their generosity towards those in need and those who lead them. Giving back to God is not limited to the confines of a traditional church. Nor is it necessarily limited to faith-based organizations. There are many organizations doing much to relieve suffering and right injustice around the world that are not faith-based. Giving to those can be akin to giving to God, provided you do your homework and are confident that your gift will be put to good use. If you are part of a church community, then a good guideline to follow would be to channel at least half of your giving to them.

For most of our married life, Elaine and I have had a separate checking account through which we channel our giving. Many people make it even easier by setting up a payroll deduction that can then be automatically paid to their church and other charitable organizations they support.

While we do have some regular monthly gifts scheduled to be paid automatically, I've purposely chosen not to have our tithe taken out via payroll deduction. Here's why. I don't ever want our giving to become an unconscious act along the lines of those insidious FICA taxes that come out of every check by governmental decree. That tax hiding in plain sight on every American's check stub has done more to destabilize our economy than any other single act of the federal government. I'm not willing to risk the same happening to one of the most significant acts of true worship that we'll ever perform…giving a little back to the One who gave it all to us.

Chapter 25

Incoming: It's Christmas morning 2014. I was up at five. No assembly required, however. Visions of sugar plums (a.k.a. the latest toy craze) no longer dance in our kids' heads. Even though every member of our extended family resides within 15 miles of one another, it's tough getting all 19 of us together at the same time. So, this year, we've divided the troops between Christmas Eve and Day. Both gatherings at B-Pa and Mimi's house, of course. This is the calm before the Christmas Day storm, though it won't be a white one this year.

Two nights ago, Elaine's last words to me before falling asleep were, "Did you *ever* like Christmas?"

BAM!

Silent night…

Unholy night…

All wasn't calm…

Elaine was right.

I knew exactly what she meant. She couldn't remember the last time I appeared to be truly enjoying the Christmas season. Nor could I. Part of the reason is, no doubt, due to the fat American Express bill that arrived two days ago. Ho! Ho! Ho! But that's really only part of it.

The bigger part of it relates to the harsh reality of the small business owner's world. A world in which holidays are both a blessing and a curse. While the business owner's customers are settling down for a long winter's nap, he rises early and goes to bed late, pondering how to get his business to the proverbial "next level." Or, in below average years, he frets about just keeping the lights on. He wants to just relax and enjoy some time off along with most of those around him, but relaxing is one of the most difficult things he ever does. There's no such thing as "Paid Time Off" (PTO) for the small business owner. It is what it is, but it isn't what it should be. At least not according to the best book I've ever read:

> *It is in vain that you rise up early and go late to rest, eating the bread of anxious toil; for he gives sleep to his beloved (Psalm 127:2).*

Since Elaine's convicting question, I've had two divinely coincidental conversations with fellow small business owners. One is a friendly competitor still in business. The other a former restaurant chain operator. Both lamented how they suffered constant anxiety while operating their businesses. So much so for the retired restaurant owner, that he had suicidal thoughts. The turning point for him came when he was driving one night (having had too much to drink) and heard a voice telling him to do himself and his family a favor by just driving into the bridge abutment up ahead. Fortunately, he was able to conquer those demons. He spent the next two years getting his four restaurants sold and is now enjoying a happy, healthy and anxiety-free retirement.

Oh yeah, one more thing. He's now the third person I've meant in the past three months whose quit drinking. Just coincidence, I'm sure. Yeah right…of the divine variety.

Elaine just finished reading *The Hardest Peace* by Kara Tippetts. In all our years together, I've never seen Elaine so deeply moved by a book she's read. Now that I'm halfway through it myself, I understand why. Barring a miracle, Kara will soon lose her battle with stage four cancer. Her disease is so advanced that she could literally be dying as I'm writing this. Determined to do in death what she may never have been able to do in life, Kara started charting her journey with cancer in her now viral blog, *Mundane Faithfulness*. I commend both the book and the blog to you.

Within her book, Kara references another author (Scotty Smith in *Objects of His Affections*) who asks two of the most provocative questions I've ever heard. First, what is the most commonly-asked question throughout the Bible from Genesis to Revelation? Second, what is the most commonly-made statement throughout the Bible that is attributed to God? Before I tell you the answers, I encourage you to take a few minutes to ponder the questions yourself. Your answers should provide you with some great insight as to where you are on your own spiritual journey.

The most commonly asked question throughout the Bible is, *"How long, Lord…how long?"* How long must I endure <fill in the blank>. How long must I endure cancer… financial hardship… depression… loneliness… hunger… injustice… oppression…???

Whatever the cause of our suffering, the human heart cries out to God…*how long*? Given the frequency of our question, it may surprise you to learn that God rarely answers it. Were He to do so, I suspect we wouldn't much care for His answer. We really don't want to hear "as long as it takes" in the midst of our pain and suffering. Maybe that's why He sidesteps the question entirely with His most commonly made statement in the Bible, "Do not fear." So, we ask "How long?" and He replies, "Fear not." What's up with that?

I turned to Kara's blog for some answers. After watching the December 12, 2014 video she made with her husband, Jason, I was completely wrecked. Ever the glutton for punishment, I read her December 22 "*Love Intentional, Love Maturing, Love Exceptional*" post to her oldest child, 13-year-old, Eleanor ("Ella"). No words. Completely undone.

Chapter 25

Blubbering...praying...confessing.

"Yes, I did like Christmas before I allowed it's true meaning to be lost somewhere between my "how long?" questions and your "fear not" reminders. Please forgive all those joyless seasons I spent under the circumstances when I could have just as easily chosen your joy to be my strength. Please don't let Kara die in vain. May our lives and the thousands of others she's touched around the world be forever changed for the better. May this and every other Christmas I'm privileged to experience this side of eternity be a time of true joy to the world...and may it start with me."

I'm pleased to report that Kara made it home for Christmas after having surgery on December 23. In sharing her December 22 post on Facebook, I simply said, "Read her blog...buy her book...Merry Christmas!"

To encourage you to read Kara's blog and buy her book, here are a few excerpts from her latest post about the special bread Ella had baked for her:

- "I get what Ella was doing – because I'm doing it too. I'm fighting to love those in my life with great intention from my little abilities."
- "And with each bite I knew she loved me. Her love was the very best ingredient. And even sweeter than all the yummy bread."
- "...the hard peace is coming – my children are and will continue to be kept long past my last breath – now that's a stunner."
- "Seeing my children grow in grace and the BIG overflowing love of Jesus – well, that's my favorite gift given this year."
- "Grace, grace, grace. We need presence not presents."

As to your "how long" question, you've probably already figured out that if you heed God's admonition to have no fear, it doesn't really matter what the answer is. Because no matter how long it takes, He's in *it* with you. Whatever *it* is...do not fear.

Now, back to being mundanely faithful with our finances. Before leaving the subject of giving, a word of caution regarding motives seems in order. While God loves a cheerful giver (2 Corinthians 9:7), He's not the least impressed with our efforts to curry His favor with our giving. God's favor cannot be bought, because it has already been paid for via the eternal exchange that Jesus made for all mankind on the cross. Thus, our primary motive for giving should be a genuine love for God and people. Anything beyond that risks being less than purely motivated and displeasing to God.

For most of us, the largest single investment we'll ever make will be in our home. This calls for wisdom beyond conventional and for young home buyers, beyond their years. Conventional wisdom, even after the significant tightening of mortgage credit since the sub-prime mortgage meltdown that brought about The Great Recession of 2007-2009, says buy as much house as you can qualify for. I beg to differ. So much so, that I have quite literally begged our children to limit themselves to a house that they believe can be paid off within 10 years. That's right, 10 years. Put it on a conventional fixed 30-year mortgage, then pay additional principal payments each month sufficient to have it paid off in 10 years. Those extra payments might be smaller in the early years then grow along with their incomes. But, I implore them (and you) to move into the home with the idea of paying it off within 10 years.

Just the other day, one of my contemporaries a few years my junior told me that he and his wife have lived in the same house (their first one) for 27 years. I didn't ask if it was paid for, but strongly suspect it is. While reconnecting with an old friend over lunch the previous week, he too shared that he and his wife are still living in their first home. Knowing them, I suspect they burned their mortgage many years ago. I greatly respect both of these couples for resisting the societal pressures to keep up with the Jones by buying bigger and bigger houses. I'm also quite jealous of the financial margin that this counter cultural approach has given them and the peace of mind that goes with it. May their tribes increase!

At this point, you might be wondering if there's anything besides a house worth going into debt for. If so, we're making progress. I don't personally think there is and I have the scars of servitude to prove it.

"But what about cars?" you ask. "New ones are very expensive" I say. "That's why you probably shouldn't own one until you've saved up enough money to pay for it…either new or used."

"But that's not being realistic," you say. To which I say, "Hogwash!"

When our youngest son was 16, we bought him a rebuilt Pontiac Vibe (a.k.a. The Moonraker) for $5,000. It was a solid vehicle that Bradley drove for almost nine years before selling it for $500. He replaced it with a rebuilt Honda Accord that he bought for $1,000. After 10 years of driving, instead of being conditioned to think that car payments are just a way of life, Bradley can't imagine having them. Why? Because he never has. That's called learning things the easy way…no fire engine red Ford Granada required.

Now that I've admitted to having bought my 16-year-old son a car, I might as well make a full confession. Despite having written into our wills many years ago that we did not want our children's guardians to buy them cars, we did just that. They were all beaters for the most part, though the girls admittedly got better quality rides than the boys. I figured the boys could more readily fend for themselves in the event of a breakdown. We never spent more than $8,000 on one of our kid's first cars and after that they were on their own...sort of. Lord knows we tried to stick to our guns, but there were more exceptions than rules.

Given a parental do-over, we'd stick to our original plan to make our kids pay for their own cars along with the insurance and maintenance thereof. Why? For a variety of reasons, not the least of which is the great opportunity it represents to instill a strong work ethic into the little bloodsuckers. Cell phones represent the same opportunity, by the way. With perfect hindsight, I can now say with authority that it is truly looney for parents to assume financial responsibility for things that their kids believe they cannot live without and will consequently be highly motivated to figure out how to get them. Hopefully, by legal means.

Seriously Mom and Dad, if you want your kids to be more responsible, then start shifting more of the burden of responsibility to them.

I know I just lost some of you, so I might as well double down. Many well-meaning parents justify picking up their kids' tabs on everything from cars and cell phones to designer jeans and spa treatments because the kids are just too busy to have jobs so they can pay for such luxuries (yes...luxuries) themselves. Right? And of course, what they're busy doing is teaching them far more about the life you want them to lead than any minimum wage job ever could. Right? Wrong. The more luxuries we allow our kids to enjoy without having made any sacrifices towards their enjoyment, the greater the risk of their growing up with the false belief that life owes them such things. Tired of your kids acting like spoiled brats? Then stop spoiling them. It's as simple and as hard as that.

I was 14 years old the summer I set my sights on a component stereo system befitting the audiophile I was determined to become. My bedroom desk drawer was overflowing with brochures from all the top manufacturers of amplifiers, turntables, cartridges, speakers and headphones. I poured over them for hundreds of hours trying to assemble the perfect system. That was 45 years ago, yet I can still tell you the make and model of every component I purchased at the end of that summer. I bought a Kenwood 7200 amp, a Dual 1218 turntable, a Stanton 681EE cartridge, KLH Model 23 speakers and Koss Pro4-AA headphones. The total system cost me 400 very hard-earned dollars. Every dollar counted nightly and secured in a locked tackle box. Perhaps most telling is the fact that I never even thought to ask my parents for financial assistance. Why not? Because I knew they wouldn't give it to me and I didn't want them to. Back then, I was the rule, not the exception. My how things have changed.

Are you wondering why I'm talking so much about children in the chapter on debt? If so, you probably have very little of either. Remember the home equity line of credit we enslaved ourselves to over 10 years ago? Virtually every dollar of the outstanding balance today can be attributed to the purchase of child-related items. Cars, tuition and a backyard swimming pool, to name a few. I'll leave this very convicting subject with a challenge to every parent reading this book. Inspect your home and garage for material things acquired with money your children earned and saved over an extended period of time. If you have anything on your list, take a bow. If you have more than one item for any child, you are hereby nominated for the Parents' Hall of Fame. If you find yourself amongst the vast majority who can find nothing meeting this criteria, please resist the temptation to mandate a new world order at the dinner table this evening. Instead, wait for the next time one of the little darlings just can't live without something and make one thing abundantly clear to them. They're going to have to live without it unless they figure out a way to earn it. Then step aside.

Now that Elaine and I have perfect parental hindsight, we clearly see that parenting, though never easy, can be made easier if parents will only heed the advice of the world's smallest instruction manual. It only contains one page and there's only one word on that page…a very small word. Most parents won't have to think long before guessing what this oft times neglected, yet incredibly useful word might be. The word, of course, is "no." It's a powerful word, provided it's backed with appropriate action or inaction, as the case may be. "No" is the nuclear option in every parent's arsenal. Use it early and often in your child-rearing years or lose the ability to do so. The idiom "stick to your guns" comes to mind. Its origin depicts a soldier who continues to stand his ground and shoot at the enemy despite appearing to be fighting a losing battle. If you have teenagers, this should sound frighteningly familiar to you. If it doesn't, then you too have a place in the Parents' Hall of Fame.

You can't say I didn't warn you. I knew this was going to be a tough chapter for author and reader alike. You may be feeling a bit overwhelmed and under the pile. Not where I want to leave you.

I have a sign in my home office that reads, "Action Conquers Fear." When it comes to dealing with your debt problems, you've already taken the positive action of reading this difficult chapter. A good next step might be to make a commitment and formulate a plan for not incurring any additional debt. It's tough to solve a problem while continuing to add to it on a daily basis. And for most of us, the reason we continue to do so is because we fail to exercise our parental nuclear option. So, when it comes to increasing your debt and indulging your children…just say no. That simple action will help conquer many of your fears.

There are no guarantees in the parenting world. The best parents can do is take every possible opportunity to stack the odds in their children's favor. Not by indulging their every whim or becoming hovering helicopter parents, but by letting their yes be yes and your no be no. By setting the boundaries and insisting that they operate within them and meting out the consequences when they refuse to.

Oh sure, they may curse you for it now, but they will thank you for it later. This is far better than enjoying a temporary store-bought peace during their formative years that can lead to all-out war during their adult years. A war with high stakes and real casualties.

But with God, all things are possible. My friend Bobby Hayden would say "amen" to that. Bobby was a child prodigy musician who lost his way early into his musical career. For 10 years, he was a hard core heroin addict living in a cardboard box on a street corner in Los Angeles. Yes, he lived in a cardboard box for 10 years!

One day a drunk stumbled into Bobby's "house" to find him passed out as usual. He woke him up to give him the startling news that if he didn't give his life to Jesus, he would die a bum in that cardboard box. It's been said that the true Gospel is simply one beggar telling another where to find bread. Another "amen" from Bobby. Shortly after those two beggars met, Bobby surrendered his life to Christ and has been drug-free since 2009. Over the last several years, his story has caught national attention and he's been privileged to travel the world telling it. His message is simple, yet incredibly powerful—God pulled me out of the pit and gave me a plan, and he'll do the same for you.

Stories like Bobby's remind us that no matter how bad things get, there is always hope. Just like there was hope for Bobby, there is hope for you and yours. Because no matter how bad "bad" gets, good has already triumphed over it. His name is Jesus. And He's as good as it gets. Good enough, in fact, to reach a hopeless addict through a derelict drunk with the cure for what ailed them both.

Chapter 25

Retoolment

> *I'm curious to see what God has planned for what I can only describe as the growing pastor's heart within me.*

With 10,000 Baby Boomers retiring every day in the U.S., you can't read a newspaper or listen to a newscast without hearing some mention of them. This morning's USA Today newspaper (December 28, 2014) offers "5 Tax Tips for Retirees" and tells us that "Volunteering Pays Off in Big Ways." I rarely read such articles, because I can't envision myself as ever voluntarily retiring in any traditional sense of the word. I prefer retoolment to retirement.

Retooling involves gearing up for a new season of productivity and creativity. As pointed out in this morning's paper, volunteering is a great way for otherwise retired folks to retool. The gentleman featured in the article happens to volunteer at one of my personal favorite non-profits. Meals on Wheels uses volunteers to deliver hot and cold meals to shut-ins around the country for a very modest charge. Our company assumed responsibility for a Thursday route near our office a number of years ago. By rotating assignments between our team of volunteers, we're able to provide a great community service to our neighbors without putting an inordinate burden on any single volunteer. My own mother took advantage of this wonderful service as her health began to decline.

Since I still need to work, I guess it's a good thing that I want to. And better yet, I'm able to. I do look forward to the day when whatever work I choose to do is voluntary, because alas we don't need the money. Absent selling the business someday, I don't really see waking up with nothing to do and asking myself, "what's next?"

I've spoken to many over the years who have found themselves in this situation. Most are climbing the walls within a year or so. Conversations with their fellow retirees while lingering over coffee and the morning paper at the local Panera Bread shift from planning their next travel adventure to "getting back in the game."

One such 72-year-old friend of mine recently purchased a Mathnasium franchise because he was so impressed with the dramatic turnaround he saw in his granddaughters' math skills. He's back in the game and is bubbling over with excitement for his new venture.

Speaking of Panera Bread, I recently witnessed the scene I just described around the corner from our office. While waiting for someone to join me, I noticed a group of a half-dozen apparently-retired guys lined up across from one another reading the paper. Once in a while, one of them would comment about something he was reading and someone else would briefly respond, then go back to whatever he was reading.

At first glance, I felt a twinge of jealousy. But as I continued to watch and listen to what, for the most part, were inane conversations, my jealousy faded to gratitude. By the time I left, I was grateful to still have all the challenges that I walked in with that morning. Grateful to still have a shot at making the news versus rehashing it with a bunch of tired "jocks" who are no longer in the game. Though the game may change from starting and operating businesses to serving others by volunteering, there's always a game to be played. And so long as I'm vertical and sucking air, I intend to suit up.

I'm curious to see what God has planned for what I can only describe as the growing pastor's heart within me. By that I mean my increasing awareness of the brokenness that surrounds us all and the desire to help restore those broken people and places.

I see it in the 60-year-old friend who's been unemployed for nearly three years now. I see it in the tired and grateful faces of the friends I'm privileged to serve at our church's food pantry on Monday nights. I see it in the testimonies of the brave young mothers who choose life for their babies after receiving compassionate counsel from a Life Centers volunteer. I see it in the daily struggles of the alcoholics and addicts to get through one more sober day. And yes, I see it in my own extended family at levels that break my heart. I see brokenness everywhere I look and hope to devote increasing amounts of my time, talent and treasure towards bringing redemption to the broken people and places I see.

Elaine's been telling me for years to get a hobby. I don't really know why. Not sure she's thought it through. With a hobby, I would spend increasing amounts of time in the garage or basement or out and about passionately pursuing whatever it happened to be. She would spend increasing amounts of time alone and we would have less in common. Although it would be fun to reciprocate by giving her a hobby memento key fob with some pithy inscription like "it's a hunter's world…adjust" or "it's a scuba diver's world…adjust" or my personal favorite, "it's a monkey breeder's world…adjust." My lovely bride has a bit of a monkey phobia. Hee! Hee!

I'm not strongly opposed to having a hobby someday. But it would need to be something that served a greater purpose than just keeping ole Brad busy. For example, should I ever learn to make anything more complex than my bed, perhaps I could create something that could make life a bit more pleasant for those who are otherwise suffering? Something like Veronika Scott's sleeping-bag coat that she created for a class project, then turned into an incredible social enterprise called The Empowerment Plan.[6] Veronika's product meets her customers' critical need for warmth, while according to ABC News her enterprise employs 13 former and current homeless people to manufacture its coats. Kudos to this once homeless entrepreneur. Show me a hobby like The Empowerment Plan and I'm all in.

I understand that former president, George W. Bush, has become quite a prolific painter in his retirement years. According to the International Business Times, when a CNN reporter asked "W" what advice he had for aspiring artists, he deadpanned, "Never paint your wife or mother."[7]

Can't you just hear Laura or Barbara saying, "That George, he's such a card." Bush's hobby got me to thinking about how he could leverage his latent talent for good around the world. I suspect an original painting of decent quality by a still-living former leader of the free world could fetch quite a price at a charity auction. Don't you? It wouldn't take much imagination to put some incredible fund-raisers together that could raise millions for causes near and dear to W's heart. What are you waiting for, Mr. President? Giddy up!

Incoming: I just returned from working out at my local fitness center. As I was leaving the pool, a neighbor friend flagged me down. He was giddy with excitement over having just signed his early retirement papers with his big pharma employer of 35 years. Imagine that, 35 years at the same company and he's two years younger than me. Maybe he's not a friend after all. In fact, I might just hate the guy. Not really, but I must

---

[6] Sleeping-Bag Coats Warm, Employ Detroit Homeless, by Alexa Valiente, ABC World News, May 9, 2013.
http://abcnews.go.com/blogs/headlines/2013/05/sleeping-bag-coats-warm-employ-detroit-homeless.
[7] George W. Bush Paintings 2014: US President Offers Advice to Aspiring Artists, by Philip Ross, December 15, 2014. http://www.ibtimes.com/george-w-bush-paintings-2014-us-president-offers-advice-aspiring-artists-1757819.

confess to being a bit envious. The dude's retiring at age 56 with a full pension plus a 401k and a myriad of other incredible benefits. Since he "took the package" as they say in Fortune 500 speak, he's sure to have at least a year's full salary before his retirement benefits kick in. Makes me want to take two Prozac and call my shrink in the morning.

Thanks, I needed that. Ever catch yourself looking back and wondering what might have been? What if you had taken that once-in-a-lifetime job opportunity? What if you had acted upon that creative business idea that you had before the person who eventually did act upon it? What if you had said "I do" to a different someone? What if you hadn't lost so much money on that bad investment? What if you hadn't blown so much money on bad choices? What if….

What if I told you that every minute you spend wondering about what might have been is stolen from what is and is to be?

We cannot change our past, but we can diminish our present and future by dwelling upon it. Time moves on and so should we. Learn from your mistakes, but don't wallow in self-pity over having made them. Truth be told, you don't know for certain what those mistakes even were. Some things you consider to be a "slam dunk" for the mistake column may be registered as miracles when the final tally is made. On the flipside, some of what you consider to be your most brilliant moves may find their way into the bloopers highlight reel. Is it a good thing or a bad thing? One day we'll know. Until then, your guess is as good as the next guy's.

Back to retooling time. The net of it is this—when you stop learning, you stop living. When you stop giving, you stop growing. When you stop caring, you start dying. Want a reason to get up every morning of your life whether your retired, retooled or just feeling like a tired old tool? Then find something (preferably more than one thing) that you care passionately about and pour your mind, body and soul into it. Live to make a positive difference in every life that you touch…or die trying. That, my friends, is life well lived. That is Live Ammo Living at its very best.

Beach Therapy (January 2015)

Due to an unseasonably cold August, Elaine began lamenting the coming of winter before summer had officially departed. Knowing neither of us could take another winter like the last one, I suggested we conduct a "working snowbird experiment." After all, when we owned the "condo from hell," those Canadian snowbirds used to migrate to the Florida panhandle to steal winter accommodations from us at bargain basement prices. Turnabout's fair play.

So, I told Elaine if she could find something acceptable to her at the same price we use to rent our condo for, we'd head south for the winter. As you might imagine, it didn't take her long. Though it was more challenging than first thought, because most owners had yet to adjust to the dog world that we lived in. Most didn't allow pets. Imagine that.

As fate would have it, we found a charming carriage house (a.k.a. efficiency apartment above the garage) with 485 square feet of open-living space, about the size of our master bedroom at home. There was no bedroom per se, but at least there was a door on the bathroom. I grilled Elaine pretty hard over just how accommodating the space would be. She assured me that we'd adjust...just like we had to the dog world. Sure we would.

After two nights of "cozy comfort," we were still adjusting. The barely functional WIFI connection wasn't helping matters. The connection went down every 20 to 30 minutes. While troubleshooting the problem with the homeowner, he casually said, "Why don't you guys just move into the main house for the rest of the month until the February renters show up? All I would ask is that you pay half of the additional cleaning fee...$110. Would that be okay?"

I was stunned at his incredibly gracious offer. Before he made it, I wasn't sure we were going to last a week in our cozy little apartment, never mind the two months we'd signed up for. I'm pretty sure Elaine was packing before I hung up the phone.

We soon found ourselves in a gorgeous three-bedroom, three-bathroom beach house with a stunning second floor balcony upon which we enjoyed full sunlight from sun up to sunset. Most importantly, our two dogs, Sky and Bentley, had their own bedroom. Come what may in February, we were living large in January, thanks to technical difficulties over the garage. Adjustment complete.

For the better part of the last decade, my business and my wife's health have been at the top of my prayer list. I've prayed more about these two things than perhaps all others combined. That's why when we prepared to head south for Rosemary Beach on New Year's Day, I packed hopes of a breakthrough on both the business and health fronts right next to my Bible. Persistent prayer is a much-discussed topic within Christian circles. Entire books have been written on how and how often to pray. I'm no expert, just another desperate relief seeker who cannot bear the weight of these burdens alone. And so...I pray:

Chapter 25

Rejoice always, pray without ceasing, give thanks in all circumstances; for this is the will of God in Christ Jesus for you (1 Thessalonians 5:16-18).

Towards the end of our first week, I met an intriguing woman during a morning walk on the beach. Given the early hour and the blustery conditions, she was the only person I saw during my walk. Wearing brightly printed flannel pajama pants and donning one of those knitted hats with ear flaps and cable yarn ties hanging loosely, she had a childlike whimsical appearance. She was collecting sea shells in a plastic sand bucket. As I approached her, she crossed my path gently holding a star fish and lovingly placed it back into the life-giving sea. "Made a difference to that one," I said, without stopping to further engage her. After the turnaround, our paths crossed again.

I had a mysterious sense that I was supposed to engage this perfect stranger in conversation. So, I removed my ear buds, but before I had a chance to say "hello" she asked, "What are you listening to?"

"Praise and worship music by a band called Jesus Culture. More than a band really. They're a movement, particularly among young people."

"Interesting," she said, "I've never heard of them. Where are you from?" she asked. And then, "What brings you here?"

When I told her that we were primarily here in an effort to break my wife's chronic pain cycle, she got a very intense, quizzical look on her face.

"Do you woo her?" she asked. Not sure I heard her correctly, I asked her to repeat the question. "Do you woo her?" she repeated. "Love on her. Do you love on her real good? She needs that. You should kiss her on the forehead like a papa. She has deep hurts causing her pain. I can feel it. It makes me cry just to think about it. She really needs you to love on her."

You could have knocked me over with a feather. Rarely at a loss for words, I was speechless after my encounter with Mary. I thanked my beach angel for her kind words and gave her a hug before moving on. The entire exchange only lasted a few minutes, but the impact of her message should last a lifetime.

That evening, I kissed Elaine on the forehead like a papa. I did my best to love on her real good, but I knew all too well that I would soon fall short of the bar Mary had set for me. That's why I decided to tell Elaine about how her Heavenly Papa had sent her a clear message through a most unusual messenger.

The following evening, I told Elaine about Mary. I wanted her to know that God felt her pain, heard our prayers and was with us even when it hurt the worst. She seemed deeply moved by my Mary story.

Towards the end, she began fumbling with her phone, looking for something. I wasn't sure what. Had the stage been set differently, I probably would have really blown it at that point. Saying something about how annoying it was trying to talk to her while she's preoccupied with her phone. Sure glad I kept that powder dry…for once.

She was soon showing me a music video of a song by Sarah McLachlan entitled, *Mary*. Here is an especially moving excerpt:

Mary walks
Down to the water's edge
And there she hangs her head
To find herself faded
A shadow of what she once was…

Oh and I would be the last to know
I would be the last to let it show
I would be the last to go

"Mary" by Sarah McLachlan

I don't pretend to know what message these lyrics might have for my lovely bride and me. Perhaps none at all. What I do know, however, is that on January 7, 2015 God answered one of my top two prayers in an extraordinary way. He didn't give Elaine the healthy 30-year-old spine I'd been praying for. Nor did He take away the chronic migraines. He simply let her know that He felt her pain, while letting me know what I should be doing about it…love on her really good. Just like He loves on us.

Four days later, I was taking the same beach walk. Again, it was early morning…Sunday morning. As usual, I was listening to worship music on my iPhone. Since I was the only one in sight, I did some rather lame worship dancing near the water's edge at the turnaround point. On the walk back, at about the same spot I met Mary the beach angel, the Spirit clearly nudged me. No voice, but the message was clear—check out Craig's latest blog on the Ransomed Heart web site.[8] Mind you, I've only read Craig's blog a couple of times and not at all within the last year or so. I knew nothing of his latest post, but clearly "heard" God tell me to read it…the latest one. Now!

---

[8] Dancing, by Craig McConnell, September 9, 2014.
http://www.ransomedheart.com/blogs/craig/dancing

Chapter 25

So, I sat down in the sand to see what God was up to. The post dated September 9, 2014 was simply entitled, *Dancing*. The picture was that of a little girl in a red tutu dancing, you guessed it...on the beach. Just as I had been doing minutes earlier. Though you could hardly call what I had been doing dancing when compared to this little ballerina leaping for joy atop the wet sand. Then, my eye was drawn to the last line which read, *"Don't let anything keep you from dancing."* Reading that post literally took my breath away. Through it, God had spoken clearly, tenderly, yet oh so powerfully to me...me! But, He wasn't finished speaking....

As I tearfully continued my homeward trek, a few minutes later the Spirit nudged me again. This time a bit more forcefully. His message was brief and business-like. The God of the Universe clearly "said" (again, no audible voice, but a clear message) to me, "I might have more interest in blessing your business plans if you had more interest in executing mine."

I knew exactly what He meant. Plan A...the one in which the God of the Universe entrusts the truth of the Gospel to knuckleheads like me. It's a simple plan really. Just tell everyone you meet about Jesus. And, it really helps if you actually know Him, as opposed to just knowing about Him.

With that, I cried "uncle" to my Heavenly Papa and my beach dancing lesson ended. I felt so loved in that moment, it was as if God had bent down from Heaven and kissed me on the forehead like a papa would. Though Elaine's health and my business challenges remain, my perspective on both has radically changed. By telling me what I needed to do about each, God had effectively told me what I desperately needed to hear—"I've got this. Just love your wife and others as I do. I'll take care of the rest. You wait...you watch...you'll see." And I believe I will.

You might be struggling, as I did, to connect the dots between my dancing lesson and the business admonition. From my experience, God never wastes a moment and He's able to fulfill multiple purposes within a single one. While lame worship dancing is better than none, it's even better to praise our great God by dancing before Him like He's the only one watching.

This was an important message unto itself, but it also set the stage for the one to follow. By confirming the first message through Craig's blog post in such dramatic fashion, God paved the way for the second message about my business to be received. Absent the first message, I may have questioned where the second one came from. Sure sounded good, but maybe I just made that one up? As it was, I had no doubt about the source of both messages.

Since the previously mentioned spiritual retreat in 2012 with Toth

Ministries in Colorado, I've been known to cut a spiritual rug or two whilst worshipping God through music. I would commend the practice to anyone who considers himself a Christ follower and desires to follow Him more closely. To encourage you, I thought you might enjoy reading Craig's entire (brief) post on the subject:

> I came across a young college student friend's Facebook post:
>
> Jon wishes that when he ran into a room and started dancing that other people would get up and dance, and not just sit and stare. Ya!
>
> Someone quickly commented: Maybe he's running into the wrong rooms.
>
> I paused, eased back into my chair, captured and wondering, "Am I dancing?" With a little reflection, I thought, "Sometimes, for some reasons, in some circles… yes and no."
>
> Soaking in the question…I'd love to run into rooms dancing and have others get up and join me… and not just sit and stare.
>
> What rooms am I running into? Lord, am I running into the wrong rooms? (Church, small group, circle of friends, etc.)
>
> After steeping a bit on my life and its effect upon others, I hear God my Father clear his throat and in tones of strength, warm invitation, and urgency, perhaps insistence, whisper to my heart, "Don't let anything keep you from dancing!"
>
> Don't let anything keep you from dancing.

Chapter 25

26. Why I'm In Business For Life

"Well, you have no choice. She has to get an abortion."

These words from my best friend were still ringing in my ears, as I searched the Scriptures for what God had to say on the matter. My head told me that I couldn't allow fatherhood to derail my college career. My heart told me that trying to convince my girlfriend to get an abortion was not only wrong, but futile. But, it was God's Word that ultimately persuaded me:

> *For you created my inmost being; you knit me together in my mother's womb. I praise you because I am fearfully and wonderfully made; your works are wonderful, I know that full well. My frame was not hidden from you. When I was made in the secret place. When I was woven together in the depths of the Earth, your eyes saw my unformed body. All the days ordained for me. Were written in your book. Before one of them came to be.* – Psalms 139: 13-16

After reading this passage, I made a note in the margin of my Bible that simply read, "NO ABORTION." It wasn't an option. God had confirmed what my heart had already been telling me. Ironically, it was a false alarm. My girlfriend wasn't pregnant. Nonetheless, the seeds of my pro-life convictions were planted deep within my soul. I didn't know it at the time, but that defining moment would one day find me "in business for life."

Over the next three decades, those seeds of life were continually watered with tears, as our extended family faced seven "surprise" pregnancies. My wife and I have seen the perils of children parenting children. We've held the precious gift of life that many times only an adopted child can be. We've seen God turn mothers' mistakes into life-saving miracles. We've heard the voice of God speak clearly on behalf of the chosen ones whose birth mothers were unable to care for them. Time and time again, we've seen mothers choose life when it was anything but an easy choice. But, it was always the right choice.

Shortly after 9/11, my seeds of life began to bring forth fruit that, to this day, unnerves me no end. In what pastor/author, Bill Hybels, refers to as "a whisper from God," I heard God calling me to play some role in helping to:

"Abolish Abortion in America in my Lifetime."

Along with this whisper came the phrase, "In Business for Life." I've always assumed this to be the name of an organization that God wants me to start and just recently I finally heard His starter's gun.

Since that first whisper, I have heard is His gentle wooing of abortion's "living victims" — the estimated 50+ million American men and women who have participated in an abortion. Setting these captives free by offering the forgiveness, faith and freedom that only God can give is essential to re-establishing a culture of life in America. Thereafter, the gates of hell will never prevail against the pro-life, soul cleansing tsunami that is destined to wash across our land. "They will know the truth and the truth will set them free" and abortion will take its rightful place as a permanent bloody stain in our nation's past.

What about "The Chosen Generations"? Since Roe v. Wade, two full generations of Americans have been born. In a very real sense, they are The Chosen Generations. Those whose mothers could have legally chosen to end their lives. Yet instead, and oft times at great sacrifice, chose to give them life. What role will these chosen ones play in convincing the nation that they were never really a choice at all, but rather a child…a defenseless, innocent child? I think it will be a huge role.

I also fervently believe that my home State of Indiana will play a huge role in leading America to victory in The War Within the Womb. Our march towards an abortion-free country starts in our neighborhoods, cities and states. Who's stopping us from shutting down the abortion clinic nearest our home for lack of demand? Why couldn't Indianapolis become an abortion-free city? What other state is more likely to become known as "The Crossroads of Life"? Where within our state capitol will we erect the official Indiana "Memorial to the Unborn"? Of course, it must be built to ensure that we never again lose our way when it comes to the sanctity of life. Now is the time to start casting that vision and planning for memorials to the unborn in every state and, most importantly, in our nation's capital.

If you think I'm dreaming…you're right. I have a dream that my five children will one day live in a nation where their right to choose will once again and forever more be constrained by the rights of all others to live. I have a dream that abortion, like slavery 150 years ago and racial discrimination a mere 50 years ago, will be legally abolished in America in my lifetime. It is a dream that must be fulfilled, for the very future of our nation depends upon it. I believe this dream emanates from the heart of God and the souls of the great leaders in our nation's past.

Yes, I know, abortion is perhaps the most divisive, politically incorrect issue in America today. But, did you know that the most dangerous neighborhood in this great nation lies within the wombs of its women? One in five who enters that neighborhood never makes it out alive. Did you know that in the America of the unborn, it's been 9/11 every day for nearly 44 years? The daily human toll within American wombs is greater than that of the fallen "Twin Towers" ...now totaling 60 million and counting. Most importantly, did you know God has much to say about it?

God's whispers are becoming louder...more like shouts at this point. He has moved us to form a non-profit entity called "In Business For Life." It seemed good to the Spirit to weave two dear Christian brothers into the fabric of IBFL. Christopher Mann of PumpJack.me Thought Leader Marketing is a staunchly pro-life father of nine, totally committed Christ-follower and brilliant thinker. His research/analytical, administrative and marketing communications skills have already proven invaluable during IBFL's formative stage.

On the creative side, we are blessed to have Tom Corey, visual storyteller extraordinaire, of CoCreate Films.[9] Tom is a deeply passionate "old soul" creative type whose work speaks to the heart and provokes the mind. In the intensely visual culture, Tom's contributions will be critical to reaching life-minded business people with the IBFL challenge.

IBFL Mission

The mission of *In Business For Life* is to reduce demand for abortion by supporting pregnant mothers in every possible way and promoting adoption as the loving option to abortion or parenting. As well, we seek to educate professionals by providing a winsome and compelling apologetic for the sanctify of human life. We will *not* do this by political advocacy, as there are already many excellent organizations who are fighting for pro-life issues in the court room and for pro-life candidates in the voting booth. IBFL is a non-profit 501 (c) 3 organization that does not have much latitude to speak politically other than general non-partisan education.

Rather, IBFL will accomplish this mission by providing a provocative platform upon which life-minded businesses and business people can take a winsomely positive stand for the sanctity of life within the markets they serve and the communities they live in. To be "in business for life" is to support and serve alongside those who are deeply committed to executing

---

[9] http://www.CoCreateFilms.com/

these four life-saving, history making strategic initiatives:

BALM

Babies—Save as many babies as possible by serving their mothers in every possible way.

Adoption—Promote adoption as the compassionate alternative to abortion.

Legislation—Provide updates and commentary on national, state and local sanctity of life legislation.

Memorial—Build a heart-stopping national memorial honoring the unborn victims of abortion.

BALM (Merriam-Webster): an oily substance that has a pleasant smell and that is used for healing, smoothing, or protecting the skin. Something that gives comfort or support.

Babies

IBFL will save babies by supporting pregnancy resource centers like Life Centers of Indianapolis around the country, those on the front lines every day supporting expectant mothers in need.[10] Saving lives now by supporting these life-saving organizations where our members live and work is job #1 for IBFL.

Adoption

Prior to Roe v Wade, 9 percent of new babies born in America were adopted. Today, it's less than 2 percent. Tragically, this precipitous drop in new baby adoptions is almost exclusively due to mothers choosing to abort their children rather than choosing adoption as the compassionate

---

[10] www.LifeCenters.com

alternative. Why? Because in 1973, seven Christian-professing men in black robes (average age 65) said it was their right to do so.

On January 22, 1973 the Supreme Court ruled 7-2 in the Roe v Wade case that a right to privacy under the Due Process Clause of the 14th Amendment extended to a woman's decision to have an abortion. Our nation owes a debt of gratitude to dissenting Justices Byron White and William Rehnquist. History will one day properly portray these brave and principled men as weeping prophets who once cried in the wilderness of a culture that effectively signed a national suicide pact by legalizing abortion on demand.

Had those seven Christian Supreme Court justices who rendered the majority opinion read their Bibles more carefully, they would have learned that adoption is the only way by which anyone can become a child of God:

"...God sent his Son, born of a woman, born under the law, in order to redeem those who were under the law, so that we might receive adoption as children" (Galatians 4:4-5).

Adoption is the central theme of the Christian Gospel. Without it, all are lost. With it, all can be saved...including those who were unplanned, unwanted and according to the confused highest court in the land...unnecessary.

Our nation is bereft of true heroes. Few American eyes can see beyond the rich, famous and flamboyant and the occasional "thank you for your service" to our men and women in uniform. By bringing to life the real American hero stories being written every day by brave birth mothers making the compassionate choice of adoption for their babies, IBFL intends to dramatically increase the national new baby adoption percentage.

Legislation

We believe that one day abortion on demand (with few exceptions) will once again and forever more by outlawed in America. This will likely occur via a Life at Conception Amendment to the Constitution, just as the 13th Amendment abolished slavery in 1865. To that end, IBFL will keep its members informed on the legislative progress.

Memorial

The number of innocent lives lost through abortion every year approximates the total number of American soldiers' lives lost in every war fought since the Revolutionary War in 1775. Our nation and every state within it have properly memorialized the 1.4 million brave soldiers who gave their lives for their country. The hundreds of war memorials throughout our land ensure that their sacrifices will never be forgotten.

IBFL's vision calls for equally-fitting memorials at both the state and federal levels to ensure we never forget the sacrifices of those whose precious, innocent lives were effectively taken by their country. We must always remember those who had the misfortune of being conceived during a dark time in our nation's history. A time when we lost our way and began sacrificing our unborn children on the altar of convenience. A time that will come to an end…in this generation. And, when it does, the citizens of our great nation will rise up and erect memorials the likes of which we've never known.

IBFL will cast a compelling vision for a heart-stopping national memorial to be built in our nation's Capital in Washington DC. Envisioning, designing, planning, funding and building that memorial will be at the forefront of all we do. We believe that by "beginning with the end in mind" (Stephen R. Covey), we can more quickly move the hearts and minds of most Americans towards a culture of life. As the design of the memorial takes shape, so will the need to be on the right side of history when the nation begins to see abortion (like slavery) as a blood-stained and shameful chapter in our nation's history that we must put behind us. Along the way, we expect every state in the union to follow suit with memorials of their own.

27. Why are You in Business?

Standing on the Life Side of History

I hope you're taking many things from this book that will help you in your life's journey. But, if I could personally choose two take-aways for every reader, the first would be this —

Wherever you stand on the issues of the day, when it comes to the sanctity of human life, be absolutely certain that you're standing on the life side of history.

I'll be standing right there with you. Resolute in *my* belief that we will win the "War Within the Womb" in America in *this* generation. Among the many tragic facts surrounding the American abortion holocaust, none disturbs me more than the fact that the majority of pro-life Americans do not believe they'll live to see the day when it's once again illegal to sacrifice our unborn children on the altar of convenience. "That would require a miracle," they say. To which I say, "Yes and amen!"

Only a miracle from the hand of the Creator of all life can save our Great Nation from itself. Only a revival, the likes of which has never been seen, will turn the cultural tide of death back to life in America. A revival which I believe is coming soon, the seeds having been planted within the hearts of America's living victims of abortion.

Yes, I say "victims" because when the leaders of the most powerful, prosperous and principled government in the history of the world grant its citizenry the right to choose life or death for their offspring, their moral compasses can no longer find true north. Little wonder that "we the people" have lost our way. Little hope of ever finding it again unless we find our way back to the One who stands with loving arms wide open:

For as high as the heavens are above the earth,

so great is his love for those who fear him;

as far as the east is from the west,

so far has he removed our transgressions from us.

— Psalms 103:11,12

So please imagine with me, that — fateful — tipping point when

America once again decides that a mother's so-called right to choose will no longer trump her child's right to live. Imagine, your great grandchildren talking around the dinner table one evening about you and where you stood on this issue — *the* defining issue of *your* generation. Like Justices White and Rehnquist, will you be counted among those who bravely stood on the life side of history OR will you be among the cowardly who said, "But we knew nothing about this...." (Proverbs 24:12). My fervent hope and prayer is that you will take your rightful place on the life side of history, thereby leaving a legacy of life for many generations to come.

    In Business For Life, an Indiana based 501c3 non-profit corporation, helps businesses and business people take a winsomely positive stand for the sanctity of life within the markets they serve and the communities they live in. At its core, IBFL stands on the inarguable truth that America will be safer and stronger, more peaceful and prosperous, as adoptions increase and abortions decrease. If this makes as much sense to you as it does to us, we'd be honored to have you join the IBFL movement.

www.InBusinessForLife.org
@InBusiness4Life

28. So What and Who Cares?

It's Sunday morning July 17, 2016. I just finished packing my backpack for the next Pacer and Buster trekking adventure. This year we're doing the 160 mile Collegiate Peaks Loop in the Colorado Rockies. We'll be joined by Pacer's lovely bride, "Desoto." It's our first serious trek in the Rockies and we're excited to see what the Creator of all things has in store for us.

Speaking of the Creator, I'll close by suggesting Him as your second take-away. If you've never seriously considered the claims of Christ, then I implore you to do so. I think C.S. Lewis said it best:

"I am trying here to prevent anyone saying the really foolish thing that people often say about Him: 'I'm ready to accept Jesus as a great moral teacher, but I don't accept his claim to be God.'

"That is the one thing we must not say. A man who was merely a man and said the sort of things Jesus said would not be a great moral teacher. He would either be a lunatic — on the level with the man who says he is a poached egg — or else he would be the Devil of Hell. You must make your choice. Either this man was, and is, the Son of God, or else a madman or something worse. You can shut him up for a fool, you can spit at him and kill him as a demon or you can fall at his feet and call him Lord and God, but let us not come with any patronizing nonsense about his being a great human teacher. He has not left that open to us. He did not intend to."
— C.S. Lewis, Mere Christianity

The choice is yours...and choose you must. Choosing to ignore the audacious claims of Jesus Christ is not an available option. So what do you choose to believe about Jesus? Is he a lunatic...a liar...or the Lord He claimed to be? He must be one of those and you must decide which one you believe Him to be.

The evidence supporting Jesus' claim to be Lord and Savior of the world is overwhelming. The remaining question then is this—when the time comes to judge, will the evidence be equally overwhelming that He is *your* Lord and Savior? To be sure, simply pray the prayer that I did on page 10 of The Four Spiritual Laws. Salvation by faith in Jesus Christ is a free gift that cannot be earned. No one deserves it, but it is freely available to all who earnestly desire it. If you're sensing that desire in your heart, don't ignore it. Act on it as I did over 41 years ago. You will never regret it. You have His word on it.

Well, it looks like we've made it. Now, it's up to you to decide if we've adequately answered the "So What And Who Cares?" questions along the way.

As the court of reader opinion prepares to render its verdict, may I remind the jury that you are to ignore anything that could not pass through your personal "So what?" and "Who cares?" filters. If you neither got it nor cared to, the fault was mine, not yours. Please disregard.

But, if something in my story connected to a dot in yours, I would be deeply grateful to hear about it. On the flipside, if I offended you in any way, I beg your forgiveness and would be equally grateful to hear about that. I take both very seriously. That's why I've included my full contact information in the preface of this book and repeat it below. In the end, if something of what I've learned about the business of life has enhanced yours, then the birthing of this book has been well worth the labor pains. With that, my book is now yours.

Brad Lindemann
In Business for Life

12400 N. Meridian Street
Suite 150
Carmel, IN 46032
317-691-6169
Brad@InBusinessForLife.org
Twitter: @blouis @InBusiness4Life
https://www.linkedin.com/in/bradlindemann
https://www.linkedin.com/groups/6665766

Chapter 28

Made in the USA
Lexington, KY
25 February 2017